*The Slumbering Volcano*

NEW AMERICANISTS

A Series Edited by Donald E. Pease

# THE SLUMBERING VOLCANO

American Slave Ship Revolts and the

Production of Rebellious Masculinity

Maggie Montesinos Sale

DUKE UNIVERSITY PRESS   DURHAM AND LONDON

1997

© 1997 Duke University Press
All rights reserved
Printed in the United States of America on acid-free paper ∞
Typeset in Trump Mediaeval with Weiss display by Keystone Typesetting, Inc.
Library of Congress Cataloging-in-Publication Data appear on the
last printed page of this book.

FOR DOROTHY, ROGER, AND TIM,

WHO FIRST TAUGHT ME HOW TO THINK

# Contents

# Acknowledgments

This book began as my dissertation, a good deal of which was written and revised during and in the aftermath of the crisis in Los Angeles in April and May 1992. As I watched events unfolding I knew that the violent, rebellious acts protested far more than the verdict that freed five police officers who had been videotaped beating Rodney King. The impetus for some of the acts may have been greed, but for most the acts were expressions of rage, disappointment, and longstanding resentment. The racialization of our legal system, as critical legal theorists are now showing, simultaneously ensures "a jury of one's peers" for white police officers brought before the court but prohibits it for any person of color. This system inherits its character from an earlier time when white supremacy was made an explicit aspect of U.S. national identity, a central theme of this study. During the L.A. crisis, I thought back to the angry responses of young black men and women, older than I, to the assassinations of Martin Luther King and Malcolm X, and to the fire bombings and marches. And I remembered, as a white kid growing up in a black neighborhood in the '60s, being both a target and perpetrator of racial violence. Here I have tried to make sense of forces that authorize the rebellions of some but not others, that differentiate and hierarchize, that challenge and claim and insist on being heard.

This study would not have been written without the invaluable assistance of many people. The University of California, San Diego, early on made possible several research trips that greatly influenced the shape of the study. The Council for Research in the Humanities of Columbia University later provided support that enabled me to devote my full attention to completing the manuscript.

My deepest debt goes to Frances Smith Foster, who guided and inspired me, who taught me what it means to do responsible research, and, perhaps most importantly, who passed on to me her love of the nineteenth century. Other members of my dissertation committee— Michael Davidson, Rachel Klein, Lisa Lowe, and, most especially, Kathryn Shevelow and Nicole Tonkovich—provided me not only with encouragement but also with that rare combination of direction and latitude that best nurtures developing scholars. My graduate cohort, particularly Ian Barnard, Megan Machinske, Anne Shea, and Mónica Szurmuk, taught me the most about collegiality, difference, and interdisciplinarity. Carolyn Haynes, Tami Joplin, Patti Orozco, Douglas Rothschild, and Shawn Smith always believed in the significance of my inquiries. Since that time, Priscilla Wald has been a most exciting, insightful, and supportive intellectual interlocutor, reader, and friend, and the source of confidence when I needed it most. Additional members of my feminist writing group at Columbia—Linda Green, Zita Nunes, Judith Weisenfeld, Karen Van Dyck, and Angela Zito—have helped to keep me sane as well as coaching and cajoling me through reshaping the dissertation into a book. The freshness and insight of students in two seminars on race, gender, and U.S. national identity enabled me to hone my overall argument. Elizabeth Blackmar and Rosalind Morris both provided helpful criticism of the *Amistad* material. Carolyn Karcher and an anonymous reader for Duke University Press gave me remarkably cogent criticism that immensely improved the final version. My editor, Reynolds Smith, helpfully persisted in thinking through the title of the work and the shape of the introduction until we reached a mutually satisfactory conclusion. Deborah Montesinos has seen me through it all, gently supporting, encouraging, and convincing me that it was worth it.

Chapters 1, 5, and the afterword in this volume are revised and greatly expanded versions of "Critiques from Within: Antebellum Projects of Resistance," *American Literature* 64 (December 1992): 695–718; reprinted in *Subjects and Citizens: Nation, Race and Gender from Oroonoko to Anita Hill*, edited by Michael Moon and Cathy N. Davidson (Durham: Duke University Press, 1995). Chapters 3 and 5 were previously published in a different form as " 'To Make the Past Useful': Frederick Douglass's Politics of Solidarity," *Arizona Quarterly* 51 (Fall 1995): 25–60. All material is reprinted with permission.

# Introduction: Rebellion and the Legacy

# of the Revolution

The Pennsylvania Constitutional Convention of 1837 provided for the disfranchisement of nonwhite men. On March 14, 1838, thousands of African Americans gathered in Philadelphia to protest this new provision. This meeting heard, discussed, and adopted an *Appeal of Forty Thousand Citizens, threatened with disfranchisement* (1838), which earlier had been prepared by a committee, and later was published in pamphlet form. Committee members, some portion of whom no doubt wrote the pamphlet, included Robert Purvis, James Cornish, J. C. Bowers, and Robert B. Forten. In their argument, the committee reviewed the first Pennsylvania Convention (1790) and a motion not carried in writing the Articles of Confederation between the States (1778).

The committee showed in each case that color had not been accepted by these legislative and judicial bodies as cause for differentiation among men. Rather the reverse: on June 28, 1778, for example, the revolutionary congress decided, eight nays to two ayes, with one divided, *not* to insert the word "white" between the words "free inhabitants" in the following phrase: "The free inhabitants of each of these States, paupers, vagabonds, and fugitives from justice excepted, shall be entitled to all privileges and immunities of free citizens in the several states."[1] This decision, the published *Appeal* argues, guaranteed citizenship of people of color, unless *otherwise* identified as "paupers, vagabonds and fugitives from justice." Similarly, in the first draft of the Pennsylvania Constitution, the word "white" appeared before "freemen." But, as the published pamphlet reports, on the motion of Albert Gallatin it was struck out, "for the express purpose of including colored citizens with[in] the pale of the elective franchise" (179). The Constitution from that time had enfranchised all free male taxpayers. By explicitly striking out the word "white," the Pennsylvania Convention of 1790 "fixed the same standard of *qualification* for all; and in fact, granted and guaranteed 'civil liberty' to all who possess that qualification" (179; emphasis in original). The present move to insert the word "white," the *Appeal* thus argues, goes against earlier policy, state and federal, whose foundations lay in the rhetoric justi-fying—and acts bringing about—the creation of the Republic. Was it the business of the Convention, the committee asks, "to deny 'that all men are born equally free,' by making political rights depend upon the skin in which a man is born? or to divide what our fathers bled to unite, to wit, taxation and representation?" (177).

The committee thus characterized the new racial provision of the proposed state constitution as a dramatic recasting of an earlier egali-tarian ideal, one that they claimed as their own legacy and historical right. Indeed, James Forten, Robert B. Forten's father, was a veteran of the Revolutionary War who left to his son not only the honor of his participation in the war, but also a considerable economic inheri-tance. They recognized and accepted the requirement of being tax-payers. This requirement drew upon the republican notion that those who participate in the body politic must be independent of mind—and therefore of means. Paying taxes was considerably less onerous a re-quirement than that of owning land. In 1790, only Vermont had a more inclusive provision for voting, providing for universal male suf-frage. New Hampshire shared with Pennsylvania the minimal re-quirement of paying taxes. Every other state called for ownership of considerable property, thus creating a body politic premised on land-ownership. Pennsylvania's requirement, so long as it was the same for all, may have differentiated somewhat in terms of class, but it did not explicitly assume, acknowledge, or create social, political, and legal strata based on racial constructions. Because the abolition of slavery had been provided for through gradual emancipation acts only ten years earlier (1780), even the taxpaying requirement for a time no doubt precluded the participation of many African and African Ameri-can men. Nevertheless, given the certainty of eventual emancipation and the possibility of gaining a livelihood thereafter, voting in Penn-sylvania was legally within their reach.

Implicitly the committee asserted that legal decisions bore a clear and significant relation to actual living conditions. This assertion obscures the extra-legal, social, and cultural factors that earlier may have prevented the actual participation of many men of color, regardless of their legal right to do so. The exclusion of men of color from Independence Day parades, duty as jurors, service in the militia, and possession of firearms, for example, all politically oriented activities through which normative masculinity was constructed, as well as from attendance at schools and seats in public transportation facilities, evidence such exclusionary practices (Baker 245). The committee's point nevertheless should be taken seriously. This shift in suffrage requirements marked the *systematic institutionalization* of racial constructs as part of a discourse of national identity.

Typically the nineteenth-century change in suffrage requirements, of which Pennsylvania's revised constitution was but a part, has been hailed as the rise of popular democracy. In the early nineteenth century, and particularly under Andrew Jackson's presidency, property requirements were excluded from new state constitutions and removed from older ones. This so-called extension of the franchise happened in tandem with the insertion of the word "white," as in Pennsylvania, into virtually all state suffrage requirements. In New York, property requirements were eliminated for white men, while they were not simply retained but increased from $200 to $250 for non-white men. This shift effectively foreclosed their access since the economic situation for African Americans in New York deteriorated considerably between 1790 and 1850.[2] Because slavery and property requirements otherwise precluded participation, in many states this shift may not have made much of a difference in terms of who actually voted. But it did matter in some states. In Pennsylvania, New Jersey, and Connecticut black men lost a vote to which they previously had had a legal right.

In some cases this change made legal what otherwise was practiced socially: the exclusion of African American men and other men of color from the political process. But more important to understand is that the shift from elite republicanism to popular democracy not only did not include men of color, but actually worsened their situation. Conversations surrounding this change illustrate the increased anxiety produced among Euroamerican men at the prospect of empowering newly freed African American men through an extended franchise. Between 1777 and 1817, Vermont, Massachusetts, New Hampshire, Pennsylvania, Rhode Island, Connecticut, New York, and New Jersey made provisions for the abolition of slavery. These acts and judicial decisions created scattered, yet increasingly substantial, free black populations in what came to be known as the northern states. Proposals to remove property requirements for suffrage raised the possibility of enfranchising the male members of these growing free black populations. Objections to this possibility illustrate the complex process of identity formation through which a new coalition of Euroamerican men—including urban artisans, the emergent working class, European immigrants, yeoman farmers, overseers, and slaveholders—remade themselves as "white," simultaneously to empower themselves as political actors and to differentiate themselves from African, African American, and indigenous men, whom they variously represented as unfit for inclusion in state and national bodies. Thus this shift should not be read as simply making explicit what was implicit or already assumed, but as actively constructing and institutionalizing a new category, "race," as the most important mode of differentiation between a newly configured national body politic and its own (racialized) others. White supremacy, or what Donald Noel (1972) defines as racism, emerged at this historical juncture precisely because of the need to justify the continued institutionalized exploitation of a major segment of an otherwise increasingly egalitarian society.

The committee that wrote the *Appeal of Forty Thousand* was not able to prevent the new Pennsylvania constitution from being ratified. Nor could its members effectively challenge the newly constructed racial categories and the rise of white supremacy. Yet they had the power to produce a critique of this process that provided the means for their own self-definition and self-generated understanding of these events. Their efforts—and the text they left behind—provide us with an important viewpoint from which to understand this defining moment in the nation's history. The committee reminds us to see this not simply as the overthrow of the class-based oligarchy that had been instituted after the Revolution and the rise of popular democracy, nor to understand this moment as even the triumph of "whiteness," a racial construct that gained new saliency as one of the defining features of the developing nation. They ask us also to consider these developments from the point of view of those at the expense of whom the "wages of whiteness" were paid.[3]

The histories of slavery and of free African Americans, the studies of eighteenth and nineteenth-century African American literature, and also the fictional and poetic works reimagining times prior to general emancipation, written largely since the sea-change in scholarship first inspired by the Civil Rights Movement, further enable such a conceptual shift in scholarly points of view. The concerted effort of more than a generation of scholars has produced an impressive corpus of work that concentrates on previously ignored, grossly distorted, or romanticized material and historical figures.[4] Visions of the happy plantation, for example, have been replaced by complex considerations of the economics of slavery, of family life under the peculiar institution, and of negotiations among slave and slaveholders. Innovative in their approaches, these studies have not only accepted as evidence slave testimony in its myriad forms, but addressed some of the crucial methodological issues facing any scholar interested in people whose extant, self-produced records are relatively scarce. In addition, the notion of complete black illiteracy has been complicated by the recent and continuing republication of novels, narratives, speeches, sermons, and appeals by blacks written prior to the Civil War.[5] The availability of these primary documents, and the growing number of literary and cultural studies that place them within their respective historical contexts, make more possible reimagining U.S. America's past at least from the public (and printed) points of view of the African Americans who lived it.

This book seeks to reconceptualize the history, culture, and literature of the United States *together with* that of chattel slavery and of enslaved and free people of African descent.[6] It sharply contrasts with the ways in which historians, politicians, literary critics, promoters of the Pledge of Allegiance, and other cultural workers since the Civil War have represented slavery as an aberration, a mistake, an unfor-

tunate inheritance from a colonial past that was successfully ex-
tinguished and should now be forgotten. As comforting as this narrative may be for a still deeply racially divided populace, splitting off
slavery from conceptualizations of the United States distorts our understanding of the nation's history, economy, political institutions,
and cultural forms. It marginalizes not only the contributions to U.S.
culture, society, and politics, but the very presence of African Americans. This process has been both a mask for continuing racial oppression and a means of discursively erasing a now embarrassing history.

My inquiry focuses on the way in which what I call the trope of
revolutionary struggle became in the nineteenth century a site of
contestation among unequally empowered groups with occasionally
complementary, but more often opposed, agendas. Produced during
the revolutionary period by a discourse of U.S. national identity, an
incarnation of liberal political theory, this trope authorized the revolt
of freeborn men against tyrannical governments attempting to enslave them.[7] It simultaneously drew upon and recast Locke's theory of
property right and classical republican notions of freedom, independence, and enslavement. At the time of the Revolution, this trope
authorized the separation of the colonies from British control. It created a new position from which many colonists-turned-patriots could
imagine themselves as citizens of a new republic rather than as subjects of a monarch. By agreeing to protect slavery in the states where it
had been instituted by positive law, the U.S. Constitution limited the
inclusionary potential of the discourse of national identity by appropriating the trope only for those *already free*, and denying it to those
enslaved *within* the U.S. population. Until well into the nineteenth
century the pervasive interpretation of the Constitution, by slavery
advocates, abolitionists, and defenders of the Union alike, was that
this founding document differentiated absolutely between appropriate behavior and ideals for those already free and those enslaved.

The specific location for my inquiry into the inequities involved in
defining revolutionary struggle is four discursive instances of slave
revolts on ships. The first two instances are constituted by the popular
press's representations and interpretations of two historical events,
revolts on the *Amistad* (1839) and the *Creole* (1841), that took place

off the Atlantic seaboard of North America. The second two instances are explicitly fictionalized accounts of historical events, Herman Melville's *Benito Cereno* (1855), based on the rebellion on board the *Tryal* in 1800, and Frederick Douglass's *The Heroic Slave* (1852), an account of the *Creole* rebellion. In focusing on these four instances, I look for the production or foreclosure of subject-positions from which to claim the trope of revolutionary struggle.[8] I map the ways in which, and the ideological purposes to which, unequally empowered groups claimed, manipulated, and transformed the statements associated with the discourse of national identity. I consider as well some of the nonrhetorical discursive practices, such as access to education and communication networks, that enabled certain groups to assert more effectively their representations and interpretations. The thematic coherency of these four events, coupled with the dramatic differences in the ways in which they were represented and interpreted, enables me to display the interaction of the discourse of national identity with a racialist discourse of white superiority.

Slave revolts provide an especially compelling starting point for investigating this large topic. Why, paradoxically, was the creation of the United States initially justified by sanctioning colonial revolt against the British Crown, yet only rarely has similar sanction been given to slave rebellion? The logic that divides so absolutely colonial revolt from slave rebellion supports, but is not congruent with, arguments that separate the United States from its own history of slavery and analyses that distinguish the republican-turned-democratic nation from its "own" racialized others.

A provisional and partial answer to this paradox may be that the rebellion at the heart of the Revolution was between people who, although they disagreed politically, considered themselves to share a relatively common heritage, culture, and religion. Although in the early years of the republic patriots such as Noah Webster called for an "American" language and an "American" literature, connections to a European, especially a British, legacy remained strong. Slave revolt within the British colonies, and the Americas more generally, disrupted more profoundly the bedrock assumptions of the dominant cultural communities because it challenged their sense of identity as Christians of European descent, and therefore their sense of divinely sanctioned superiority. In the eighteenth- and nineteenth-century United States, *revolution* could be conceptualized as the necessary spur against the community's backsliding practices, a spur that ensured continual progress, the dictum of the chosen nation. The term *rebellion*, by contrast, characterized the insurgency of the unfit, the unruly, the untamed, against the better government of a civilized people (Bercovitch). The perceptual chasm between Euroamericans and the supposedly heathen and uncivilized Africans they had enslaved—regardless of the actual character or behavior of enslaved people—made the violent assertion of those enslaved not simply frightening, but earth-shattering. The metaphor in this book's title, "The Slumbering Volcano," illustrates the sense of the disruption of the natural order typically used to characterize the upheaval of slave revolt.[9]

Although during the colonial period Euroamericans had for generations enslaved and subordinated Africans and African Americans, and "removed" and committed genocide upon the indigenous populations, differentiation based on perceived *racial* characteristics was only one among several important modes of stratification. Indenture particularly, but also apprenticeship and, for women, marriage, created significantly hierarchical and often oppressive interpersonal relations. Indeed, during the Revolution, "Americans" used icons of the indigenous populations to differentiate themselves from the British and to create themselves anew—for example, ironically dressing as Mohawk warriors in their attack upon tea in Boston Harbor.[10] But as the revolutionary promises of a more egalitarian society began to reshape the political and social terrain of the colonies-now-states, race became an increasingly significant means of differentiating among the U.S. population (Noel 163–64). In the early years of the republic, in fact, U.S. national identity increasingly was formulated as different from various racialized groups residing within the nation's expanding geographical boundaries, as different and separate from its "own" racial others. In the second quarter of the nineteenth century, the newly emergent, then increasingly dominant, Democratic Party, proudly led by Andrew Jackson, created a powerful new process of appropriation by challenging "the politics of deference" (Saxton) to the upper class that had supported the National Republican Party (which had dominated the political process from 1801 until 1829) and championing the working common man. The party did so by adopting a racialist discourse of innate Anglo-Saxon superiority that empowered all men recognized as white, creating for the first time an *explicitly* racialized subject-position, "all [white] men," from which to claim the discourse of national identity. The Pennsylvania Constitution of 1837 is but one example of this change. The rise of racialist discourse and white supremacy in the nineteenth century constituted a new way—different from distinctions between those already free and those enslaved—in which the inclusionary potential of the discourse of national identity was simultaneously expanded and limited.

The history I have told and the vantage point enabled by recent scholarship disrupt historical visions of the United States as moving along a teleological path toward greater freedom and equality. Traditionally this vision asserts that the Pilgrim fathers left England to found a new society based on freedom, the U.S. Revolution set forth the promise of political liberty, Jacksonian democracy extended it, and then the Civil War completed another portion of the promise by abolishing slavery. In this mythical narrative, the Puritans' chosen people become the chosen nation, tied together inevitably by a sacred history produced not only by theologians, but by politicians, rhetoricians, historians, educators, and other cultural workers. This vision imagines progressive change as the inevitable result of America's mission as a providential nation, committed to continual improvement, open to all who share it. Yet not only the fact of slavery, but protests against a wide range of exclusionary practices, such as native genocide and removal, illustrate both the partial character of citizenship and the marked *deterioration* of conditions for indigenous Americans virtually since the onset of colonialization, and for African Americans during several historical periods.[11]

Sacvan Bercovitch (1978) has perhaps best traced the myth of America as a providential nation. In his study of the American jeremiad, the political sermon of exhortation and celebration, Bercovitch argues that the American Puritan legacy provided first eighteenth-century revivalists, then republican revolutionaries, and later nineteenth-century empire-builders and industrialists, with a sense of themselves as first God's chosen people, then the forward flank of a Christian army, and finally the cutting edge of human progress. Bercovitch's study connects across several centuries many disparate writers who make use of similar rhetoric for not entirely dissimilar ends. Its sweeping power lies in its ability to explain the continuing significance of the rhetoric. He argues that later generations recast earlier notions of New England as a sacred place set aside by God for the fulfillment of the millennium as the destiny of the entire continent for an errand in sacred history, and they elevated the first emigrants to the status of mythic heroes, to whom Yankees would turn as the progenitors of the nation. Not only this, but they created what Bercovitch calls a "genetics of salvation" (64), by which they ensured the passing of grace from generation to generation, a move that eliminated the requirement of displaying election in behavior, and that later enabled the extension of the Puritan vision to the growing immigrant population.[12] This argument goes a long way to explain the myth of progress as self-realization as well as improvement, that so deeply undergirds U.S. national identity.

Yet Bercovitch's focus on the continuance and transformation of rhetorical traditions cannot explain, and, indeed, masks the importance—and uniqueness—of the U.S. Revolution, particularly for African Americans. His study figures the Revolution as simply a stage in a more general movement that began generations prior to the creation of the republic. Lockean political theory enters in only as a supportive character in his play of the jeremiad. This fact, he implies, explains why the U.S. Revolution "succeeded" while so many revolutionary movements elsewhere in the world, particularly in Latin America, did not. Rather than actually embracing the universalistic claims of liberalism, U.S. Americans, bolstered by their Puritan heritage, kept a tight rein on their revolution, keeping its benefits for the Anglo-American middle class. Rather than degenerating into bloody factionalism, U.S. Americans created a social and political order that precluded most violent conflict by privileging rather than challenging the burgeoning middle class, maintaining a clear differentiation between included and excluded populations, and requiring conformity to the myth of the providential nation. Bercovitch's argument, therefore, explains much about the religious and cultural underpinnings of U.S. national identity and their continuing significance over time. Yet it also tends to marginalize those for whom liberal political theory held out an important—and in some ways very real—promise.

The revolutionary period, a defining moment in the history of the nation, has long been evoked and valued by many African American writers and activists as a moment of promise. It is precisely the radically egalitarian *potential* of liberal theory, which Bercovitch cites as the reason for the conservative reaction against and the subsequent failure of revolutionary movements elsewhere, that appealed and continued to appeal to African Americans. My emphasis on liberal political theory derives not from a desire to reinstate the free-willed individual as the subject of history, or from a belief that it was hegemonic during the revolutionary period, but from a recognition that its inclusionary potential—and the exclusionary practices that limited that potential—was and has been most significant for African Americans.[13] This same potential first embarrassed then discomforted colonial-turned-national policymakers as they faced a variety of radical movements making use of this rhetoric. Virtually every document of political protest written by African American men—and some by white and African American women—between the Revolutionary and the Civil Wars laid claim to the authorizing notion that "all men are born equally free" (*Appeal of Forty Thousand*).

And no wonder. After all, this egalitarian assertion had served the colonists well. Although many historians emphasize the classical republican underpinnings of revolutionary rhetoric, invocations of Locke's natural right to "life, liberty, and estates" indisputedly were commonplace.[14] This notion of natural rights enabled elite policymakers of colonial America not only to lay claim to representation—which they had been denied in Parliament—but to create a new political process. In the context of European history, this move was radically inclusive. It not only challenged the notion of the divine right of kings and the dominance of the aristocracy, which were the original targets of Locke's formulations, but asserted the equality and significance of populations of European, particularly British, descent in the Americas. Typified by the Declaration of Independence's claim that "all men are created equal," this rhetorical strain of the U.S. Revolution emphasized the inclusionary aspect of this political theory. Despite its opening clause, this claim was far from self-evident, asserting as it did a notion of equality among men unparalleled in European history.

The rhetoric created a new identity which drew the colonists together, that of free men endowed with natural rights resisting political slavery at the hands of British authorities. It produced what I call "righteous masculinity," a meeting point of Locke's notion of natural rights and a Christian ideal of correct moral action. This rhetoric drew upon Locke's version of the natural world, in which individual human entities ("Man") have property in their "Lives, Liberties, and Estates." Locke presents as axiomatic the notion that before the organization of society, all men are in "a *State of perfect Freedom*," which is "a *State* also *of Equality*" (II, 4).[15] In Locke's schema, the notion of property is used to describe a wide range of nonequivalent and unlike things: the biological and spiritual concept of "Life"; the philosophical and legal notion of "Liberty"; the physical and economic concept of "Estates"; and one's relation to some of the physical acts of one's body, such as one's labor or work. Governments are then instituted among men in order to protect the property of individuals. Locke argues that men cannot justly be subjected to the "Political Power" of another, whereas individual men may agree to give up some of their liberties in order to form a "*Body Politick*," "for their comfortable, safe, and peaceable living amongst another, in a secure Enjoyment of their Properties" (II, 95). Because governments are based on the consent of the governed, they also may be dissolved and reestablished with the consent of the governed. The notion that this collection of individualized masculine entities, "the People," have such rights, a right to political revolution, is what Locke was most famous for in Europe (Ryan 16), although he considered revolution extreme behavior. In the context of the U.S. Revolution, Locke's right to rebellion against an unjust government became the positive duty of "all [free] men," such that an at least rhetorical willingness to die in the cause of liberty became the mark of being "American."

The apparent openness of this identity, which required only one's willingness to rebel in the twinned cause of liberty and property, made it possible for a wide range of men to imagine themselves to be part of, and thereby to dedicate themselves to, this alliance. Indeed, it provided the basis for solidarity not only among merchants, farmers, apprentices, and artisans, but also among planters, overseers, frontiersmen and yeoman farmers, men from different colonies, with different ethnic heritages and different linguistic traditions who otherwise did not see themselves as having much in common. Because the Declaration of Independence, only the most famous example of this, represented "unalienable rights" as belonging to "all men," even men who did not own property, and so did not have the independent status otherwise valued by classical republicanism and Lockean political theory, could imagine themselves to be newly made citizens rather than subjects. This despite the fact that most of them would not meet the property requirements for suffrage.

Yet this rhetorical emphasis on—and certain practices of—inclusion was accompanied by other exclusionary practices. The Declaration's proclamation that "all men are created equal" and that governments are instituted "among Men" made visible what many already assumed, and what was later made explicit in virtually all of the requirements for suffrage, that *only men* participate in the social contract. This gendering was reinforced by the Declaration's characterization of the colonists as having defended their rights with "manly firmness" and by its threat that these rights will now be defended in one of the most masculine of ways—on the battlefield.

The masculinity of the revolutionary subject reproduced and reasserted in a new social and political context the gendered structure of Locke's treatises on political power. Locke axiomatically defined "Political Power" as the power of a magistrate over a subject, as opposed to that of "a *Father* over his Children, a *Master* over his Servant, a *Husband* over his Wife, and a *Lord* over his Slave" (II, 2; emphasis in original). This split between "Man" and these "dependent" others also was justified by the theory's logic because these auxiliaries' so-called dependent status made them beholden to "Man" for sustenance. These "dependents" therefore are "not free" because they supposedly do not have the means necessary for self-determination. Thus, even within

Locke's abstract schema, children, servants, wives, and slaves are not naturally free, equal, and independent, so they do not have a power to protect their "property," defined by Locke as their "Lives, Liberties, and Estates." They therefore have no "natural" rights. This split largely was reproduced in the colonial context, although the matter was more complex when it came to servants because of the ability of most Euroamerican men to learn a trade, to escape indenture if necessary, and to become self-sufficient artisans even if not landowners. Thus children, wives, and slaves, as auxiliaries of free men, might enable the rebellion of "all men" against the specter of political slavery, but not create one of their own in *opposition* to those "free men" because they are not authorized to wield "Political Power." The logic of this schema dictates that these supposedly dependent entities could claim the title "American" only by supporting the rebellion of "free men."

In addition, the colonists' rejection of their own *political slavery* did not necessarily translate into an identification with enslaved people of African descent. The colonial rejection of political slavery, defined by them as the imposition of taxation without representation in the political bodies imposing the levies, has been extensively documented. Recently connections between the colonists' notion of political slavery and chattel slavery within the colonies has received more attention. David Roediger, for example, argues that "the special force [of the metaphoric use of slavery] in the American colonies derived in large part from proximity to chattel slavery. American revolutionaries consistently exhibited terror of being treated, as one of them said, 'like *Guinea slaves.'* "[16] Thus the collateral existence of chattel slavery in effect prodded the colonists to resist more forcefully what they termed British attempts to enslave them. In the Northern states, the use of the rhetoric of slavery and freedom led to an at least partial identification on the part of Euroamerican colonists with enslaved people, which resulted in the abolition of slavery. In what became the South, most newly empowered "Americans" did not make, recognize, or honor the potential connection between political and chattel slavery, although some individuals did make private acts of manumission. Indeed, as Edmund Morgan (1972) has shown most convincingly, to most Southerners the freedom and equality of white men depended upon a large enslaved class.[17] In the years that followed, the Southern states and territories instead expanded and extended chattel slavery.

Thus the revolutionary potential of the notion of natural rights was, in the emergent United States, attached to a particular agenda, that of a Euroamerican male colonist rejecting British authority. In contradistinction to Bercovitch, I would argue that the rejection of political slavery and the protection of property that included African and African American slaves, as much as the myth of America as a providential nation, limited the radical potential of liberal theory in what became the United States. Patrick Henry's famous call to revolt—"Give me liberty! or give me death!"—did not and was not intended to authorize the revolt of, for example, enslaved Africans and their descendants living in the colonies. Nor did it sanction a wife's murder of an abusive husband. It had a specific meaning within the context of its utterance that was attached to the position of the subject speaking, a Euroamerican male colonist—and in this case a slave-holder—rejecting what he thought of as political slavery. This is not to suggest either that free women and enslaved people did not identify with the cause of national independence or that they did not partici-pate in acts that enabled separation. Many did. But the character of that revolt did not facilitate the expression of their concerns *if they ran counter to* the revolutionary agenda: the protection of the property of "free men," property that included, in addition to "Life, Liberty, and Estates," enslaved *people.*

During the Revolution, enslaved petitioners in Connecticut and Massachusetts argued for their right to emancipation using reasoning similar to that of the colonists-turned-patriots. "Your petitioners," they argued, "aprehind we have in common with all other men a natu-ral right to our freedoms . . . as we are a freeborn Pepel and have never forfeited this Blessing by aney compact or agreement whatever" (Ap-theker 1965, 8–9; original spellings). In an attempt to subvert the colonists' definition of and limits on revolutionary struggle, the pe-titioners represented themselves as, like the colonists, "a freeborn Pepel." In doing so, the petitioners were not trying to assimilate to the "American" agenda so much as to rewrite that agenda so that it would include their own emancipation. They assert, according to Lockean logic, that as freeborn people they cannot justly be enslaved because they have not agreed to any social compact, thereby obscuring Locke's provision of the enslavement of prisoners of war. Other petitions argued the colonists' and enslaved's common masculinity and religion to be more important than differences in their racial and cultural backgrounds.[18] Although they referred to and implicitly supported the colonists' struggle with Britain, they did not claim for themselves the trope of revolutionary struggle, the right to revolt against an unjust oppressor. As I have argued elsewhere, this claim would have too obviously set them against those with whom they were attempting to identify—their colonial masters—and from whom they were hoping to win concessions.[19]

After the war was won, the Continental Congress that produced the U.S. Constitution limited the use of the trope of revolutionary struggle by agreeing to protect slavery in the states where it had been instituted by positive law. Although this founding document made no explicit reference to race or slavery, it recognized the subordinate status of "persons held to service," counting them as three-fifths of those free for the purposes of taxation and representation in the national legislative bodies, and it provided for the suppression of domestic insurrection (art. 1, sec. 2; art. 4, sec. 4). These constitutional clauses limited the inclusionary potential of the discourse of national identity by appropriating the trope of revolutionary struggle only for those *already free*, and thereby denying it to those enslaved *within* the U.S. population. Until well into the nineteenth century, the pervasive interpretation of the Constitution, by slavery advocates, abolitionists, and defenders of the Union alike, thus differentiated absolutely between appropriate behavior and ideals for those already free and those enslaved.

Still, it was precisely the potential for inclusiveness, which enabled the actual (if slow and uneven) abolition of slavery in the Northern states, that made and continued to make revolutionary rhetoric appealing to African Americans. This was particularly true for men, whose gender enabled them to imagine themselves, to identify themselves, as citizens of the emergent republic, and which in some cases actually did enable them to participate in the political process.[20] All this is to emphasize that *race* was not generally an explicit part of revolutionary rhetoric, although slavery, which had come to be associated with certain perceived racial characteristics, and normative gender constructions were the basis for important divisions within the colonial and national populations. Nineteenth-century African Americans often harked back to the revolutionary period in an effort to renovate and extend the inclusive potential of liberal theory, which, for them, was being foreclosed at exactly the moment when—and precisely because—Jacksonian democracy was extending it more fully to "all [white] men."

This vantage point is crucial for understanding why activists and writers like Frederick Douglass, whose only piece of fiction is the subject of chapter 5 below, returned to the revolutionary period to claim—and thereby transform—its authorizing legacy.[21] While it was common for rhetoricians of all kinds to claim to be the true inheritors of the revolutionary fathers, most did so with a collateral assumption and/or assertion of white supremacy as the norm. As the work of revisionist historians such as Ronald Takaki, George Frederickson, Reginald Horsman, and especially David Roediger and Alexander Saxton has shown, the nineteenth century witnessed the emergence of white supremacy and the myriad ways in which race came to code relations of power in the United States. Given this shift in signifying relations of power from the Revolutionary to the Jacksonian period, the claim to the authorizing legacy of the Revolution by African American men had a different meaning in the later period than in the earlier one. Their attempt to renovate and extend the inclusionary potential of liberal political theory was more explicitly and dangerously oppositional in the later context because they had more explicitly been created, recognized, and identified as other, and thereby more explicitly excluded from the national body.

Too often African American claims to U.S. citizenship and to the inclusive potential of liberal theory more generally have been dismissed as false consciousness, or as capitulation to a hegemonic political, social, and cultural order designed to oppress them. Such dismissals, I suggest, read back into the past a later knowledge of, for example, the failure of Reconstruction and the reign of terror that followed, or the recent dismantling of the gains of the Civil Rights Movement. This anachronistic perspective flattens our understanding of the past, rendering it an inevitable path to current conditions. Further, comprehending pervasive political and social structures and cultural forms as intrinsically serving the interests of a ruling class figures those structures and forms too monolithically and simplistically. Undoubtedly people do internalize values and modes of understanding that limit and oppress them. Yet it is equally true that others claim such structures and forms and transform them and their meanings in the service of their own often oppositional concerns and interests. This process is uneven, partial, often confusing and conflicted. In order to discern and analyze this process, we need not only historical specificity, but a conceptual apparatus that enables us to understand the claims of African American men, or of women from any background, to liberal theory as other than futile attempts to become empowered by acceding to another class's interests, as other than attempts to assimilate to an agenda that is predicated on and therefore reproduces their exclusion and degradation.

A way out of this dilemma may be to think of liberal theory as a *discourse of natural rights*, and its incarnation in the United States in the period between the Revolutionary War and the Civil War as a *discourse of national identity*, in the Foucaultian sense of discourse.[22] Discourse is marked by a polyvalent series of statements (including rhetorical and narrative forms) that appears and reappears at different historical moments and in different cultural and political contexts. The notion of freedom in the natural world, for example, which appears in early European writings about the lifestyles of indigenous Americans, became part of a discourse of natural rights when made into a political theory by John Locke.[23] This notion reappeared in the rhetorical forms of the U.S. Revolution, and again in nineteenth-century abolitionist and proslavery rhetoric. This notion of natural rights was dispersed not only in the United States, but in revolutionary documents throughout the Americas. But statements such as "all men are created equal" and "all men have a natural right to Life, Liberty, and Estates," which were produced by the discourse of natural rights, were not *intrinsically* attached to a particular political agenda or class. As my examples suggest, and as I will demonstrate in the chapters that follow, such discursive statements rather may be mobilized and deployed for different and often opposed ideological purposes. At issue then is not the *unity* of an ideology, such as Bercovitch found with the American jeremiad, but rather the way in which discourse *disperses* the series of statements associated with it, thereby producing differently authorized subject-positions.[24]

Ideology historically has been used by leftists and progressives in two ways: to describe values, narratives, and practices, produced by and for the ruling class, that are naturalized and imbibed by those they oppress; and, in a more neutral sense, to describe a system of ideas appropriate to a specific class or group, such as "feminist ideology," or "working-class ideology."[25] The notion of ideology, particularly as developed by Louis Althusser (1971), has been a powerful tool for understanding the influence of what he calls "ideological state apparatuses," the largely private institutions of church, education, communications, and family. While recognizing their diversity, Althusser argues that these apparatuses operate in tandem to inculcate ruling-class ideology. He thus asserts that on a structural level prior to the distinction between public and private, the range of ideological state apparatuses serves a unified set of interests, that of the ruling class. This formulation has been very useful in explaining how capitalist selves are (re)produced and oppressive practices internalized. But in contradistinction to this assertion of *unity*, I offer the term *discourse*. For Althusser's notion of ideology not only attaches rhetorical forms to a specific political agenda, it also creates a sense of overwhelming and totalizing coherency that threatens to preclude any other than already doomed attempts at resistance, transformation, and (re)creation. Instead I use *ideology* to speak about the way in which rhetorical forms and discursive practices are given different *ideological import* under different conditions. Analysis then focuses on determining not the way in which such forms and practices contribute to a ruling ideology, but rather the particular interests they serve in the context in which they appear and operate.

A discursive field is governed by certain rules of formation that

produce and disperse the objects of which they speak, be they an identifiable series of statements, subject-positions, character-types, issues, or facts. Yet the identification of the rules of formation of a
discursive field does not alone provide information about the ideological work performed by the statements associated with it. To discern
what is at stake and for whom, we need to analyze the specific context
in which the series of statements appears and the kinds of subject-
positions created or foreclosed. Meaning changes depending upon the
position of the speaking/writing subject. Indeed, intrinsic to discursive formations are certain processes of appropriation that ensure that
not all subject-positions made possible by the productive logic of the
discourse will be authorized to articulate or claim it. Thus additional
work needs to be done to determine the action of these appropriative
processes, and so to understand the uneven production and authorization of subject-positions.

The rules of formation of the discourse of U.S. national identity, for
example, a specific incarnation of liberal political theory, made possible many more positions than actually were—or have been—realized.
The inclusionary logic of the discourse made possible a wide range of
potential positions from which to claim natural and equal rights and
to articulate progressive agendas, some of which we have considered
thus far. John Adams's dismissive response to Abigail Adams's famous
request that the new policymakers "Remember the Ladies" gives a
sense of the range of possible positions:

We have been told that our struggle has loosened the bands of Government
everywhere. That Children and Apprentices were disobedient—that schools
and Colledges were grown turbulent—that Indians slighted their Guardians
and Negroes grew insolent to their Masters. But your letter was the first Inti-
mation that another Tribe more numerous and powerfull than all the rest were
grown discontented.—This is rather too coarse a Compliment but you are so
saucy, I wont blot it out. (930; original spellings)

Adams uses "Government" here as a metaphor for any hierarchical
relation. He facetiously hints at the potential of liberal theory to include women, children, apprentices ("servants" in Locke's terms),
Negroes, and Indians, potential that he attempts to foreclose with his

mocking tone and assumed prerogative. Uday Mehta (1990) argues that liberal theory distinguishes between the universal *capacities* of all people, and the conditions for their *actualization;* that is, all potentially may be capable of being free and equal, but all may not be situated such that this potential may be realized. In addition, Mehta posits such exclusionary practices as proceeding from a level of social convention that psychologically precedes abstract formulations of universal equality.[26] For example, in the passage quoted above, John Adams dismisses on the unstated basis of social convention Abigail Adams's claim to abstract formulations of equality. Socially constructed at an earlier time, and now under Abigail Adams's challenge, limited though it was, such convention might be thought of as the residue of an older political and social order, other aspects of which were then effectively being challenged by men such as John Adams. Mehta's suggestion that such convention psychologically precedes theorization in some cases may be useful in discerning internalized oppression; yet as our example suggests, John rather than Abigail Adams still internalized the residual convention of male supremacy. Conceptualizing residual convention and emergent theory as operating on different but collateral registers may help us skirt any notion of a psychological realm that precedes its construction in culture. Thus, in addition to the provision within liberal theory for the necessary conditions for the realization of equality, residual conventional forms, operating on a register different from explicitly theoretical formulations, may inhibit the inclusionary potential of liberal theory. Adams calls upon residual elements of hierarchy in order to reinforce certain specific relations of power, even as he in different arenas contests others.[27] He and his cohort were relatively successful in limiting the extent of "their" struggle.[28]

Yet Mehta's formulation does suggest that such limits on inclusion may be disrupted by further challenging the residue of social convention, internalized boundaries, and naturalized hierarchy, the bedrock of this political theory. With this insight, it is possible to see that the *specific* limits Adams and his contemporaries imposed were not an intrinsic part of the discourse of national identity they helped create. Rather, these limits resulted from residual assumptions of hierarchy and a preexisting uneven allocation of power, both of which granted greater authority to elite colonial-turned-national policy-makers. Their power enabled them to foreclose the authorizing of—and in some cases the mere production of—many of the subject-positions hinted at above, such as women, children, "Indians," and, for the most part, "Negroes." That is, they were able to normalize their own use of liberal theory while simultaneously making other attempts to claim it seem outrageous, ridiculous, irrational, or dangerous. They successfully kept largely in place the distinction between dependent and independent entities, thereby obscuring the actual dependence of "individuals" or "Man" upon "their" supposedly dependent "children, servants, wives and slaves." Yet their ability to do so was not settled once and for all. The productive and foreclosing process remained open to contestation because it was their specific appropriative strategies, not the productive logic of the discourse itself, that limited subject-positions in *this particular way*.

Understanding liberal theory as a *discourse* rather than as an *ideology* allows us to understand the ways in which various groups have claimed this theory for their own—and often opposed—ideological purposes. For if liberal theory is understood as a single ideology, then it must be fundamentally connected to the interests of a particular group. In the United States, this group would necessarily be the elite policymakers who appropriated and recast it as the discourse of national identity at the time of the Revolution. Yet, as scholars such as Alexander Saxton have shown so well, liberal theory was given different ideological import at different historical moments. Jacksonian Democrats used it in the early nineteenth century to split the National Republican Party and thereby unseat the Northern upper-class heirs of the Revolution. The free-soil coalition that became the Republican Party appropriated it yet again and thereby fragmented the Democratic Party. If liberal theory is conceptualized as a single ideology, then these contestations must be understood as mere variations within an agreed-upon structure. Bercovitch makes a similar point about the different kinds of people who used the American jeremiad, that their conflicts "were divisions, antagonisms, *within the culture*" (158; emphasis in original). Such a conception leads to a monolithic and hermetic vision that homogenizes and privileges the actors in these struggles, figuring them all as competing members of an otherwise unified ruling class. It thereby minimizes the significance of issues, such as slavery, Indian removal, and the national bank, about which these groups disagreed. In addition, any claim to liberal theory by African American men, for example, or by women from any background, or by indigenous peoples, none of whom played defining roles in the struggles of the major political parties outlined above, can only be understood as futile attempts to become empowered by acceding to another class's interests. Their efforts, then, appear as attempts to assimilate to an agenda that is predicated on their exclusion and degradation.

But if liberal theory is instead understood as a discourse, then dispersion rather than unity governs its operation. This mode of conceptualizing emphasizes heterogeneity, proliferation, fluctuation, contestation, differentiation. It asserts that, despite the uneven allocation of power, including the power of discourse itself, no one group may completely control the meanings produced by the invocation of discursive statements. Thus the nineteenth-century production and reconfigurations of political parties indicate truly important changes in relations of power, changes that, at times, centered on and centralized slavery. In addition, because meanings are not set, each time the statements associated with the discourse appear, the specific ideological purposes to which they are deployed must be discerned. Therefore less empowered persons and groups not only may lay claim to discursive statements, but in doing so they may produce meanings that are not already determined by or attached to the interests of another, more powerful group. Groups with greater and lesser power *all participate* in the creation and re-creation of meanings according to their differing agendas. All may recast discursive statements with different ideological consequences.[29]

The success or failure of a particular group's assertion of meaning lies not so much in the particular statements deployed, as in the various groups' dramatically differing degrees of access to communication networks, to economic and educational opportunities, to modes of cultural production, to legislative and judicial bodies. Jacksonian (white) Democrats succeeded in part, again as Saxton has shown, because their mass, race-based politics made use of and was supported by the emergent penny-press, blackface minstrel shows, and western/frontier literature. Their political coalition developed out of and became large enough to propel further the racialization of suffrage requirements. Their access to media, culture, and politics enabled them to limit, *in a different way* from their elite predecessors, the inclusive potential of liberal theory. They were largely successful, as we shall see in the chapters that follow, in *normalizing* their version of natural rights and national identity, in normalizing differentiations based on perceived racial characteristics and white superiority, and in allocating to themselves the authority to define.

But it is crucial to understand that, if the logic of the discourse of natural rights and the logic of the discourse of national identity were not potentially more—or in a different way—inclusive, there would not have been a need for a racialist discourse to limit it. The creation and appropriation of racialist discourse, and its attachment to the discourse of national identity, solidified limits on national identity in a way that the earlier class-stratified structure had not. By drawing in the active and imagined participation of a far larger segment of the population, working- as well as middle- and many upper-class white men, racialized and masculine mass democracy created a basis for participating in politics that lasted well into the twentieth century.

The successful conflation during the nineteenth century of white supremacy and national identity does not mean that the inclusionary potential of the discourse of national identity, or of liberal theory, was exhausted by Jacksonian democracy. Nor has it been exhausted today. This discourse contains within its productive logic, as many have either exalted or worried over time, the potential for far more inclusion than historically has been realized. Dramatically uneven distributions of power have prevented fuller realization than is theoretically possible. In addition, it may be, as Mehta's analysis suggests, that residual—and I would add, newly emergent—social hierarchies will always limit *in some way* the inclusionary potential of this discourse. Yet as Ann Laura Stoler and Frederick Cooper (forthcoming) have recently argued, postmodern critiques of "bourgeois democracy give insufficient weight to the possibilities that universalistic notions of rights and participation can be deployed against the exclusions and oppression historically associated with them" (58).

Rather than accepting the common twentieth-century view of slavery as a mistake, an aberration, an institution peripheral to the real identity of the colonies, the republic, the nation, I view slavery—and later race—*as becoming integral to* U.S. national identity. Although I argue (following many others) that slavery—and later racialist discourse—was the means by which inside and outside were determined, this does not mean these are the necessary and inevitable ways in which inclusionary and exclusionary practices must operate. My focus on the changing meaning of the trope of revolutionary struggle and its authorization of rebellion enables us to perceive the historically specific purposes to which the discourse of national identity was invoked and deployed. Most significantly, I seek to recast what may be called dominant formulations of U.S. national identity from the at least published perspectives of those once enslaved and in other ways excluded from the national body.

This project grows out of and contributes to four distinct yet overlapping fields of critical and historical inquiry: African American studies, American studies, gender studies, and studies of colonialism. Recent histories of slavery and of free African Americans, scholarship on eighteenth- and nineteenth-century African American literature, and fictional and poetic works reimagining times prior to general emancipation provide the fundamental backdrop for my work (Blassingame, Bradley, Chase-Riboud, Foster, Giddings, Gilroy, Gutman, Genovese, Johnson, Jones, McDowell, McLaurin, Morrison, Peterson, Tate, Williams). Positing this field as central to conceptions of the United States contributes to recent developments in American studies, which increasingly seek to understand the United States as the coming together, often within dramatically uneven relations of power, of many different cultures, broadly categorized as European, African, indigenous American, and Asian (Castronovo, Karcher, Limerick, Nash, Nelson, Sundquist, Wald, Wiegman). In addition, my project provides another angle from which to understand the nineteenth-century rise of white supremacy, already well documented in relation to mass culture, democracy, and working-class identity formation (Noel, Roediger, Saxton). Further, I use modes of analysis developed in gender studies to ask, both of all of this secondary scholarship and of the primary materials that form the foundation of this book, how and on what terms are "men" created at different historical moments and in different cultural contexts, and how does gender operate separately from descriptions of human beings to code social, political, and geographical spaces, and relations of power (Leverenz, Scott)? Similarly, I draw upon modes of inquiry developed over the last decade by students of colonialism to ask in what ways was the United States fundamentally shaped by its dual status as an imperial and as a post-colonial power, by its relations with indigenous peoples and the descendants of Africans, its "own" internally colonized populations (Lowe, Said, Stoler and Cooper)?

Chapter 1 analyzes two competing myths of national development, both published in 1839, in the *Democratic Review* and the *Southern Literary Messenger,* that disagreed on slavery but nevertheless drew upon racialist discourse and supported the Democratic Party. I compare these accounts with documents written by African American men that protested their exclusion from political, social, and economic structures, the enslavement of their compatriots to the south, and the systematic racialization of suffrage requirements. In this and subsequent chapters, I trace the way in which various writers, almost exclusively male, seek to expand or delimit the inclusionary potential of the discourse of national identity by producing or foreclosing subject-positions from which to claim, speak, and act upon the statements associated with the discourse of national identity, particularly the trope of revolutionary struggle. My focus on male writers, Euroamerican and African American, accurately represents who used the trope of revolutionary struggle as recorded in the historical record. In analyzing the masculine character of this trope, the following chapters suggest why so few women laid claim to it. In the afterword, I consider the few instances in which women, African American and Euroamerican, engendered new meanings of this trope in the service of their own oppositional agendas.

By analyzing the newspaper press accounts of and debates concerning the *Amistad* and *Creole* rebellions, in chapters 2 and 3 I have created an archive of cultural material that indicates what it was possible to say publicly and in print about slave rebellion on ships. This archive contains not only accounts of the revolts and editorial interpretations, but records of court proceedings and judicial decisions, congressional debates, and diplomatic correspondence. These events provided opportunities for journalists, politicians, activists, religious leaders, diplomats, and lawyers—all of whom published in the newspaper press, and virtually all of whom were white men—and their readers and listeners to develop, articulate, and debate the appropriate role of slavery in the formation of U.S. national identity. In creating this archive, I have been influenced by recent scholarship that posits the newspaper press as a particularly significant mechanism for political and national identity formation (Anderson, Saxton).

Focused on Herman Melville's *Benito Cereno* (1855) and Frederick Douglass's *The Heroic Slave* (1853), chapters 4 and 5 build upon the previous chapters by situating these literary productions, which were originally published at least in part in the newspaper and periodical presses, in the same discursive field with other kinds of texts based on their thematic similarities. Emphasizing themes and rhetorics of a specific historical moment, rather than an author's intentions or biography, my method of cultural criticism brings forth new meanings from the literary texts under analysis. The questions that guide my inquiry were generated from debates regarding the salient issues at the texts' moments of production, publication, and reception. I ask, for example, how does each of the stories respond to the widespread prohibition of the authorization of slave rebellion? Does the text support the prohibition either by figuring slavery as a non-issue (as did the Constitution and supporters of the Union), or by drawing upon racialist logics of white supremacy as did slavery advocates? Or does the text create a way by which U.S. Americans might imagine the slave rebels to be righteous rebels, that is, both morally correct and endowed with natural rights such that they become worthy enough to claim the trope of revolutionary struggle? How do the stories handle the anxiety produced by the specter of slave rebellion? What kind of alliances and identifications are produced and foreclosed, and with what consequences? I recognize, in addition, differences in genre in order to ask: In what ways did the fiction operate differently from the newspaper archives? What cultural work did the stories perform that journalism could or would not? What issues did the fiction writers centralize that were not evident or were marginal in the newspaper press? How did they differently address social conventions and assumptions of hierarchy? Did they expand or contract the inclusionary potential of liberal theory?

My focus on shipboard rebellion particularly illuminates contradictions within formulations of national identity. Ships by their very nature are liminal spaces that move between state and national boundaries. Their involvement in trade and transportation, especially the international and domestic slave trades, complicates the legal and diplomatic issues raised by rebellions on board the ships. In international relations, the United States was conceived of as a nation among a community of nations, represented by the president and his administration. But in relation to matters such as slavery, which was a state rather than a federal institution, the United States was thought of as a confederation of sovereign states, administered by Congress. Thus slave rebellions that involved more than one national entity brought into conflict these two versions of U.S. national identity, posing to it a challenge of a special nature. But before pursuing these issues, first we turn to important developments of the historical moment under consideration in this study.

# Chapter One

# 1839: Rhetorics of Nation, Race, and Masculinity

## THE EMERGENCE OF WHITE SUPREMACY

It was a nation of *white men*, who formed and have administered our government, and every American should indulge that *pride* and *honor*, which is falsely called prejudice, and teach it to his children. Nothing else will preserve the *American name*, or the *American character.*   JUDGE ANDREW T. JUDSON in the case of Prudence Crandall vs. the State of Connecticut (1833)[1]

The increasing importance in the nineteenth century of a new notion of "whiteness" has now been well documented. Reginald Horsman (1981), for example, has traced connections between formulations of the "manifest destiny" of the United States to take over the North American continent and new scientific notions of innate and immutable racial differences and Anglo-Saxon superiority. He argues that otherwise diverse and myriad groups of light-skinned, largely European peoples joined together under the rubric of "white" in order to justify their appropriation of native lands and their subordination of peoples of color.[2] In contrast to the views of many New Englanders, who no longer lived along a frontier, the beliefs of Euroamerican southerners and westerners, formulated in their experiences of conflict with indigenous and enslaved peoples, created a fertile environment for the acceptance of or adherence to the racial hierarchy developed by phrenologists. Horsman nostalgically juxtaposes this absolute and inflexible version of racial inequality with earlier Enlightenment conceptions that understood racial difference as environmentally produced and theoretically changeable through education. Horsman presents the ideals of the Revolution and the Enlightenment as lost opportunities for more equitable relations between the races.

While largely agreeing with this general thesis, Alexander Saxton

(1990) refined specific aspects of Horsman's argument. Saxton offers the concepts of "soft" and "hard" racism as a corrective to Horsman's position that an earlier, more optimistic view of race relations was later replaced by a more pessimistic view. He argues that the "soft" racism of Enlightenment and New England thinkers, perpetuated into the nineteenth century by the National Republicans and later the Whigs, was in practice no less oppressive and exclusive than the "hard" racism of the Democrats, which figured peoples of color as of different species than Euroamericans. This formulation enables Saxton to avoid the trap into which Horsman fell, that of romanticizing the Enlightenment and the revolutionary fathers. But he also explains that the "soft" racist view was part of a larger system of republican thinking that conceptualized racial inequality as one among several important, and largely naturalized, hierarchical relations. This republican thinking had institutionalized a class oligarchy in the wake of the Revolution, and so long as it held sway, racial difference did not gain an independent saliency. By contrast, the "hard" racist view operated in tandem with an egalitarian impulse among Euroamerican men that challenged republican hierarchy, and with a federal policy that called for the rapid takeover of the territories. The racial character of the Democratic "white republic" that Saxton documents so well arose as a bulwark against people of color (of African and indigenous descent), particularly African American men, many of whom were newly freed, and who theoretically might otherwise have been incorporated into a society in which class divisions were substantially being challenged and reorganized.

Following on the heels of Saxton, David Roediger (1991) has best explained the racialization of the emerging working class. Roediger argues that the U.S. Revolution began a contestation of traditional hierarchies that enabled working Euroamericans to reconceptualize themselves as of a kind with those for whom they worked, to be "help," for example, rather than "servants." In the northern states, industrialization in the nineteenth century further eroded old economic relations even while slaveholding continued to expand to the south and west. Roediger argues that the U.S. working class was the only working class to develop in the context of a slaveholding society, and this proximity to racialized slavery helped produce a psychological benefit, which he calls the "wages of whiteness," among Euroamerican workers otherwise facing potentially oppressive new forms of wage labor. Whiteness enabled Euroamerican workers to differentiate themselves not only from those still enslaved, but from those dark-skinned people whom they now enthusiastically excluded from economic and educational opportunities, and political practices. Thus these workers helped to bring about and perpetuated the "hard" racism of the Democratic Party because it enabled them not only to conceptualize themselves as more free and independent than slaves, but to create meaningful differences between themselves and those whom they actively marginalized. These three important studies agree that the headlong expansion into the territories, sought by immigrant, agricultural, slaveholding, and industrial interests alike, fundamentally transformed class relations in the United States, and gave new and primary saliency to the idea of "whiteness."

What interests me is the way in which the tenuous coalition that made up the Democratic Party, together with a range of others to whom white male supremacy if not party affiliation was paramount, was able to transform the initial ideological import of the discourse of national identity. Let us reconsider for a moment John Adams's disdainful remark that apprentices, along with children, "Indians," "Negroes," and women, should have thought their bonds loosened by the revolutionaries' proclamations of liberty. Clearly Adams's assumptions of hierarchy had been challenged by the time of the election of Andrew Jackson in 1829, such that men who in earlier generations would have been apprentices or indentured were now often wage laborers and voting Democrats. These previously unenfranchised white men were able to lay claim to the inclusive potential of the discourse of national identity in order to become active participants in the political process. They successfully recast the notion of natural rights in the service of different interests—thereby with different ideological import—from that which predominated during the Revolution. Race figured significantly here because, although economic structures dramatically shifted and re-formed during the early nineteenth century, considerable differences in economic status among the Euroamerican population remained the norm. Now whiteness rather than property—all along with masculinity—determined one's access to political participation and economic opportunities.[3] In fact, masculinity gained a new visibility and an abiding significance as the conjoining figure that bridged the shift from class to race.[4]

Thus the Democrats and their allies brought forth a new subject-position, "all [white] men," from which to claim, articulate, and transform the discourse of national identity.[5] This subject-position, this authorized yet limited position from which to speak, write, and act, had always been potentially available, but had not yet been a realized aspect of the discourse. Yet it is crucial to understand that many other subject-positions also were potentially available, most of which had not been realized, and some of which were further foreclosed by the emergence of white supremacy. That the Democrats were successful in changing so dramatically the subject-position that would be authorized illustrates the way in which those who are empowered may change given a new set of conditions, rather than because of something intrinsic to them.

This chapter considers the way in which a range of writers claimed and sought to transform the discourse of national identity by asserting competing versions of national development. The first section analyzes two articles published in 1839 in major periodicals, unsigned but no doubt written by white men, that represent rival, but for that particular moment compatible, interests. The second section examines three pamphlets published independently in 1829, 1837, and 1840 by African American men whose political perspective lay more clearly in their opposition to slavery and the explicit racialization of the discourse of national identity than in any party affiliation (although they typically supported the Whigs). Their claim to the authorizing legacy of the Revolution was more dangerous and oppositional in this period than it would have been earlier because in this context they had been more explicitly excluded from citizenship; new assertions of white supremacy had more explicitly identified them as other. Crucial here is not the unity of these articulations, but rather the dispersal of the statements associated with the discourse, and the clearly conflicting ideological purposes to which they were invoked.

The writers discussed in the pages that follow fundamentally disagreed about what constituted true, relevant, or factual information, about what information to include, about the character of relations between peoples, about what had happened and why. Yet they each produced and meditated upon narratives of identity for the developing nation. Benedict Anderson's suggestive coda to *Imagined Communities* (1991), "The Biography of Nations," illuminates the process of identity formation for nations, comparing it to that for people. He argues that "[a]fter experiencing the physiological and emotional changes produced by puberty, it is impossible to 'remember' the consciousness of childhood." And because such a time "can not be remembered, [it] must be narrated" (204). But unlike persons, "[n]ations . . . have no clearly identifiable births, and their deaths, if they ever happen, are never natural" (205). In the case of nations, then, a narrative of identity needs to account not only for "childhood," as it were, but for birth itself. This narrative creates identity, not only from what is remembered, but—because such a time "can not be remembered"—from that which is forgotten. The forgotten—or as often that which is pushed aside, obscured, erased—shapes the identity as surely as the remembered, haunting the story told. Further, such a narrative produces a functional identity only so long as its structure is not too closely examined. For in revealing the narrative's constructed character, analysis disrupts that which makes the story compelling—its drama, heroism, and seeming inevitability and naturalness.[6] By juxtaposing several competing versions of national development, this chapter exposes what one narrative elides through what others "remember," revealing much of what is at stake in the story's telling.

Identifying some of the rhetorics of nation, race, and masculinity for this historical moment will enable us to discern the discursive fields in which debates regarding slave revolts on ships, considered in subsequent chapters, took place. As we have seen, the commonly invoked terms "rebellion," "revolt," and "revolution" were inflected with varied and often opposing meanings depending upon the contexts and populations under consideration. As we will see in the pages that follow, as the United States extended its influence across the North American continent, categories of race increasingly were attached to formulations of national identity, such that the legacy of the Revolution became the province of "all [white] men." How then to argue for the righteousness—natural rights and moral correctness—if indeed it was, of rebels under slavery?

## COMPETING MYTHOLOGIES OF NATIONAL DEVELOPMENT

In the two and a half decades following the War of 1812, massive increases in controlled territory and population and dramatic technological developments transformed the United States. The geographical area officially under the control of the U.S. government (in the form of states rather than territories) more than tripled in size, while the general population more than doubled. This quick and massive growth far exceeded any previous efforts at colonization by Europeans in North America. In 1803, President Jefferson had paid the French government for transferring to the U.S. government its claims to the native lands between the Mississippi River and the Rocky Mountains, some 823,000 square miles known as the Louisiana Territory. Jefferson intended his "purchase" to bring about his dream of the United States as a republic of independent yeoman farmers by providing sufficient land for the appropriation of the growing populace. In 1818, General Andrew Jackson aided the further expansion of the United States into the southern regions when his army invaded and took control of the Floridas. One year later, in the Adams-Onís Treaty, Spain ceded its claim to this land mass to the U.S. government, and the representatives of these two national entities agreed upon a boundary between their territorial claims in North America (Blum et al. 164, 178). The U.S. government represented these agreements as authorization for what became an aggressive campaign to populate the territories, evident, for example, in the increasingly easy conditions under which land claims could be purchased by farmers.[7]

In contrast to Jefferson's dream of a republic of self-sufficient farmers, most who pursued the appropriation of native lands were interested in acquiring greater wealth through planting cash crops (Blum et al. 162). In areas to the south and west of Virginia and the Carolinas, the creation of new slaveholding states accompanied the "removal" of the indigenous populations and the planned increase of the enslaved population by as many as ten times.[8] In the "free" states to the north, the agricultural population increased dramatically from five to fifteen million in forty years, with a similar corresponding decrease in indigenous populations.

One of the most crucial sources of conflict among rival Euroamerican groups in the second quarter of the nineteenth century was the question of whether slavery would be allowed to expand into the territories or would be confined to the states where it already existed. This question pitted northern industrial interests and western agricultural interests, which wanted to preserve the territories for white labor, against those of southern slaveholders, who wanted to extend slavery in order to protect their numbers and their influence in national politics.[9] They all agreed, however, upon the need for the rapid takeover and "development" of the territories.

## A Free-Soil Mythology

"The Course of Civilization" (1839), an article published in the *Democratic Review,* the periodical organ of the Democratic Party,[10] creates an extensive mythology concerning the origins of the Anglo-American race.[11] After 1815 the term Anglo-American—used interchangeably with Anglo-Saxon—was ethnically shorn from its roots in pre-1066 Britain and was used increasingly in the United States to describe almost any person of European descent who was willing to identify with the label (Horsman 94). This term masked ethnic and "racial" differences among light-skinned peoples and drew them into an alliance based on notions of their own "racial" superiority. Indeed, by the 1850s, many defined democracy and an innate desire for liberty as "racial" rather than political or social in origin, as part of an Anglo-Saxon essence, and therefore as realizable only by people with those hereditary traits (Frederickson 101).

The mythology produced by "The Course of Civilization" represents the teleological development of "man from a state of savage individualism to that of an individualism more elevated, moral, and refined," from primitive organizations, through various intermediary forms of society, until finally reaching "the last order of civilization" (209)—the democratic. Each state of previous society is but a stepping-stone to democracy, which in the United States signifies the equal meeting of individuals. Thus, like Locke's construction of the natural world, this mythology posits in the colonial past the necessary conditions for the fulfillment of its argument, the rise of democracy in the United States:

The peculiar duty of this country has been to exemplify and embody a civilization in which the rights, freedom, and mental and moral growth of individual man should be made the highest end of all social restrictions and laws. To this result the discipline of Providence has tended from the earliest history of the Anglo-American race. (211)

Notice first the assertion that the needs and desires of "individual man" have been at the center of civilized development in "this country" since its inception. Even a quick review of the communal project of the Puritans is enough to problematize this assertion (Miller). In addition, the economic and physical conditions under which Europeans created colonies in every area of North America demanded communal rather than individual effort. These repeated assertions of individualism as the path of development in the United States obscure the fundamental dependence of Europeans and their descendants on one another in their appropriation of native lands in North America, as well as their dependence on the assistance of indigenous peoples and the labor of African Americans.

The centrality of natural rights to "the peculiar duty of this country" and in the service of "all men" (Declaration of Independence) was not an aspect of colonization prior to the Revolution, but rather was produced by the discourse of national identity. More remarkably, this passage allocates this duty and its rewards solely to the "Anglo-American race." In this schema, a racially coded community made up of individualized entities undertook and created a legacy of teleological development toward "the last order of civilization." Thus, not only does the assertion of individualism obscure the interaction of different communities (European, indigenous, African American), but the privileging of the "Anglo-American race" discursively erases the very presence, as well as the acts, of these non-European, non-Anglo peoples.

This paradoxical assertion of individualism and community ("Anglo-American race") marks the free-soil appropriation of the discourse of national identity. On the one hand, this appropriation emphasizes and expands upon the Enlightenment notion of the individual as the source of argument and government to include the source and foundation of economic structures and cultural forms. This appropriation supports the development of the free market system, in which each individualized entity competes for access to raw materials, capital, technology, labor, and so forth, and ascends or descends according to its ability to compete. On the other side of the paradox, this appropriation constructs the "Anglo-American race" as the community from which these individualized entities emerge. The specific racializing of this community discursively excludes members of differently coded communities from being "individuals," and by implication, from participation in economic, cultural, and political structures.

"The Course of Civilization" also figures the earliest members of the "Anglo-American race" in North America as men "of the pilgrim stock" (211). This construction privileges the people of New England over those of Virginia as the originators of this rise to democratic institutions, and it posits the trope of revolutionary struggle as descended from and the product of the "peculiar duty" of New Englanders. In addition, the discursive erasure of racialized slavery takes on additional meaning in this new set of conditions. As I discussed in my introduction, earlier factions with opposing positions on slavery were able to come together by excluding slavery from the Constitution, and in so doing they formed not just a confederation of states, but a new kind of nation. But now the erasure of racialized slavery marked a split between what, since the Missouri Compromise (1820),[12] had become known as the North and South. The erasure of both black people and slavery in the mythology of "The Course of Civilization" marks the emergence of a new set of interests, one that desires the absence of both black people and slavery. This desire explains why these assertions of Anglo-Saxon superiority often appear in isolation rather than together with assertions of African or indigenous inferiority. This text thus offers an authorizing mythology for this new alliance, later organized into first the Free-Soil Party, and later the Republican Party. The doctrine of free-soil defined freedom anew as the absence of both African Americans and slavery.

## A Slaveholding Mythology

In contrast to the mythology of the "Northern" text, "The Course of Civilization," by the late 1830s powerful slaveholders and their supporters, far from discursively erasing the existence of blacks and slavery, represented their "peculiar institution" as a positive good for slave as well as slaveholder. The South's conception of itself as a slaveholding society was complex, with two divergent yet compatible branches of thought. One position asserted that a patriarchal model was best for all societies because it was based on a clear hierarchy that bound all together through relations of responsibility and dependence. This position recognized the inherent humanity of the African race, despite its supposed inferiority, and defended slavery as an institution aside from racial slavery. The second position was that of Herrenvolk democracy, which posited a democratic and egalitarian society among the master race and cast Africans as subhuman and therefore unfit for membership in the republic (Frederickson 61–64). While disagreeing to some extent as to the appropriate social structure among white men, these ideological constructions agreed on both the supposedly innate inferiority of African Americans to Euroamericans and the supposed contentment of African Americans with their enslaved status.

An article from the *Southern Literary Messenger* entitled "Domestic Slavery" (1839) takes up the second of these two positions by presenting a vision of slavery as an institution, both political and domestic, that creates liberty and equality among white men and "contentment, cheerfulness and even gaiety," among the "negro laboring class" (686). This text creates a different kind of mythology, which represents the United States as descended from the "great" slavehold-ing republics of Greece and Rome and as having in common with them a people whose virtuous character befits them for republican government. For "[i]t does not depend solely upon constitutions and laws, whether a people shall be free or not. They must desire liberty in order to win it, and they must understand and appreciate, in order to preserve it. . . . It depends on the character of a people, and on that alone, whether they can live under free institutions or not" (677–78). A central element of the discourse of national identity, the once-thought inalienable rights to life, liberty, and the pursuit of happiness (the basis of free institutions), far from being endowed in "all men," were now dependent on "the character of a people." Yet this character is also in part formed by the system of slavery, which purportedly prepares the mind and feelings of the master for the enjoyment of liberty and participation in republican institutions.

In the United States this mutually constitutive system of freedom and slavery is particularly advanced (so this argument goes) because the unmistakable distinction of racial difference creates a deep bond among the master class:

[This distinction] is certainly well calculated to inspire the humblest white man with a high sense of his own comparative dignity and importance, to see a whole class below him in the scale of society. . . . All classes of white men are alike interested to maintain this distinction. . . . Hence arises a sympathy among white men, extremely favorable to republican equality. . . . Color alone is here the badge of distinction, the true mark of aristocracy; and all who are white, are equal, in spite of the variety of occupation. (678–79)

By asserting the superiority of "white men," this argument makes visible slaveholders' understanding of the interdependence of white freedom and black slavery. Notice that the important color in this quotation is "white," rather than "black"; whiteness is figured as "the badge of distinction," the mark of equality. Rather than erasing the presence of enslaved people, as in "The Course of Civilization," this text welcomes them in their subordination, which is presented as serving a higher cause. The enslaved are in turn figured as "contented from necessity" because "the eternal brand is upon [their] face" (686), the mark of caste that would deny true freedom even to those emancipated (as in the North).

This assertion of unequivocal racial difference functions ideologically in at least three important ways: first, it obscures class differences among the racialized master class in order to make light-skinned people think of themselves as equal "in spite of the variety of occupation," thereby pulling poor whites into an alliance with wealthy slaveholders. Second, this assertion naturalizes the system of enslavement by referring to a supposedly innate and immutable category such as "race," with purportedly clear subcategories. And third, this assertion masks the presence of mixed-race people and any supposed evidence of sexual relations among people of different races, including the rape of enslaved women by slaveholders.[13] Yet the existence of mixed-race people undermines the very notion of immutable race. This naturalized system of enslavement, based on the premise of dominant and subordinate races, presages both the often-cited *Negroes and Negro "Slavery": The First an Inferior Race: The Latter Its Normal Condition* (1853) by John Van Evrie and Alexander Stephens's "Cornerstone Speech" (1861) heralding the foundation of the Confederacy.[14] Despite these important differences in regard to the representation of the appropriate fate of African Americans, the mythologies of "The Course of Civilization" and "Domestic Slavery" agree on the superiority of the Anglo-Saxon race and the supremacy of "whiteness."

Also published in 1839, Samuel Morton's *Crania Americana* led the phrenologically derived ethnology, the vanguard of new scientific theories of racial difference. It developed a clear hierarchy, from the Anglo-Saxon/Caucasian race to the indigenous peoples of the New World (the Toltecan race) to the native inhabitants of Africa (except ancient Egyptians who were classified with the Toltecans), from measurements of skulls. These theories were popularly debated in many cultural arenas during the antebellum period; by the 1850s periodicals such as *Harper's* and the more progressive *Putnam's* were publishing discussions exploring the possible number of original human races.[15]

This hierarchy of races was also gender coded in order to naturalize further and thereby mask the inequalities of power. For example,

Francis Parkman's comment that the "Germanic race, and especially the Anglo-Saxon branch of it, is peculiarly masculine, and, therefore, peculiarly suited for self government" (qtd. in Horsman 184) adds masculine gender to the notion of democracy as part of an Anglo-Saxon essence. It makes explicit the masculine coding of the republican subject and indicates how this articulated assumption about gender may then be used to bolster an argument for white supremacy. Similarly, "The Course of Civilization" argues that, in the development of democratic institutions, the highest form of civilization, "the men sufficient to accomplish the work needed to be peculiar men," not "striplings made effeminate by the luxuries of courts," but men with "the manly spirit of courage and endurance" (211). The notion of "manly spirit" takes on an especially aggressive and acquisitive quality when viewed in the context of Andrew Jackson's campaigns of "removal" of the indigenous populations from what became the southeastern United States and the formulations of Manifest Destiny that appeared in the context of the war with Mexico.

Racialist discourses constructed Africans and their descendants in opposition to this masculine Anglo-Saxon model, figuring them as naturally brutal, savage, even cannibalistic, but as becoming submissive, cheerful, and productive under the proper training of a superior race. Slaveholders calmed their own fears by representing African Americans as an unresisting, feminized race, then positing that supposed lack of desire for liberty as justification for their enslavement. In a very different context, T. B. Thorpe, writing for *Harper's Magazine*, characterized enslaved people as prone to the feminine faults of imitation, jealousy, and "wrangling." Thorpe also argues that "the religious feelings of the negro are easily touched and excited," but he cautions that they can lead to superstition if not firmly directed (461), a fate to which women are purportedly prone. In a society that increasingly came to associate masculinity with economic gain and at least minimal political participation, the denial of the right to vote and exclusion from virtually all but the most menial jobs served to exclude African American men from the realm of recognized manhood, and thereby to deny them normative masculinity in relation to the increasing numbers of empowered white men.[16]

A powerful new process of appropriation, deployed largely but not solely by supporters of the Democratic Party, interfaced this gender-coded hierarchy of races with the discourse of national identity, thereby bringing forth a new subject-position: "all [white] men." This process gave divided and increasingly opposed Euroamerican men, and the white women who supported them, a unifying factor that was meant to ensure that, whatever else happened, the United States would remain as it mostly had been, a white man's country. It added a new naturalizing force, supported by scientific research, to the Compact between the States, which recast and further complicated the limits and erasures of the discourse of national identity.

### OPPOSITIONAL MOVEMENT

I must observe to my brethren that at the close of the first Revolution in this country, with Great Britain, there were but thirteen States in the union; now there are twenty-four, most of which are slave-holding States, and the whites are dragging us around in chains and in handcuffs, to their new States and Territories to work their mines and farms, to enrich them and their children—and millions of them believing firmly that we being a little darker than they, were made by our Creator to be an inheritance to them and their children for ever—the same as a parcel of brutes. Are we MEN!!—I ask you, O my brethren! are we MEN? . . . How could we be so submissive to a gang of men?
WALKER'S *Appeal* (1829)

The pervasive authority of the discourse of national identity meant that those men seeking inclusion within the nation were most likely to base their arguments on its masculinist logic. As I have argued, those largely agrarian, Euroamerican male workers who supported and benefited from the so-called extension of the franchise argued for their political empowerment by asserting that the Declaration of Independence authorized common men.[17] They reemphasized a supposedly common masculinity as they challenged class distinctions and invested race with a new salience. Their arguments, while proceeding according to the logic of the discourse of national identity, also transformed that discourse by changing the rules of inclusion and exclusion, by successfully removing the property clauses from and adding the word "white" to suffrage requirements (in the newer western states universal white manhood suffrage was adopted from the beginning). Similarly, African American men who argued against this change, and who protested against slavery and racial prejudice and discrimination more generally, typically did so, at least in their public and published declarations, according to the logic of the discourse of national identity. The remainder of this chapter will be concerned with their arguments. But first we need to account for the specific context of abolition out of which those arguments emerged.

Abolitionist rhetoric during the revolutionary period posited the ethical and theoretical equality of all peoples in the eyes of God, despite any perceived differences in culture, level of development, or achievement. Many abolitionists of European descent drew upon the racial theories of Samuel Stanhope Smith, who argued that Africans' lower level of development could be remedied, and the darker race thereby regenerated, through education and conversion to Christianity. Although a few, such as James Otis, Thomas Paine, and Isaac Skillman, called for immediate emancipation on the basis of the natural rights of man, more common was concern for the sin of enslaving committed by Europeans-now-Euroamericans. New England clergy led the fight for abolition as part of the colonies-now-states' redemption from servitude to Britain.[18] After the Revolution, Northern policymakers, judicial and legislative, applied to the enslaved population the notion of freedom as merely the absence of slavery. Thus, although slavery was gradually abolished, the notion of racial regeneration was abandoned, the material conditions for most African Americans did not change dramatically from that under slavery, and racial prejudice and discrimination continued unabated, and later, as we have seen, increased.

During these early years, African and African American men, such as Benjamin Banneker, Prince Hall, Absalom Jones, and Richard Allen, published pamphlets that, according to Herbert Aptheker (1965), outlined nearly every argument against slavery to be developed in the later abolitionist movement. Working from the premise that differences in development resulted from differing access to education, religion, and resources, these writers argued particularly vociferously against any notion of innate racial inferiority and denied the supposed complacency of the enslaved. Free African Societies sprung up in Philadelphia, Newport, R.I., New York City, and Boston, all of which organized against slavery and the kidnapping of free blacks (Aptheker 1965, 27–30).

Although African American women participated in these societies, in the early nineteenth century women like Mary Battys, Grace Douglass, Clarissa Lawrence, and Hannah Morris began to form their own organizations.[19] Benevolent societies for the relief of the needy and informal insurance companies were common. In the 1830s, women organized literary circles both for their own edification and to demonstrate their abilities, and they founded the first antislavery societies for "females of color" (Sterling 113). In the years that followed, African American women organized with African American men, with Euroamerican women, and within multiracial antislavery societies, putting on lectures and fairs, raising money, and getting petitions against slavery distributed, signed, and collected. Thanks to Dorothy Sterling (1984) and Dorothy Porter (1970), collections of organizational documents and manuscript letters record the major roles these women played in activist movements against slavery. The class and gender politics of free black communities in the North, and of the broader U.S. society of which they were a part, help explain why the surviving historical record is less rich with antislavery rationales by women. I will return to this issue at some length in my afterword. What needs to be understood here is that, although many women organized against slavery, African American women—and Euroamerican women for that matter—did not publish many treatises against it, nor attempt to recast the discourse of national identity in the service of their own agendas.

Largely in response to emancipation acts in the Northern states and the increasing number of organizations founded by African Americans both against slavery and for their own edification, many prominent Euroamerican male leaders across the Northern and Southern states together established the American Colonization Society in

1816. With men such as Henry Clay, senator and then Speaker of the House, and John Randolf, the leading Virginia politician, as its founders, this society was the leading proponent of the proposed institution of colonies in Africa for African Americans emancipated by the new laws. It received endorsements from a variety of groups, such as reform clergy, gradualist antislavery societies, several Protestant denominations, fourteen state legislatures, and many prominent white political figures, including James Madison, James Monroe, and Daniel Webster (Ripley 5).

The American Colonization Society (ACS) developed an abolitionist discourse that called for private and gradual manumission and the expatriation of the freed slaves to Africa, with the intention that the freed slaves should create Christian missions and so bring religion to the "dark continent." This discourse figured African Americans as undeserving of enslavement and as capable of acquiring and disseminating Christianity, but as also unfit for membership in the U.S. republic. Consider, for example, these words of Henry Clay:

From [the freed slaves'] condition, and the unconquerable prejudice resulting from their colour, they never could amalgamate with the free whites of this country. It was desirable, therefore, as it respected them, and the residue of the population of the country, to drain them off. [While] Various schemes of colonization had been thought of . . . [I have] a decided preference for some part of Africa.[20]

Clay argues that since free blacks could never be fully incorporated into society, because of the "unconquerable prejudice" of white U.S. Americans, it would be better for them to go somewhere else. The more generous proponents of this proposal argued that it would enable the expatriates to develop a separate society under their own direction. Clay's argument illustrates that within colonization proposals antislavery is linked to "unconquerable prejudice." It was this connection, and not only the tolerance but tacit support for such prejudice, that was most strongly attacked by free black people.

In the 1820s, abolition among white people was dominated by evangelical Christians, often drawn from the New England clergy, who were missionary in spirit and interested in reform, descendants of those clergymen who helped create a conducive environment for antislavery during the Revolution.[21] The discourse of the ACS appealed not only to these evangelicals; it offered a solution to a number of differently empowered white groups, with seemingly conflicting interests. By calling for emancipation and for the development of missions, this discourse appealed to the reformers' missionary tendencies and to their desire to end slavery. Yet it also calmed more general fears among Euroamericans about the growing number of free black people in Northern society (Ripley 5). In addition, it appealed to two different factions in areas without emancipation acts and with large enslaved populations. It provided an outlet for those whose antislavery feelings were too strong to be kept entirely silent and a potential solution for those who wanted to rid slaveholding areas of free blacks (David Brion Davis, 1975, 199–200).[22]

Building upon their already considerable history of opposition to slavery and racial prejudice, free black men and women opposed the colonization schemes of the ACS. As early as 1817, James Forten, the veteran of the Revolutionary War whose son helped to write the *Appeal of Forty Thousand*, discussed in my introduction, led a protest meeting of three thousand African Americans in Philadelphia to oppose colonization (Davis 1975, 34). This meeting was held under the auspices of Richard Allen's Bethel African Methodist Episcopal Church, illustrating the particular opposition of black Christians to the ACS.[23] This meeting was followed by at least three others in the following two years (Ripley 6). This spirit of opposition to what black convention leaders, newspaper writers, and pamphleteers later figured as the plans of white reformers and slaveholders to maintain slavery while deporting free black people was a crucial impetus to the further development of black abolitionist discourse. This newly inflected discourse challenged the ACS's claims that African Americans would be better off in Africa by asserting their claims to citizenship in the United States, much as the African American men who protested their exclusion from the elective franchise did in subsequent years. Rather than being an activity that supported only their own interests, C. Peter Ripley argues, "For free blacks, asserting their citizenship, opposing colonization, and creating a place for themselves in American society were acts that threatened slavery" (7).

Indeed, black abolitionist discourse continued fundamentally to challenge the "unconquerable prejudice" named by Henry Clay, while further refining itself in response to the new threat of deportation. During the late 1820s and the 1830s it was produced and disseminated, not only as earlier, in the pages of various pamphlets, but in the new venues of the first newspapers owned and edited by African Americans, such as *Freedom's Journal*, *The Rights of All*, *The Weekly Advocate*, and *The Colored American*, and in speeches at the increasing number of antislavery meetings and national and state conventions.[24] It was then further transformed in the 1840s and 1850s as the goals of many white abolitionists and black activists diverged, as often more militant, formerly enslaved people increasingly became prominent spokespeople within the abolitionist movement (Ripley 23–29), and as sectional tension increased over the extension of slavery into the territories. Despite the pervasiveness of new discourses of white supremacy, and despite the political and economic power supporting the dissemination of these racialist discourses, Northern free black people, primarily but not exclusively men, continued publicly to challenge dominant assertions of their inferiority and their unfitness for membership in the republic.[25]

These rhetorical challenges usually drew upon statements associated with the discourse of national identity. They had different emphases at different historical moments, but tended to take one of three forms: appeals to the logic of racial regeneration, assertions of a common masculinity, or claims to the trope of revolutionary struggle. The first accepted the republican virtues of morality, industry, and moderation as indicators of man's natural state of being free, equal, and independent, and encouraged African Americans to acquire or replicate these virtues. It largely acceded to assertions of their inferiority, but also argued that their degraded condition had been forced upon them by slavery and was now maintained through the system of racial prejudice that denied them access to quality education, public services, and other means of improvement. This argument drew upon the Enlightenment belief in one set of original parents, Adam and Eve, explaining cultural and physical differences by way of different environmental conditions. This belief did not include or accept the notion of immutable difference, but instead cast all along collateral but not equally developed trajectories toward perfection. Thus this first argument challenged any assertions of *innate* and immutable inferiority of African Americans by casting their condition as socially, economically, and culturally determined. It called for free people of color to improve themselves through the acquisition of literacy and Christianity, and to aid others in doing so, in order to develop and to prove their innate capacity for learning and morality. This attempt to prove their natural equality seemed particularly cogent at a time when so many forces within the United States were producing and disseminating the model of an immutable hierarchy among races. This black abolitionist discourse, encouraged and supported by powerful white abolitionists such as William Lloyd Garrison, was most prevalent until the early 1840s.

Before the alliance of black activists and Garrison abolitionists was formed in 1831, and then again after many of these activists began to lose faith in their strategy of moral and intellectual improvement in 1840, African American men often figured their exclusion from political and economic arenas as an incorrect or unjust application of the discourse of national identity. They frequently charged the U.S. government with being contradictory and argued that the Declaration of Independence's assertion of the equal and natural rights of "all men" should apply to them as well. This rhetorical strategy based their right to inclusion on the assertion of a common masculinity, which they figured as innate and which they sought to demonstrate, despite the fact that they were largely excluded from the means through which normative masculinity was constructed, such as service in the militia, bearing of firearms, duty as jurists, and casting ballots (Baker 245). Emphasizing gender over race and status, they created the subject-position "all MEN," which the various rhetorical, theoretical, and discursive appropriative strategies of Euroamericans had denied to them.

This second strategy employed by African American men paralleled that of the largely agrarian and Euroamerican male population, which successfully had translated their claims for inclusion into changes in suffrage requirements. That these Euroamerican men were more successful than African American men in translating their claims into actual political power does not signify that Euroamerican men had a more sophisticated or even a significantly different argument. Rather, it indicates two different but related factors. First, it points to the great disparity between the material conditions of most African American men and most Euroamerican men who were enfranchised by the changes in suffrage requirements; the satisfaction of this second population was much more crucial to the welfare of the growing nation because of their larger numbers and because they wielded considerably greater economic power, both individually and collectively. And second, it indicates the growing power and pervasiveness of discourses of racial hierarchy and white superiority throughout the Euroamerican population.

The third rhetorical challenge of African American men was based on the trope of revolutionary struggle, and it was thereby threatening both to Southern slaveholders and to the national alliance. During the Revolution, the most economically and politically powerful Euroamericans, such as merchants, lawyers, and slaveholders, were able to come together because of the exclusion of racial slavery from their revolutionary agenda, which ensured the further exclusion of the enslaved population from the national community. When black activists claimed the right to revolt for the enslaved population, or, similarly but more moderately, the right of resistance for themselves, they not only challenged the dominance of slaveholders, they disrupted a fundamental principle of the Compact between the States—the agreement to keep slavery a state rather than a federal issue. By claiming the authorizing rhetoric of the Union, these activists gave that rhetoric new ideological import. For their invocation of the right to revolt threatened rather than supported the Compact between the States, and sought a reconfiguration of the political, economic, and social structures undergirding the nation.

In 1829 David Walker wrote *An Appeal . . . to the Coloured Citizens of the World,* the first sustained, published challenge to slavery and white supremacy authored by an African American man in the United States. Drawing upon a by all accounts deeply felt and lived religiosity, Walker challenged colonization, counseled moral and intellectual improvement, appealed to the manliness of enslaved men, and called for an end to what he called the "submissiveness" of the enslaved population. Walker successfully distributed his pamphlet not only in the Northern states, but to various sympathizers through sailors on trade routes to the South. His arguments—and their appearance in written form among persons of different statuses and racial backgrounds—were deemed so incendiary that the governors of Georgia and North Carolina convened special sessions of their legislatures to discuss how to deal with the situation. Many repressive laws regarding literacy, assembly, and the mobility and status of free blacks subsequently were passed in Georgia, North Carolina, Mississippi, and Louisiana (Aptheker 1965, 45–50). A year after his pamphlet's publication, Walker was found dead under mysterious circumstances, possibly the victim of poisoning.[26] Southern planters had offered a reward for his murder. His probable murder further demonstrates the disruptive power of the positions he articulated and disseminated, and the nonrhetorical discursive practices deployed to mute them.[27]

Walker's *Appeal* includes a preamble and four articles, devoted respectively to "our wretchedness in consequence of slavery," "ignorance," "the preachers of the religion of Jesus Christ," and "the colonization scheme." This structure situates the *Appeal* within a rhetorical tradition of political pamphleteering and argumentation related to the founding national documents to which he explicitly refers, the Declaration of Independence and the U.S. Constitution. Although our focus on rhetorics of nation, race, and masculinity precludes a thorough analysis of this document, not only the breadth of learning Walker marshals, but his sense of the interconnectedness of the issues he examines are worthy of note.[28]

In the passage that heads this section, Walker presents a vision of U.S. development that differs fundamentally from and is opposed to both of the mythologies of development analyzed earlier. He notes the predominance of slaveholding among states newly added to the Union and foregrounds the dependence of the burgeoning U.S. economy on enslaved labor: "the whites are dragging us around in chains and in handcuffs, to their new States and Territories to work their mines and farms, to enrich them and their children" (55). Thus Walker "remembers" some of which has been forgotten or elided in "The Course of Civilization"'s and "Domestic Slavery"'s narratives of nationhood. Like "Domestic Slavery," the *Appeal* makes evident and disrupts the erasure of African Americans and their labor in "The Course of Civilization." And like "Domestic Slavery," the *Appeal* figures African Americans as subordinated, "in chains and handcuffs," but as still crucial labor. Perhaps dangerously close to the vision presented by "Domestic Slavery," the *Appeal* here marks its perspective primarily by way of its tone.

Indeed, the overwhelming tones of the *Appeal* are outrage, indignation, and frustration. Walker's ubiquitous use of underlining and multiple exclamation points marks his attempt to translate into print what he would otherwise do with his voice in orating, to make inert paper writhe with his emotional critique. One can imagine his voice becoming louder and more forceful as he moves through the passage that heads this section, changing from relatively calm observation to a shouted outrage. Walker's explicit address to "the Coloured Citizens of the World, but in particular, and very expressly, to those of the United States of America," may account for his approach. Although he draws upon all three of the rhetorical strategies outlined above, Walker articulates them with a special challenge to African American men.

For example, Walker argues for self and communal improvement through "education and religion": "You have to prove to the Americans and the world, that we are MEN, and not *brutes, as we have been represented, and by millions treated. Remember, to let the aim of your labours among your brethren . . . be the dissemination of education and religion*" (68–69; emphasis in original). His use of "brutes" betrays his dismay at and discomfort with the status of enslaved people—and many free blacks—and urges the creation of proof of the status of African Americans as human beings. His equation of the human category with "MEN" reproduces the discourse of national identity's privileging of masculinity. It challenges assertions by both the free-soil and slaveholding mythologies of the racialized subject-position "all [white] men" with another, emphatically gendered position: "all MEN." By challenging the explicit racializing of the community constructed by the discourse of national identity with an assertion of nonracially coded masculinity, Walker's *Appeal* thereby challenges the appropriative strategies of Euroamericans.

Walker quotes all of the first and most of the second paragraph of the Declaration of Independence, but he singles out the opening of the second paragraph for particular attention: "ALL men are created EQUAL!! that they *are endowed by their creator with certain unalienable rights;* that among these are life, *liberty,* and the pursuit of happiness!!" (114; emphasis in original). In singling out the words "all," "equal," and "liberty," Walker claims the trope of revolutionary struggle by asserting that this sentence has an obvious, self-evident meaning that can be located in the specific words of this phrase, aside from the historical circumstances in which the phrase was written and understood. Further, by emphasizing the "creator" as the source of "unalienable rights," he simultaneously supports the universal and transhistorical nature of the Declaration's assertion and challenges any limits placed on who may claim those rights. Some U.S. Americans did find their rhetorical and discursive practices contradictory. But for many others, the "obvious" meaning of the Declaration did not apply to the enslaved population, whose condition was the foundation of both slaveholders' freedom and the new republic's economic prosperity. Ironically, Walker's strategy was thus to limit the numerous possible interpretations of the Declaration's assertion that existed at the time of the Revolution—interpretations that included the right to hold property in persons—by asserting "all MEN" to be its self-evident meaning.

Walker then reproduces that section of the Declaration articulating the colonial policymakers' appropriation of Locke's right to rebellion: "But when a long train of abuses and usurpation, pursuing invariably the same object, evinces a design to reduce them under absolute despotism, it is their *right,* it is their *duty,* to throw off such government, and to provide new guards for their future security" (114; emphasis in original). But rather than trying to explain to a white audience why slaves are justified in throwing off their bonds, Walker chastises what he sees as the submissive behavior of enslaved men and calls on them to assert themselves: "O, my God!—in sorrow I must say it, that my colour, all over the world, have a mean, servile spirit. . . . Oh! my coloured brethren . . . when shall we arise from this death-like apathy?— And be men!!" (100). In specifying a choice between "aris[ing]" or having "death-like apathy," Walker articulates a version of the revolutionary choice between liberty and death. Recall that in Locke's schema, rebellion was a last, desperate if justified, action, but when translated into the trope of revolutionary struggle, rebellion became commonplace, the duty of every true "American." In claiming the trope and appealing to a common notion of masculinity, this passage uses the same logic: to "arise" is a duty and the mark of manhood. While Walker's desire to inspire and even to incite makes sense given his aims and the context in which he was working, this stance obviously is problematic in relation to those, particularly women, who chose not to flee or overtly to resist slavery because they constituted the primary support system for others. Walker's logic makes no provision for this population, defining refusal to resist as "a mean, servile spirit," or even worse, brutishness and semihuman stature.

The conflation of manhood and resistance that characterizes the trope of revolutionary struggle is more evident still in this passage from the *Appeal*: "Now, I ask you, had you not rather be killed than to be a slave to a tyrant, who takes the life of your mother, wife and children . . . [why do we] so meanly submit to their murderous lashes, to which neither the indians nor any other people under Heaven would submit?" (64, 66). Walker constructs the status of the male persona in terms of the condition of his female family members, his mother, wife, and children. Locke formulates "Man" as the protector and provider for supposedly dependent "children, servants, wives and slaves" (II 2). Walker similarly argues that to be a slave is not to be able to protect one's female "dependents" from a "tyrant." Although this may well have not been Walker's intention, the logic of both scenarios positions female family members as the rightful property of the active male persona. Freedom and manhood are produced through and dependent upon his right to this female "property."

A primary tone of the *Appeal* is its frustration with the supposed lack of fortitude and resolve, implicitly the lack of manliness, of enslaved men. Of course numerous scholars in the last century and a half have worked to document the resistance of the enslaved population. But what is needed here is not a refutation of the submissiveness of the enslaved population, but rather an awareness of the pervasiveness of natural rights theory and its assertion that "all men" are innately endowed with an uncrushable desire for liberty. Walker's evident frustration with what he perceives to be the submissiveness of the enslaved population may, for him as for many if not most of his era, indicate that liberal theory formed part of the discursive system by which he made sense of the world. Or his representation of frustration may simply be a rhetorical device to spur new thinking and action. Whichever the case, it is important to understand that if one accepts the logic that all humankind is endowed above all else with a desire for freedom, then those who are subordinated—especially those who are or who appear to be willingly subordinated—must not be fully human. This logic, of course, underpins slavery advocates' discourse of white superiority and apparently represents David Walker's fear.

But if one sees the desire for liberty as an aspect of liberal political *theory*, as part of a pervasive discursive system rather than as an aspect of the natural world, then it need no longer appear as a requirement for being human. From this vantage point, the supposedly submissive behavior of enslaved people need no longer be understood as a sign of their inferiority; the representation of this behavior, in a wide variety of texts, including Walker's *Appeal* and those of slavery advocates, may be seen as part of the hegemonic functioning of liberal theory rather than as an accurate representation of the behavior of enslaved people.[29] Although only a small number of large-scale rebellions were either planned or executed in the United States, scholars have documented virtually constant resistance by enslaved people in less visible forms. Rather than reproducing the work of these scholars, and so accepting the terms set by natural rights theory, I have chosen to focus on the discursive conditions that made resistance the mark of humanity and manhood. I emphasize this point not to construct David Walker as a dupe of his society, but to foreground the power and pervasiveness of natural rights theory and the discourse of national identity that was based upon it. By detaching the grid of natural rights from our critical strategies, we can develop an awareness of the ways in which others have disrupted and manipulated its hegemonic functioning.

I turn now to two texts written some ten years after the death of David Walker. As explored in the introduction, *The Appeal of Forty*

*Thousand* argues the case of African American men who had been either disfranchised or not enfranchised by the Pennsylvania Constitutional Convention of 1837. This text asserts their right to citizenship by noting that earlier attempts to include the word "white" in the Constitution had not been successful. There is no justification, they argue, for the insertion of this word at this time but for the influence of slaveholders. "We are constrained to believe," the *Appeal* reports, "that [the Convention] have laid our rights as a sacrifice on the alter of slavery" (184), that disfranchisement of "men of color" is being used as a method of wooing the favor of the slaveholding states by "political aspirants." This text thus directly addresses the link between the rise of slavery's importance to the economic and political structures of the United States and the rise of white supremacy in non-slaveholding areas.

In arguing against their exclusion, these men represented solidarity among white and black men through a narrative of common gender, history, and genealogy: "Our fathers," they asserted, "shared with yours the trials and perils of the wilderness. . . . Our fathers fought by the side of yours in the struggle which made us an independent republic" (183). This commonality produces a shared narrative of identity in which Euroamerican and African American men collectively and cooperatively create the nation that is the United States. This narrative of nationness forgets as much as it remembers, particularly the dramatically different circumstances under which these "fathers" worked and fought. This passage also obscures the historical fact that much of the population in 1838—of European and African descent alike—were relatively recent immigrants (voluntary or forced), and therefore would not have actually participated in either "the trials and perils of the wilderness" or "the struggle which made us an independent republic." Rather it creates yet another mythology of development, not unlike that of "The Course of Civilization," this time with African as well as Anglo-American "fathers" as central players in the building of the nation.

The *Minutes of the State Convention of Colored Citizens*, held at Albany, New York, in August of 1840, creates a similar narrative of identity:

Again: we are the descendants of some of the earliest settlers of the state. We can trace our ancestry back to those who first pierced the almost impenetrable forests . . . when the vast and trackless wilderness, that had alone answered to the fierce roar of the roaming beast, or the whoop of the wild native, spread itself before the earlier settlers, our fathers were among those, who, with sinewy frame and muscular arm, went forth to humble that wilderness in its native pride. (200)

Like "The Course of Civilization," this mythical narrative of advancement rhetorically subordinates the indigenous population, by "humbl[ing] that wilderness," including "the wild native." Thus in making their claim to an "American" identity, these African American men reproduced the hierarchy of civilization that Euroamericans used to justify their appropriation of native lands. In addition, they laid claim to what Priscilla Wald has shown to be a central narrative of U.S. development produced and deployed by figures as diverse as the literary nationalists of the *Democratic Review*, Ralph Waldo Emerson, and Justice Benjamin Curtis (who wrote the *Dred Scott* decision). According to this narrative, " 'America' inheres not in the physical space of the continent, but in how the collectivity transforms that landscape—and in how that newly politicized landscape attests to the presence of 'the American people' " (Wald 111). The convention-goers insert themselves into this narrative of development by articulating a history in which their fathers, "with sinewy frame and muscular arm," fundamentally participated in transforming the landscape into the terrain that later became the United States.

This passage thereby transforms the logic of "The Course of Civilization" by asserting the centrality of the labor of African American men. By obscuring their "father's" status—as either slave, indentured servant, or free—this argument asserts the right of these men to be recognized for the fruits of their labor, and so implicitly asserts their right to property. The value of their labor then becomes the basis for a solidarity among black and white men. Gender is a crucial factor here: "We base our claim upon the possession of those common and yet exalted faculties of manhood. WE ARE MEN" (202). Thus "manhood" and one's labor form the foundation of these claims to the subject-position "all MEN."

The racialization of the masculine discourse of national identity characterizes the historical period of the remainder of this study. Many different groups and persons, with various or no party affiliation, internalized, actively supported, and/or opposed this process, taking competing stands on what constituted the developing nation. The discourse of national identity did not present a unified vision of the United States, but rather provided the terrain upon which rival forces struggled for authority. Indeed, the pervasiveness of the discourse illustrates not the existence of a particular national identity, but rather the importance of the *idea* of national identity to a diverse and divided population attempting to define itself and its internal and external relations. The chapters that follow trace the complex articulations of these attempts in relation to four slave revolts on ships. Slave rebellion brought together two of the most powerful, meaningful, and volatile topics of the antebellum United States—slavery and the legacy of the Revolution. To these topics we now turn.

# Chapter Two

# "The *Amistad* Affair" (1839)

Ships have a unique character that makes revolts on board them differ from those on land. Ships are bounded spaces with limited and relatively set, though changeable, populations, characteristics that increased the likelihood of successful revolt. Slave ships typically carried many, many more enslaved people than crew. If they could get free from chains and the hold, a relatively small number of determined and armed rebels, equipped with surprise, could take over a ship. As the first mate in *The Heroic Slave*, the subject of chapter 5 below, states, "It is one thing to manage a company of slaves on a Virginia plantation, and quite another to quell an insurrection on the lonely billows of the Atlantic, where every breeze speaks of courage and liberty" (62). Douglass's romantic characterization of the sea bespeaks as well the much greater opportunity for a shipboard rebellion—those in command do not have immediate access to reinforcements. Not only this, ships are mobile—at that time the fastest means of transportation—and, despite the large number of ships then at sea, relatively solitary. This meant it was possible, once the ship was taken over, for the rebels to move quickly and secretly to another place, perhaps one of safety for them. But being able to make use of this maritime advantage, as we will see in the *Amistad* incident and *Benito Cereno*, depended upon the ability to navigate.

The confined space, limited population, and mobility of ships made them also an unusual symbolic space in which fiction writers were able to imagine situations that could not be posed as plausibly on land.[1] In *Benito Cereno*, Melville uses these and other features peculiar to ships to heighten the sense of uncertainty experienced by the central character and the reader, and to suspend the eventual outcome. In particular, the isolation of the ship enables Melville to explore relations among the ship's inhabitants. Taking another approach, and with a remarkably different intent, Douglass finds in a shipboard rebellion a way to create a dramatic and successful leader who does not need to take many lives in order to secure his own and others' liberty. Unlike revolts on land, which required either violence or stealth, and probably both, on board the *Creole* Douglass may have his rebel leader act and speak heroically, asserting an ideological explanation for his acts. In addition, the ship's mobility enabled Douglass to choose a historical antecedent in which the captives not only rebelled, but successfully *got away.*

Such ships were masculine spaces, despite the occasional presence of women, historically always "manned" by men, who played the gender counterpart to the vessel they commanded, always referred to as "she." Ships facilitated adventures, explorations, and invasions, naval and commercial, participated in virtually exclusively by men. Women did travel as passengers on ships, but they did not join or aid the crew, a job reserved exclusively for men. And although a few became pirates, they no doubt had to perform tasks gendered as masculine, such as "manning" the rigging and fighting (Cordingly). These ocean-going ships were also European or Euroamerican in origin, descendants of those vessels that first took Europeans to Africa, Asia, and the Americas and that made possible a new international economy driven by the trade of slaves from Africa and rum, tobacco, sugar, chocolate, and coffee from the Americas.

Yet the ships' very mobility and part in trade often embroiled shipboard rebellions in international conflict. Each of the four incidents considered below brought together members of different European and/or Euroamerican nations, and in the *Amistad* and *Creole* cases provided the context for them and their governments to interact and spar over international laws governing the international and domestic slave trades. By the mid–nineteenth century, Britain had successfully signed treaties with most—but not all—European and Euroamerican nations abolishing the trade in slaves recently taken from Africa. These treaties slowed but did not stop the capturing and transporting of Africans to slave-based societies in the Americas. Further, they said and did nothing about domestic slave trades, trading within a nationally configured community, which could mean transportation across vast distances between the colonies—or states—of a given imperial power. The *Amistad* case, for example, hinged on the difference between the international trade in natives of Africa, and the slave trade within Spain's colonial possessions. In addition, incidents on board ship were governed differently depending upon whether it fell under international law, as did piracy but little else, or whether the nations had an extradition agreement, which potentially could apply to any crime. Although the British Parliament agreed that the rebels on the *Creole*, then in custody in Nassau, had committed murder, the absence of such an agreement between Britain and the United States meant that they could not be extradited. All of these factors impacted the eventual fate of rebels on slave ships, for once they took over, they all had to find somewhere to land. Whether or not that somewhere recognized property-in-persons had a lot to do with what happened next.

International incidents involving slavery created uncomfortable and uncertain situations for the United States. In international relations, the United States was conceived of as a nation within a community of nations, governed by the president and his administration, particularly the secretary of state and diplomatic liaisons. But questions having to do with slavery raised another conception of the United States, that of a confederation of sovereign states, governed by three separate branches of government, of which the executive was only one. Because the states differed in their positions on the legality of slavery, debates within Congress also played a particularly important role. In addition, within the United States, the judiciary, rather than the executive branch or Congress, was empowered to judge questions of law. Because slavery was such a vexed issue, and because slavery brought into conflict conceptions of the United States as a nation among a community of nations or as a confederation of sovereign states, decisions about what fell under which branch of government were not clear cut. Finally, state and federal jurisdiction over incidents at sea differed depending upon locale, which, because the states differed on the legality of slavery and the federal government did not officially recognize slavery, caused further complications in regard to insurrections in the domestic trade. All of this legal maneuvering makes evident not just the way in which state and national borders created limits on freedom and slavery. It also reveals *the very production of these statuses* by the organization of state and national entities, by their systems of documentation and litigation, by their geographical configurations, and by their recognized status under the law of nations.

"The *Amistad* Affair" (1839) and "The Case of the *Creole*" (1841), considered in the following chapter, are the names given by the popular press to two rebellions, names taken from the slave vessels on which the rebellions occurred. The *Amistad* (*Friendship*) was a Spanish-owned schooner that had been sailing between two ports in Cuba when the captives on board took over the ship. The schooner left Havana with a captain, cook, crew of two, two passengers, and the captain's enslaved servant, in addition to the fifty-four captives whom the passengers claimed to own as slaves. The captain and cook were killed during the rebellion, along with two of the captives, and the two crew members either escaped in one of the boats or were killed. For a period of two months, the rebels and their former "owners," José Ruiz and Pedro Montez, competed for control of the vessel's final destination. The schooner eventually was captured off the coast of Long Island and brought into port in New London, Connecticut. During the trials that ensued, the district court judge acknowledged that the rebels were natives of Africa, mostly from the country of Mendi, who had been taken from their homeland in violation of the international abolition of the African slave trade.[2] After three trials and some two years in jail, the Mendians were released.[3] They were visited during this time by more than four thousand U.S. Americans anxious to "acquaint themselves with the African character, as developed before the natives have been corrupted by intercourse with the white man" (letter from Lewis Tappan, qtd. in *Eman* 10/10/39:93,6).[4]

The *Creole* was a U.S.-owned vessel that had been sailing from Richmond, Virginia, to New Orleans, Louisiana, when the slaves on board rebelled and took over the ship. The rebels demanded that the crew take them to one of the islands in the Caribbean where slavery no longer existed. Upon arriving in Nassau, in the British Bahamas, British officials boarded the vessel, determined who had been responsible for the rebellion (according to the white passengers and crew), detained those so identified, and allowed all the others to leave the vessel. Some weeks later those who had been detained also were released by the British courts for "lack of evidence." The U.S. secretary of state vehemently opposed the action of the British, and demanded reparations from the British government for the economic value of the "lost cargo." Events on board the *Creole* were the subject of extended debate in the newspaper press throughout the United States.[5]

The second two instances, considered in chapters 4 and 5, are fictionalized accounts, Herman Melville's *Benito Cereno* (1855) of the historical revolt on the *Tryal* (1800), and Frederick Douglass's *The Heroic Slave* (1852) of the *Creole* rebellion. *Benito Cereno* tells the story of a Spanish ship (whose name Melville changed to the *San Dominick*), which had, prior to the opening of the text, been taken over by its enslaved passengers. According to Don Benito Cereno's deposition, the *San Dominick* had been sailing from Valparaiso, on the coast of Chile, to Callao, near Lima, Peru, when on the seventh day "the negroes revolted suddenly" (105), and took over the ship. And like those of the *Amistad*, the rebels wanted to go to Africa, but they too were ignorant of navigation and sailing techniques, as well as being short on supplies. When stopping for water at the isolated island of St. Maria, as the *Amistad* had stopped at Montauk, the *San Dominick* meets and is eventually retaken by the U.S. ship the *Bachelor's Delight*. At Lima the rebels are tried and remanded to slavery, their leader beheaded. In contrast, *The Heroic Slave* recasts the *Creole* rebellion as the life story of an enslaved man who, only at the end of the text, leads the shipboard rebellion.

Any public discussion of slave rebellion disrupted arguments, such as that of "The Course of Civilization," that obscured the existence of an enslaved population in the United States. The mere incident of physical resistance by enslaved people also disrupted slavery advocates' mythology of a natural hierarchy of races that figured dark-skinned people as naturally docile and subservient in their relations with light-skinned people. Most powerfully perhaps, the abolitionists' invocation of the trope of revolutionary struggle in the service of en-slaved rebels threatened the national alliance. By representing black men as participating in the physical battle for self-liberation, aboli-tionists claimed space for them in a national community that, in the nineteenth century, was increasingly constructed in opposition to them. The abolitionists' use of the trope of revolutionary struggle, especially in the service of enslaved people *within the United States,* disrupted both the original alliance of "all [free] men" and the alliance of "all [white] men" solidified in the 1830s, and claimed the discourse for an alliance of "all MEN." Thus these abolitionists, primarily white men, reproduced a discursive strategy begun earlier but developed most thoroughly by David Walker, the assertion of masculine gender as the most salient characteristic of the subject-position authorized to claim the discourse of national identity.

Events on the *Amistad* and *Creole* are only two of the better-known acts of resistance by enslaved peoples in North America.[6] Slaveholders' fear of retaliation by enslaved people, and the anxiety of many white people throughout the United States who feared the vio-lence and bloodshed that would result from a general uprising, funda-mentally shaped dominant attitudes toward slave revolt. Slavery ad-vocates suppressed knowledge of such rebellions whenever possible, or represented them as the reemergence of the supposedly innate sav-ageness of dark-skinned people, a masculine-coded savageness that had been subdued but not eliminated by their subordination to so-called civilized people. When forced to do so, they typically employed images of volcanic eruptions, earthquakes, and other natural disasters to describe slave rebellion, which they viewed as a cataclysmic disrup-tion of the natural order. The forms of repression generated by this anxiety are strikingly evident, for example, in this statement from a Virginia lawmaker, a response to Nat Turner's insurrection of 1831: "We have closed every avenue by which light might enter their minds. If you could extinguish the capacity to see the light, our work would be complete: they would then be on a level with the beasts of the field, and we should be safe" (qtd. in Gross and Bender 492).

Given this environment of anxiety, the representation of slave re-bellion was a particularly charged site of ideological struggle. Abolitionists applauded acts of resistance by enslaved people and represented them as evidence of their innate desire for liberty. Antislavery advocates used every opportunity to raise moral, ethical, political, and legal questions regarding slavery, recognizing that public debate on these subjects was crucial to their goal of transforming the United States into a non-slaveholding society. In response to both the planned and enacted rebellions listed above and the increasing action of abolitionists in the Northern states, lawmakers in the slaveholding states instituted a variety of measures to suppress agitation against slavery, and called upon state legislatures in the Northern states to do the same (Aptheker 1989, 24). As a result, official censorship of, as well as public sentiment against, abolitionist texts, speech, and meetings became the norm in slaveholding states, and was not uncommon in the Northern states. For example, a regulation known as the "gag rule," in effect between 1836 and 1844, prevented the reading of antislavery petitions on the floor of Congress. John C. Calhoun argued that the right of petition was unnecessary in a democratic society where all people are represented in government. Yet the "gag rule" was used primarily against antislavery petitions, which were gathered largely by black and white women on behalf of enslaved women and men, all of whom were excluded from direct political participation and representation.[7]

Such censorship of antislavery discourse was possible in the public and supposedly open forum of Congress because abolition was deeply disruptive not only of the institution of slavery and discourses of white supremacy, but of the Compact between the States. One newspaper writer called abolition "disorganizing in the extreme" (*SMN*, qtd. in *Eman* 9/12/39:77,4), while a naval officer called abolitionists a "faction" that, as a U.S. American, he "could wish to see destroyed" (qtd. in Jones 1987, 116). Antislavery advocates had to contend with supporters of the Union as well as with defenders of slavery.

In examining the popular press coverage of these incidents,[8] I do not intend to write a detailed history of events in the sense of creating narrative accounts of "what happened."[9] Rather, I am interested in analyzing the discursive strategies employed by differently empowered groups as they produced, debated, and limited the possible range of meanings of the rebellions in the popular press. I am interested in the way in which these discursive struggles disrupted the discourse of national identity and posited or foreclosed subject-positions for enslaved peoples. I focus on the popular press (newspapers, pamphlets, and periodicals) because it offers the most diverse and extended range of textual representations and interpretations available, and therefore provides the broadest sense of what it was possible to say and argue publicly and in print at that historical moment.

In addition, the character of the popular press played its own role in the dramas of the *Amistad* and the *Creole*. The *Southern Quarterly Review* remarked that the "power [the newspaper] has exerted on popular opinion, and the information it has diffused through all classes of society upon subjects of vital interest, political, commercial, statistical, literary and religious, is great beyond calculation."[10] The 1830s witnessed the rise of the "penny press" in New York City and later Boston, papers that promoted the very notion of "news" as recent significant happenings. Asking "what's the news," disseminating the news to semi- and non-literate friends and family members, and discussing and debating the meaning(s) of the news provided urban dwellers with new reasons for interacting and a new language with which to do so. In writing about the dissemination of political ideas regarding freedom and slavery, Harriet Beecher Stowe notes that "discussions were printed in the newspapers," and what was printed was further discussed "at the post-office door, in the tavern, in the bar-room, at the dinner-party" (1856, I 248). These papers were sold by boys on the street rather than through subscription, and they sold for a fraction of the cost of the mercantile and political papers. They extended the concern for "news" to an economic class previously unable to participate in the imagining of a national community afforded by such reading.[11] The first successful penny press, the New York *Sun*, whose reporting figures prominently in this chapter, contributed a new angle to news reporting by focusing on local happenings, particularly criminal trials. Sensationalist in style, the *Sun* made for compelling and provocative reading, especially when compared with the stylistically dry reports of national politics that filled the mercantile and political papers. Although the *Sun,* and other presses like the *Morning Herald* that sprang up in the wake of its success, was often in questionable "taste"—not to mention accuracy—its flamboyance not only created a new reading audience, but provided a new perspective to those who were already avid news readers.[12]

This increased interest in and prominence of news developed before standards of objective reporting came into vogue in the late nineteenth century.[13] Newspapers actively and openly interpreted happenings and issues from a particular perspective; readers expected to hear and valued editors' and writers' views on what they reported. These conventions produced a dynamic discursive world of news reporting in which "what happened" was debated as obviously and fiercely as the matter of how to interpret it. This is not to suggest that truth was not an issue, but rather to point to the different way in which truth was arrived at and understood.

### PART ONE: THE EYEWITNESS ACCOUNTS

The initial reports regarding the *Amistad* were published before any person in the United States—either the sailors who reported sighting the vessel or the journalists who wrote the newspaper articles—knew who was on board or where they were from. The *Amistad* archive begins with a series of eyewitness accounts that implicitly assert that the truth of what was happening could be determined through direct observation. Yet with primarily hearsay and little visual information to go on, the initial reports most startlingly reveal the bedrock assumptions of those who represented them. With so little to go on, their "common sense" filled in the blanks.

### The Initial and "Official" Accounts

On August 24, 1839, the New York *Advertiser and Express* and the New York *Morning Herald* ran similar articles reporting that "a vessel was discovered off our coast on Wednesday under very mysterious circumstances." The schooner's first appearance was so incongruent with what the U.S. sailors who saw it considered normal that they reported it to the newspapers. Called "the Long, Low Black Schooner" and "a suspicious sail—a pirate," the schooner was barely seaworthy, its sails torn, its hull covered with barnacles and grass.[14] But what really drew the sailors' attention were the scantily clothed, dark-skinned men wielding weapons up on deck. Although sailors of African descent participated in many voyages, naval and commercial, ships did not typically have a majority black crew, nor were they usually controlled by black captains, mates, or officers. In addition, the schooner had apparently been built in Baltimore as a slaver and the U.S. sailors who reported their sightings of it assumed that it was such. Why should they think otherwise? Although an official but poorly enforced ban of the international slave trade had been in effect since 1806, the coastal slave trade among slave states within the United States was still legal—and brisk. And yet here they were, off the coast of Long Island, leagues from any port in a slaveholding district. No wonder the sight of the ship and crew was at first deemed "mysterious."

Both articles include the following description, apparently based on word from the pilot boat *Lafayette:*

[A] number of negroes, twenty-five or thirty, were seen on deck. Some were almost or quite naked, some were wrapped in blankets, and one had on a white coat. . . . The strange crew on board were armed with muskets and cutlasses. One of them had a belt of dollars round his waist; another, called the captain, had a gold watch. They could speak no English, but appeared to talk in the negro language.

At this point the inhabitants of the ship appear threatening to those who sighted them. Their nakedness threatens, not so much because their bodies are visible—enslaved people often were stripped of clothing as a sign of subordination—but because, combined with weapons, their nakedness resonates as aggressive, potentially violent sexuality. Even more important, their possession of "muskets and cutlasses," weapons common enough when held—and used—by Euroamerican sailors, makes them threatening because within the United States—and certainly on slave ships—men of African descent were routinely prevented from having any, at least publicly. Thus the proscription

against weapons for dark-skinned people not only marked power relations, but operated as a sign of racial distinctions. The myriad trans-
gressions of normalcy combined here together were of a greater mag-
nitude than they would have been individually. The appearance of the
"suspicious sail" produced enough anxious interest that at least three
ships of varying sizes set out to capture it.

The description's last remark is most telling. The crew's "negro
language" makes them culturally different from and incomprehensi-
ble to the sailors who heard them. Yet the very concept that all Africans speak only one "negro language" homogenizes a heterogeneous
population and presents the racial marking of "negro" as that population's most salient characteristic. One of the ways in which slavery
operated in the United States was to attempt to erase memories of life
in Africa, religious, cultural, economic, political—and linguistic. Unlike slavery in much of Latin America, where many African lifeways
were maintained under slavery, eradication of ethnic heterogeneity
and an enforced homogeneity based on skin color characterized U.S.
slavery. The notion of a "negro language" positions the crew as outside
the admittedly diverse range of language groups represented by Euroamericans and European immigrants. The inhabitants of the schooner
must have appeared as radically different from those who sighted
them, though not in the same way as, say, Irish or German people who
spoke only their native languages would have appeared, but as subtle
challenges to the sailors' notions of racial character and hierarchy.
Ironically, the fact that the blacks spoke "no English" or Spanish was a
crucial part of the evidence that eventually secured their freedom,
because their lawyer, Roger Baldwin, argued it to be an irreducible
signifier of their condition as native Africans.

Four days later both papers again ran articles on the schooner. The
*Advertiser and Express* reported on a meeting between "The Long
Low Black Schooner" and a purported "Mr. Seaman":

He states that he run the pilot boat a few yards of her, with the intention of
putting a pilot on board. Two or three of the blacks, who appeared to be the
ringleaders and who kept the others in awe, made signs to them not to come on
board. One of them had a pistol in one hand and a cutlass in the other, which
he flourished over the head to keep the others down, who appeared very anx-

ious to receive a pilot, and when the eyes of the fellow who had the pistol was off them, would beckon to the pilots to come on board. (NY *Ad & Ex* 8/28/39)

This passage marks the first stage in a process of separation of the "ringleaders" from their awestruck and undifferentiated followers, a process that will continue in some form through virtually all of the writing about the Africans. The (ring)leaders are presented as tyrannical overlords who constantly have to survey their fellows or they will ally themselves with the white sailors. Thus the authority of the leaders is thrown into question, and Mr. Seaman and his pilot are represented as possible rescuers of these oppressed fellows, who are held at bay only through terror. Given this, the taking of the vessel by Mr. Seaman and his pilots could be justified by arguing that they had been called upon for help by those oppressed fellows who desperately desired their freedom from the ringleaders, but who did not have the resources to obtain it.[15]

First its (re)capture, then its representation in the popular press diffused the threat posed by the *Amistad.* On August 28, the New London *Gazette* reported that "The Suspicious Looking Schooner," which was "full of negroes and in such condition as to lead to the suspicion that she was a pirate," had been captured and brought into New London. Lieutenant Thomas R. Gedney, a U.S. naval officer in charge of the USS *Washington,* apparently smelling a reward for salvage on the *Amistad's* "cargo," boarded the schooner off of Montauk, the far end of Long Island, and brought it into port in Connecticut. The "official account" of the capture was provided "by one of the officers" to the press. It is unclear who wrote or approved the document, which is written in third person; it may have been "official" only because it was written and/or delivered by an "officer." This account describes the *Washington's* crew first sighting the *Amistad,* the identities of the Spaniards and schooner, the rebellion itself, and the sixty-three-day journey of the *Amistad* between the time of the rebellion and the schooner's capture. Appended to the account is an anonymous report of a visit to the *"Washington* and her prize."

Given that this official account characterizes the rebellion as "murder," assumes the ownership of the rebels by the "two white men," and emphasizes that "the situation of the two whites was all this time truly deplorable," the Spaniards no doubt were its primary source. The appended report's description of the current condition of the schooner and its crew confirms and is confirmed by the official account. It characterizes José Ruiz as "the owner of most of the slaves and cargo," "a very gentlemanly and intelligent young man," who is "the most striking instance of complacency and unalloyed delight we have ever witnessed." In addition, "we also saw Cingue, the master spirit of this bloody tragedy, in irons. . . . His countenance, for a native African, is unusually intelligent, evincing uncommon decision and coolness." "Phrenologically speaking," the report continues, "Cingue" "has considerable claim to benevolence," yet "the backs of several poor negroes are scored with scars of blows, inflicted by his lash to keep them in subjection." Elsewhere on the deck of the *Amistad* "were grouped amid various goods and arms, the remnant of her Ethiop crew, some decked in the most fantastic manner, in silks and finery, pilfered from the cargo, while others, in a state of nudity, emaciated to mere skeletons, lay coiled upon the decks." Finally, the report describes "the most horrible creature we ever saw in human shape, an object of terror to the very blacks, who said that he is a cannibal. His teeth projected at almost right angles from his mouth, while his eyes had a most savage and demonic expression." The article concludes by expressing the hope that Lieutenant Gedney will receive either prize or salvage money for the ship and its cargo, said to have been worth forty thousand dollars when it left Havana.

The details included, the temporal narrative frame, and the point of view of the "official account" and report are consistent in identifying with and authorizing the Spaniards, while presenting the Africans as fantastically different from both Spaniards and U.S. Americans, and their actions as illegitimate. Although the Africans were near starvation, the report describes the white men rather than the Africans as in a "truly deplorable" condition and emphasizes the Africans' supposed severity, both in relation to the Spaniards and among themselves. Apparently the scars on the backs of the "poor blacks" were inflicted by "Cingue," although the report presents no reason as to why he might have done so. Read in relation to the earlier report of the New York *Advertiser and Express,* in which the (ring)leader "flourished [a cutlass] over his head to keep the others down," this assertion works to invalidate both "Cingue's" leadership and the rebellion itself. The description of "the cannibal" represents him as the most alien of all the racial others; his ritual mutilations demarcate the outer limits of possible difference in human form. Similarly, the description of "Cingue" as "the master spirit of this bloody tragedy" separates him from the rest; he and "the cannibal" denote either end of the possible range of representations within this schema, what is most familiar and most different, respectively. The remainder of the Africans are an undifferentiated mass of "fantastic" suffering, whose "coiled" posture suggests non-human, possibly reptilian or hemp-like form.

On August 31, 1839, the New York *Sun,* the largest and most successful penny press in the country, published the first extended account of the rebellion. Selections from this lengthy article were subsequently republished in newpapers from Boston to New Orleans.[16] The *Sun's* coverage took up nearly the entire second page of the Saturday morning edition, with a two-column-wide square etching of the *Amistad* introducing the piece and text filling five columns. The picture of the *Amistad* was one of two procured "at a most enormous expense" from a locally known artist, James Sheffield, Esq., of New London, Connecticut. The second was "a most accurate likeness" of "Joseph Cinquez," which was lithographed, bound with two of the African's speeches, and advertised at the end of this long article as for sale from the *Sun's* office. Also included were a narrative of the "mutiny"; a description of "Joseph Cinquez" and the text of two of his purported speeches; a report of the judicial investigation, which took place immediately after the schooner's capture on board the USS *Washington* and on the *Amistad;* "A Card" from the Spaniards, expressing their gratitude, first to Lieutenant Gedney and his crew, and then to "that nation whose flag they so worthily bear," "for their most unhoped for and providential rescue from the hands of a ruthless gang of African bucanneers"; and an advertisement for a special *Weekly Sun* compiling the newspaper's articles on the *Amistad* saga, which it characterized as "a history unparalleled for atrocities and horrors in the history of navigation."

This anonymously written article begins not with the rebellion, but with the story of Don José Ruiz, "a wealthy and noble Spaniard," who had left his estate at Principe and had gone to Havana to buy slaves. At Havana, the article reports, Ruiz purchased forty-nine men from "a cargo which had just arrived from the Coast of Africa." He then chartered the *Amistad*, owned and under the command of Ramon Ferres, and loaded it with both his newly bought slaves and assorted other cargo, such as crockery, dry goods, and fancy articles "for amusement or luxury." With him sailed Don Pedro Montez, who had bought and now brought with him four slaves from the same cargo as that of Ruiz, three girls and one boy, between seven and twelve years old. According to this article, all of the slaves were "Congolese negroes, only six weeks from the coast of Africa." The account of the rebellion begins with the captain being awakened from sleep by "Joseph" stabbing him with a sugar knife, which the article describes as "about 28 inches long, and 3 broad at the end. From that width it tapers off to the handle, where it is simply a piece of bar steel, about an inch square." The captain called to Antonio (his enslaved servant) to "get some bread and throw it among the negroes, hoping to pacify them," and although he "defended himself bravely," he was overpowered by "Joseph," "who split his head open." While "Joseph" was engaged with the captain, three others were attacking the other white men and the mulatto cook, and "the other negroes were making the most dreadful noises imaginable." Soon two were dead, and the two remaining crew members purportedly "let down the stern boat and escaped."[17] Then Joseph and his three unidentified comrades lashed together Ruiz and Montez, and pointing to their sugar knives and the sun, they expressed their desire to head eastward. Though "dangerously wounded," Montez controlled the schooner so that it made little headway, steering the vessel over the subsequent weeks to the northeast during the day, and to the west at night. The article interpreted the rebels' attempt to return to Africa in this way: "The poor wretches knew that they had come from where the sun appeared to rise, but they understood nothing of navigation, and were easily deluded." Throughout their journey, the demonic leaders purportedly "brandished their knives over the head of Montez in the most horrible manner."

By beginning the narrative with Ruiz's trip to Havana, this article presents the young Spaniard as the subject of the story. In giving an individual name to the captain and to Ruiz's companion, Montez, the article adds them to the roster of central characters. In contrast, the Africans are figured as part of an undifferentiated mass of slave "cargo," which receives only the geographical designation "Congolese." Like the "official" account and first report, this article emphasizes the violence and cruelty of the Africans and the victimization of the Spaniards. The implied sneakiness of the attack, while all were sleeping, and the details about the size and shape of the sugar knives, sensationally encourage readers to feel themselves in danger. Interestingly, the descriptions of the Africans' sounds and actions as "the most dreadful imaginable" and "the horrible manner" function similarly though they may be imprecise; these descriptions needed only to evoke racialist tropes of heathen rituals to call forth a "common sense" that linked readers with those attacked. In another vein, the narrative detail that the captain ordered bread to be thrown to the rebels in the hope of pacifying them implies both that the Africans had not been receiving enough food, and that the Africans are creatures of the body, driven by the body's needs, and satisfied when those needs are met. How the Africans were treated on the *Amistad* became a crucial factor in one of their court cases, which will be considered later in this chapter. The representation of the Africans as primarily visceral categorizes them as animal-like, a theme common to contemporary racialist discourses that appears in much of the subsequent negative writing on the *Amistad.*

The article goes on to narrate events once the *Amistad* reached the vicinity of Long Island. Apparently the *Amistad* "was boarded by several vessels," one of which supplied them with water, and "[w]hen any vessel came alongside Joseph would stand by Ruiz, the only man who speaks English, and watch him with fearful intensity." Between the fifteenth and twenty-fourth of September the schooner anchored off the coast about thirty times. At Culloden Point several of the Africans went ashore in search of water. According to the article they were "almost naked, and the inhabitants were exceedingly alarmed." Although the locals' alarm seems to have made bartering difficult, for the Africans purportedly only made two successful exchanges, yet they were in the area for two days "without any attempt being made to arrest them." Then Captain Henry Green stumbled upon them during a hunting expedition, and "immediately [seeing] that all was not right," "gave them to understand that they should be taken care of." What kind of care I will leave it to my reader to imagine. Indeed, Green apparently asked if they had money (asked how, the newswriter wanted to know, unless Green knew Congolese, since the Africans knew no English), and they supposedly presented him with two trunks filled with four hundred doubloons. At about the same time that this was happening on shore, the small boat of the (much larger) USS *Washington* boarded the *Amistad.* Immediately upon seeing a man in a uniform, Ruiz approached him and said in English: "These negroes are my slaves; they have taken the vessel; that is the leader (pointing to Joseph) and I claim your protection." Lieutenants D. D. Porter and Richard W. Meade subsequently disarmed the Africans and took the schooner in tow.

Although the *Sun*'s narrative identified with the Spaniards, it also included an admiring description of the rebels' purported leader and the text of two of his purported speeches. Notice first the terms in which this passage praises "the master spirit of this bloody tragedy":

Among the slaves purchased by Ruiz was one called, in Spanish, Joseph Cinquéz, who is the son of an African Chief. This Cinquéz is one of those spirits which appear but seldom. Possessing far more sagacity and courage than his race generally do, he had been accustomed to command.... His eye is that of a Spaniard, and can express every variety of thought, from the cool contempt of a haughty chieftain, to the high resolve which would be sustained through martyrdom. His lips are thicker and more turned up than those of his race in general, but when opened, display a set of teeth rivaling in beauty the most regular of those which we praise so in Caucasian beauty. His nostrils are the most remarkable feature he possesses. These he can contract or dilate at pleasure.... [M]any white men might take a lesson in dignity and forbearance, from the African Chieftain, who, although in bondage, appears to have been the Oseola of his race.

The assertion that Cinqué[18] is the son of an African chief singles him out, not only from his companions on the *Amistad,* but from the vast majority of Africans. Phrases such as "one of those spirits which appear but seldom" and "possessing far more sagacity and courage than his race generally do" reinforce Cinqué's individual status. This process of separation echoes the earlier descriptions of the "ringleader," but recasts the tyrannical overlord into a figure identified with his (white) observer. Rather than being part of a community of black people (Africans) or an overlord, Cinqué is now a superior exception.

Nevertheless, this gendered process of individuation supports rather than challenges discourses of racial difference. If Cinqué can be shown to be unusual, out of the ordinary, then his masculine bravery and leadership need not disturb the cultural logic that emasculated black men and constructed black people as inferior to white people, particularly when it came to such issues as reasoning and fighting. Rather, this logic of identification constructs an identity for Cinqué as an honorary "Caucasian" (or at least an honorary Spaniard). He has physical as well as personality traits usually reserved for light-skinned people: "His eye is that of a Spaniard" and his teeth rival "in beauty the most regular of those which we praise so in Caucasian beauty." Yet he is also oddly hyper-African, his lips even thicker than most, and his nostrils especially pronounced. This description attempts to domesticate what is unfamiliar by equating it with what is familiar, and yet its inconsistency registers the difficulty of that process. This racialist logic shears the force of Cinqué's acts and leadership from the context in which they were originally produced, that of captured Africans rebelling against their Spanish captors, and appropriates them into a discourse that supports a hierarchy based on race. This appropriation lessens the psychological threat to white people in the United States presented by an example of a successful slave rebellion. So long as Cinqué is an exceptional—and masculine—individual, the threatening aspects of both the solidarity of the "blacks" and their physical resistance will be minimized.

Yet Cinqué most resembles not a Caucasian or a Spaniard but the Seminole chief Oseola.[19] Oseola resonates here only in the truncated form of being known for being captured and executed by U.S. military forces yet never surrendering, a central feature of the trope of the noble savage. The passage's suggestion that "many white men might take a lesson in dignity and forbearance, from the African Chieftain," situates Cinqué firmly within this racialist and gendered discourse of savagism that at once admires and glorifies the wisdom, bravery, and "natural" independence of indigenous men, and relegates them to a savage world sadly but necessarily receding in the face of advancing civilization.[20] This characterization operates in at least three directions at once: it uses gender to separate Cinqué from and elevate him above his companions, it uses the noble savage tradition to create a hierarchy between African(s) (Americans) and indigenous Americans, and it uses racialist discourses to figure its writer as civilized and knowledgeable in relation to them all.

The *Sun's* version of two speeches reportedly delivered by Cinqué on the *Amistad* after its capture develops still further the characterization of Cinqué as a masculine, noble savage. Although other accounts confirmed that Cinqué made two speeches, the printed text of the speeches is deeply suspect. The speeches were reported to have been given in Congolese, translated into Spanish by Antonio, and then translated into English and transcribed by John Jay Hyde, an editor of the New London *Gazette.* Yet the language the Africans were supposedly speaking was not in fact a language they spoke, and, in addition, a later news article reported that Antonio spoke no African languages (New Haven *Record*, qtd. in *Eman* 11/7/39:110,2–3). It seems likely, then, that these speeches were primarily Hyde's constructions.

After one attempt to escape the USS *Washington*, Cinqué reportedly delivered the following speech:

"Friends and Brothers—We would have returned but the sun was against us. I would not see you serve the white man, so I induced you to help me kill the Captain. I thought I should be killed—I expected it. It would have been better. You had better be killed than live many moons in misery. I shall be hanged, I think, everyday. But this does not pain me. I could die happy, if by dying I could save so many of my brothers from the bondage of the white man."

This speech displays Cinqué's "natural" desire for liberty, his preference for death over enslavement, and his willingness to die in the pursuit of freedom. He even more forcefully asserts this theme in the second speech, which he delivered minutes later after an escape attempt:

"My brothers . . . you have only one chance for death, and none for liberty. I am sure you prefer death, as I do. You can by killing the white men now on board, and I will help you, make the people here kill you. It is better for you to do this, and then will you not only avert bondage yourselves, but prevent the entailment of unnumbered wrongs on your children. Come—come with me then."[21]

This rendition of Cinqué's words—"you have only one chance for death, and none for liberty. I am sure you prefer death, as I do"—resonates with two traditions, one that represented indigenous Americans as too noble to be enslaved, and the other of the U.S. Revolution and Patrick Henry's paradigmatic phrase "Give me liberty! or give me death!" On the one hand, this representation figures Cinqué as like male heroes from the revolutionary period in his desire and willingness to die for liberty. It grants him the rights accorded a masculine individual. This similarity signals and undergirds the hegemony for U.S. Americans of natural rights discourse. By presenting Cinqué this way, his translator constructs himself as part of a righteous community that recognizes liberty and values the struggle for it above all. The translator thereby disarms one potential threat of Cinqué's words, that Cinqué and the other Africans have another motivation for their behavior that he doesn't understand, a motivation, for example, that perceives their captors not as men like themselves but as devils.

This translation is sympathetic in that it grants to Cinqué the one discourse known to his translator that could justify in his mind and the minds of *his* countrymen the Africans' aggressive actions toward their captors. Its significance lies in its equation of the Africans' aggressive gestures with justified rebellion. But singling Cinqué out from the rest supports a logic of racial difference which asserts that black people, especially enslaved people, only rebel when convinced to do so by someone braver and more intelligent than they. Often such a purported agitator was a white man, an abolitionist. But by reporting that he had "deceived the enemy of our race," this speech racially differentiates Cinqué from the officers of the USS *Washington.* Such language was commonly deployed in white-generated representations of indigenous Americans, linking Cinqué once again to figures like Oseola. Thus the racial stratification deployed here separates Cinqué from both his African companions and his white captors, locating him somewhere in between on a plane with indigenous Americans. This construction thereby undermines Cinqué's call to rebellion because it also figures his compatriots, so inferior to him, as unworthy to rebel. It also mediates the dangerous possibilities produced by Cinqué's individual and exemplary behavior by characterizing him as a savage hero. This representational back and forth, and back again, illustrates the unstable workings of racialist and gendered discourses as they sought to identify—that is, create an identity for—Cinqué.

Thus the New York *Sun* paradoxically figured the rebellion as a "massacre" and characterized Cinqué as an admirable leader. This paradox illustrates precisely the dilemma of the noble savage. Though brave, eloquent, freedom-loving, and independent, the violent self-assertions of this masculine, even virtuous heroic savage will be characterized as a massacre by his civilized "superiors" whenever they are pitted against them. Subsequent interpretations of the *Amistad* rebellion obscure and mediate the anxiety produced by this combination of massacre and heroic rebel, an anxious undercurrent of U.S. public discourse wrought not only by slavery but by Indian removal in a republic founded on freedom. Here the way in which Cinqué is separated from the rest of the rebels, individuated, and masculinized glosses this paradox by suggesting, however unconvincingly, that the actions of the group, but not those of their leader, were a massacre. Even given the additional mediating factor of the noble savage tradition, this incoherence cannot be maintained, and never again in discussions of this incident are the two presented together.

On the same page, the *Sun* also printed a report of the judicial investigation that was convened on board the USS *Washington*, with the Honorable Andrew T. Judson, U.S. district judge, presiding, and C. A. Ingersol, Esq., appearing for the U.S. district attorney. This was the same Judge Judson who had presided over the trial of educator and activist Prudence Crandall. Together Ruiz and Montez lodged a complaint against "Joseph Cingue (the leader in the alleged offense), Antonio, Simon Lacis, Peter, Martin, Manuel, Andrew, Edward, Caledonis, Bartholomew, Raymond, Augustine, Evaristo, Casimiro, Mercho, Gabriel, Santaria, Escalastio, Paschal, Estanilaus, Desiderio,

Nicholas, Stephen, Thomas, Corsino, Lewis, Bartolo, Julian, Frederick, Saturnio, Lardusolado, Celistino, Epifanio, Tevacio, Ezidiquiel, Leon, Julius, Hippoloto, 2d, and Zinon, or as such of the above as might be alive at that time." An indictment was framed, based on the complaint, charging them with murder and piracy on board the *Amistad*. The court examined and took into custody as evidence the papers of the *Amistad*, which included two licenses from the governor of Havana, one for three slaves owned by Pedro Montez, and another for forty-nine slaves owned by José Ruiz, to be transported to Principe. Regular passports were produced for Ruiz and Montez, and licenses for the now deceased mulatto cook, enslaved to the captain, and for each of the sailors. Custom House clearances dated May 18 and June 27, 1839, together with several licenses for goods to be shipped, "were read and decided to be regular." Testimony was taken only from Lieutenant Meade, whose testimony was quite short and referred only to the schooner's capture, and from Ruiz, Montez, and Antonio, with Meade acting as interpreter.

Considerably shorter than the separate narrative in the *Sun*, the testimonies of Ruiz, Montez, and Antonio each mention the darkness of the night the rebellion broke out, that a storm had just passed, and no moon shone. The discrepancy in length was explained by the following note: "Many of the events which are detailed in the narrative, were omitted in the evidence as having no bearing on the guilt or innocence of the accused." This aside indexes differences between news reporting (in the admittedly sensational penny press) and evidence accepted by an official U.S. tribunal. (Neither here nor elsewhere does the *Sun* acknowledge its source for the "narrative.") Like the "narrative," Ruiz's testimony begins with his purchase of forty-nine slaves in Havana, but focuses on the rebellion itself. On the fourth day out, everyone was asleep except for the man at the helm; he was awakened by the noise and saw "This man Joseph." It was dark; Ruiz took an oar, shouting "no!" and tried to "quell the mutiny." He heard the captain call to the cabin boy to get some bread to throw to them, "in hopes to pacify the negroes." He went below and called to Montez to follow him and told them not to kill him. He did not see the captain killed. They called Ruiz on deck, told him he would not be hurt, and he "asked them as a favor to spare the old man." They did so. The next day Ruiz noticed that all the crew was missing except Antonio, who was kept alive to act as interpreter and was now on board the schooner.

In his testimony, Montez asserted that when awakened by the noise of the mulatto cook being killed he took up a stick and knife to defend himself, but he "did not wish to kill or hurt them." He was wounded severely on the head and arm, then ran and hid himself below. The prisoner ran after him and attempted to kill him, but someone else prevented him. He recognized his attacker but was too weak to know who saved him. He was taken on deck and tied to Ruiz; then, he reported, "they commanded me to steer for their country. I told them I did not know the way." On the second day after the mutiny, when a gale struck, he still steered, having once been the master of a vessel. When the storm passed, he steered away from Havana, "in the night by the stars, but by the sun in the day, taking care to make no more way than possible." They passed by several ships. "Every moment [his] life was threatened." Having been asleep, all he knew of the murder of the mulatto was that he heard the blows. They were all glad the next day about what had happened. At several times, he would have been killed but for the interference of others. They had lost track of days when the officers came on board. They anchored at least thirty times. "I had no wish to kill any of them," he commented, "but prevented them from killing each other."

The court then adjourned to the schooner *Amistad* in order to inspect the ship and to question Antonio, specifically to see if he could identify who "murdered" the captain and the cook. Antonio was addressed in Spanish by Lieutenant Meade, who asked him about the nature of an oath. He replied that he was a Christian, was sworn, and then testified. After the storm, he said, the captain and cook lay down on some mattresses that they had brought on deck. Four of the slaves came up, armed with sugar knives, and they struck the captain across the face and the mulatto "oftener." By this time the rest of the slaves had come on deck armed in the same way. "Joseph, the man in irons, was the leader," Antonio stated; "he attacked Senior Montez." The captain ordered him to throw some bread to them, and he did so, but "they would not touch it." Antonio's testimony ended with his going below and identifying two men who "conspired to kill the captain and the cook."

After considerable deliberation, the court apparently decided that "Joseph Cingue, the leader, and 38 others, as named in the indictment" were to be held for trial until September 17. The three girls and Antonio were ordered to give bonds in the sum of one hundred dollars each to appear before the said court and give evidence in this case, and to be committed to the county jail if they were unable to furnish the bonds. These four were not indicted. Lieutenant Meade, Ruiz, and Montez also were to give a bond of one hundred-dollars each to guarantee their appearance to give testimony in the case. The court adjourned, giving the captives into the hands of the U.S. marshal, to be transported to jail in New Haven.

The court's focus on the killings exemplifies "narrow time-framing," an interpretive method common to much substantive criminal law.[22] This method limits legal examination to usually one specific incident and excludes from consideration any other events, either prior or following, or any other issues that might create a larger context for understanding that specific incident. The incident at stake in the court's initial examination was the killing of the captain and the cook, not, for example, the fact that one of the Africans had been killed or the wounding of Montez, or even the takeover of the ship. Though the questions themselves were not recorded, clearly the three witnesses were asked to identify who perpetrated the killings. All agree that "Joseph" was the leader, and it seems odd, given the degree of concern about who helped him, that the two men whom Antonio identified were not named, either here or in any subsequent court proceedings. The method of narrow time-framing focuses upon whichever incident the court accepts as under its consideration; it thereby implicitly privileges the person from whose point of view that incident is a crime. In hearing testimony primarily from Ruiz and Montez, with Antonio being questioned mostly as to the identity of who killed the captain and cook, the court implicitly structured, on a register different from testimony, which incidents would be examined. Thus the court's narrow time-framing limited its focus to the incidents presented as crimes by the Spaniards, and privileged the Spaniards' point of view without seeming to do so.

The narrow time-framing also excluded details about character, status, and the rebels' history, presented in the *Sun*'s narrative, that give a different construction to the *Amistad* affair. In the official testimony, "Joseph" appears only as the perpetrator of at least two murders and the takeover of the ship. Despite its use of racialist and gendered discourses, as we have seen, the *Sun*'s narrative does hint at reasons for the rebels' actions. It emphasized that the Africans were recently taken from their homeland and enslaved, and that they rebelled when urged to do so by their charismatic leader. Although the narrative concluded, "Now most probably [Joseph] will be hanged as a murderer and a pirate," thus acknowledging the likely legal decision, it also asserted that "had he lived in the days of Greece o[r] Rome, his name would have been handed down to posterity as one who had practiced those most sublime of all virtues—disinterested patriotism and unshrinking courage." In presenting this perspective, the *Sun*'s narrative opened up an interpretive possibility that the narrow time-framing of the court obscured. Thus the court initially asserted its legal objectivity by focusing on a specific set of actions and implicitly denying the relevance of character, status, and history.

In addition to time-framing, the matter of identity—the question of who the players "were"—also structured the court's perspective. When Ruiz approached Meade on board the *Amistad* and claimed his protection, Ruiz hoped that Meade would accept his characterization of the circumstances. His hopes may have been dampened by the fact that the *Amistad* had apparently come in contact with many vessels over the previous week or two, with sailors even spending time on board, and yet he and Montez remained under the control of the rebels. But in approaching Meade, a man he trusted because he wore a uniform, Ruiz was looking to an authority that would recognize that the current relations of power on board the schooner were not compatible with what that authority would consider "normal." Ruiz hoped, even assumed, that in stating to Meade, "These negroes are my slaves; they have taken the vessel," the truth of his statement would be obvious to the lieutenant, as indeed it apparently was. But what made this truth obvious to Meade? As we have seen, sailors and newswriters assumed virtually from the beginning that the *Amistad* was a slaver taken over by its cargo. Thus Meade's reaction was in keeping with general opinion. According to this opinion, dark-skinned men with weapons and in control of a ship can only be something outside the law, dangerous at the very least, and perhaps piratical. Thus, cultural assumptions about status and race—about who each of these men "could be"—determined Meade's reaction to Ruiz's statement.

The assumptions undergirding Meade's actions, illustrative of general opinion, in turn informed the actions of the court. Meade acted as the authority not only in disarming the Africans and bringing the schooner into port, but in shaping the circumstances to be considered by the judicial investigation. His testimony presented his actions as "common sense," thereby within a legal setting at once relying upon and giving voice to larger cultural assumptions. Ingersol, the district attorney, implicitly accepted Meade's characterization of the circumstances, evidenced by his asking for testimony from only Ruiz, Montez, and Antonio. Similarly, the court granted the official papers of the *Amistad*, produced by authorities in Ruiz's homeland of Cuba, a slaveholding state, the authority to confirm Ruiz's statements. Judge Judson in turn implicitly agreed to these proceedings by accepting an indictment against all of the Africans, except the three girls, and remanding them to jail. Each of these actions depended upon those in authority accepting without question Ruiz's initial statement of who they all "were," either slave or slaveholder.

Ironically, in the weeks that followed, it was the question of who the rebels actually "were," more than any other, that captivated newswriters and the public more generally. Representations of the rebels' identity, especially Cinqué's, as I have suggested in my reading of the initial and official accounts, were already complicated and unstable. As newswriters, activists, politicians, and the rest of the interested populace entered into the process of interpreting the *Amistad* affair, assertions about their identity became more diverse, inflexible, contested, antagonistic. Most obviously at stake in this debate was the fate of the rebels: who they were determined "to be" would in turn determine the laws under which their actions would be judged. Also at stake was who the people participating in the debate understood themselves "to be," for every assertion about the identity of the rebels carried within it an implicit characterization of the person making the assertion. The following section analyzes the various ways in which the Africans themselves, their abolitionist supporters, and their Spanish antagonists represented the rebels.

### The Partisan Narratives

Immediately upon being captured and brought into port, where they were jailed for murder and piracy, the Africans were approached by some "friends of freedom" from the city of New York, who had decided to take up their cause. A committee was appointed, consisting of Simeon S. Joselyn, Joshua Leavitt, and Lewis Tappan, authorized to "receive donations, employ counsel, and act in other respects as circumstances might require, for the protection and relief of the African Captives" (*TPA* iv). The *Trial of the Prisoners of the Amistad*, in which this information is recorded, does not say who did the appointing, but Tappan and Leavitt in particular were active members of the white-run American Anti-Slavery Society, and it seems likely that some portion of this society (perhaps themselves?) "appointed" them. Leavitt and Tappan were evangelical abolitionists: Leavitt was a minister and editor of the *Emancipator* newspaper of New York City, while Tappan was one of the wealthiest supporters of abolition in the United States. During the first week following the capture of the schooner, many New York newspapers published an "Appeal to the Friends of Liberty" from the newly formed *Amistad* Committee. It stated that "[t]hirty-eight fellow-men from Africa, after having been piratically kidnapped from their native land, transported across the seas, and subjected to atrocious cruelties, have been thrown upon our shores, and are now incarcerated in jail to await their trial for crimes alleged by their oppressors" (NY *MH* 9/6/39:2,2, qtd. in *Eman* 9/19/39:2,3; *CA* 9/14/39:2,5). The committee employed various experts who wrote and published their own observations or eyewitness accounts of the captives' activities. These accounts were published throughout the duration of the

Africans' time in jail, but were most numerous during the first few months.

A little more than a week following the New York *Advertiser and Express* article reporting the capture of the schooner, Leavitt and Tappan published three letters in New York papers regarding the Africans. The committee's initial rhetorical strategy challenged earlier representations of the captives' violent agency by creating a sense of their passivity. Joshua Leavitt's letter in the *Commercial Advertiser* argues that "they were not as destitute of clothing when taken near the shore, as has been represented in the papers," and that "they all appear to be persons of quiet minds and a mild and cheerful temper; there are no contentions among them; even the poor children, three girls and one boy . . . seem to be uniformly kind and friendly" (9/6/39:2,2). The abolitionists reiterate this description of the Africans as quiet, mild, and cheerful throughout their accounts: "their demeanor is altogether quiet, kind and orderly. . . . [they are] intelligent and docile Africans" (Tappan's letter, NY *Sun* 9/10, qtd. in *Eman* 9/12/39:78,4); "some of them are not only cheerful, but merry" (Tappan's examination of Cinqué, *Eman* 9/12/39:78,4); "the sober truth is that they are just what in the south would be called a likely lot of young Negroes—very few of them seeming to be much if anything over twenty. . . . The 'cannibal,' or 'man with the tusks,' is a good-tempered fellow, and I venture to say never ate a morsel of man's flesh in his life" (*Com Ad* 9/19/39:2,1); "a more harmless, peaceable, good-tempered set of men was never got together than these same Africans" (*Com Ad* 11/1/39:2,2). These descriptions of the captives not only oppose and challenge earlier representations of them as dangerous and demonic pirates; they also domesticate the Africans by echoing "soft" racialist notions of "happy darkies."

These characterizations mediate the potential threat posed by the rebellious acts of the Africans in yet a third way: not through separation and individualization or through demonizing, but by implicitly challenging representations of their agency in any but the most benign and domesticated form. Of course, the "Appeal" turns the Spaniards' story on its head, presenting these "fellow-men" as the hapless victims of piratical kidnappers. Rather than active agents willing to be violent in the service of their own liberation, the Africans appear here as happy-go-lucky children in need of protection. Thus these characterizations also subordinate the Africans to their abolitionist supporters, who, through these notices to the press, construct themselves as active, authoritative, articulate, and benevolent. At least two of the *Amistad* Committee construct a new hierarchy, with themselves on top, based on language, culture, and as will become evident later, religion.

Tappan's two letters to New York papers also contain the first of several versions of "what happened," purportedly from the Africans themselves. The recording, collecting, and publishing of the Africans' accounts should be considered in the context of a more general movement among abolitionists to publicize firsthand accounts of slavery by former slaves. In the 1830s, the rise of abolition brought about an increasing demand for slave testimony, which was widely recognized as a powerful critique of the "peculiar institution." Testimony of the horrors of life in bondage, especially from those who had experienced it personally, could be used to disrupt the increasing number of positive representations of slavery produced by slavery advocates in journals, novels, and newspapers. Such testimony, sometimes in the form of written narratives, sometimes in the form of as-told-to memoirs, was greatly influenced by the context of its production. The purpose of challenging the representation of slavery as a divinely sanctioned institution gently resting on the labor of contented slaves, as in "Domestic Slavery," considered in the previous chapter, demanded both accounts of physical and emotional torture and evidence of the inherent humanity of enslaved people.[23] The accounts of the Africans, all of which come to us through the mediation of abolitionists, should be considered not only as evidence produced for their own defense, but as material gathered in a more general fight against slavery.[24]

Because the Africans did not speak English, did not read or write English, and at this time had no direct access to print, their version of events comes to us first through interpreters and then through abolitionist writers. This version may very well be more reliable than the New London *Gazette*'s copy of Cinqué's speeches, given that Tappan's first letter also notes "the joy manifested by these poor Africans when they heard one of their own color address them in a friendly manner and in a language they could comprehend." The *Amistad* Committee was able to find first John Ferry, a native of the Gissi country who interpreted the passage below, and then James Covey, a native Mendian and sailor in the British navy, who became the captives' principal interpreter.[25] The ecstatic meeting between Covey and the captives in October demonstrated that the captives also were native Mendians, hailing from Mendi, in what is now Mali. Tappan's first letter goes on to recount "the following statements, nearly in their very words, as translated by the interpreter":

They demanded of the slavers where they were going to take them but received no satisfactory answer. In one and a half moons, they said, we arrived at Havana. Here they were put on board the schooner which brought them to this country. . . . [T]hey agreed to take the schooner and go back to their own country. Previous to this the Captain was very cruel and beat them severely. They would not take it, to use their own expression, and therefore turned and fought for it. After this they did not know where to go.

In contrast to the initial and official reports, this brief story creates a longer temporal frame by extending back into the time prior to their sale to Ruiz and the rebellion. This frame brings into play not only the question of the captives' point of origin, but a new narrative starting-point. Thus, not simply the meaning of "what happened," but the very elements of the story changed dramatically depending upon the story-teller. Similarly, "they said they were forced to drink a great deal of salt water, on board the slaver, and that made them sick. . . . The captain of the schooner . . . kept them nearly starved" (*Eman* 9/12/39:78, 4). Now who appears to have been kept in a "truly deplorable" condition?

Some weeks after the capture of the *Amistad*, the *Amistad* Committee filed three affidavits as part of a lawsuit against Ruiz and Montez for assault, battery, and false imprisonment. Like the Mendians' own accounts, the affidavits focus on their journey on the *Amistad* prior to their decision to rebel. The affidavits of two of the Mendians, Fonni and Kimbe, are written in first-person and expand upon the earlier accounts of the Spaniards' treatment toward them. As Kimbe stated,

> I did not have enough to eat and drink, two potatoes and one plantain twice a day and half a tea-cup of water morning and evening. When I asked for more water I was driven back with a whip. The Spaniards washed their own clothes in fresh water. For stealing water I received a severe beating. I was held down over a piece of timber, and beaten with twenty three lashes on the back. This was done by Pepe and the cook. This was repeated morning and evening for two days and powder and rum were rubbed into the wounds. Pepe told the sailors to do this and the marks are still visible. Yaboi, Fonni, and Burnah were beaten in the same manner. (NY *Ad & EX* 10/19/39:4,2)

The affidavits emphasize not only the cruelty of the Spaniards, but the abundance of their resources, which they refused to share with the Mendians. The assertion that the Spaniards "washed their own clothes in fresh water" suggests that they had a reason other than scarcity for withholding adequate water from the Mendians. Starvation and withholding water, like the severe beatings, likely were part of a strategy to accustom the "imported" Africans to their new lives as slaves. Details of the beatings reported here challenge the assertion made in the *Sun*'s account of a visit to the *Amistad*, that "the backs of several poor negroes are scored with scars of blows inflicted by ["Cinqué's"] lash to keep them in subjection" (NL *Gaz*, qtd. in *HAC* 4). While the earlier account attributes the condition of the Mendians to Cinqué's cruelty, these affidavits allocate all physical torture to the sailors upon the orders of the Spaniards.

On the one hand, the Mendians' accounts figure them as the hapless victims of first the international African slave trade, which "all civilized nations" had agreed to abolish, and then of the cruel captain, implicitly at the behest of the Spanish slaveholders. This representation opposes those in which they appear to be violent, uncontrolled, even demonic figures. Yet the Mendians' accounts also return the larger context of the violence of slavery and the violence of the African slave trade to our understanding of the violence of the rebellion. The "initial and official accounts" (and the Spaniards' account) neither include nor speculate about what went on before the rebels took over the schooner. Their narrative framing only allows for information that supports the construct of the Spaniards as the victims of an unprovoked attack by irrational, out-of-control pirates. In contrast, the narrative framing of the Mendians' accounts, which chronologically precedes that of the other accounts, disrupts this construction by providing specific evidence of the previous violence of the captain, the cook, and the Spaniards.

Although the case against the Spaniards was eventually dismissed, this insertion of the Mendians into the U.S. legal system as plaintiffs in a civil suit was nevertheless significant.[26] Under ordinary circumstances it was not possible for slaves to sue their masters in civil court; nor was it possible, in most cases, for black people to testify against white people in any kind of suit.[27] The fact that the Mendians' legal status as slave or free was unclear undoubtedly influenced the decision of the judge to hear their case; had they been proven to be slaves by the laws of Spain they would not have been able to file a suit. The significance of this case lies in the *Amistad* Committee's and the Mendians' attempt to force the legal system to recognize them, if not as righteous rebels, at least as individuals with the ability to enter the social contract. The case thereby sought a more inclusive interpretation of liberal theory and the discourse of national identity, one that challenged not only racial slavery, but racial hierarchy more generally.

Another account by the Spaniards, Don José Ruiz and Don Pedro Montez, different from that taken during the judicial investigation, was published over a month after the schooner was first brought in, and some weeks after the preceding accounts of the Mendians had appeared in newspapers throughout New York and Connecticut. Several papers explained this delay as resulting from their physical exhaustion and their emotional duress after their ordeal on the *Amistad* (NY *Ad & Ex* 9/18/39). While this may well have been true, it is also the case that, upon arriving in the free states of the United States, the Spaniards did not receive the kind of treatment that they would have had they landed either in the slaveholding states of the United States or in Cuba, where the Mendians would have been given up to the Spaniards immediately, probably without a trial.[28] Although the Mendians were taken into custody, it was not at all clear whether they would be "returned" to the Spaniards who claimed them as their property.

The Mendians were fortunate enough to have the *Amistad* Committee provide them with excellent legal counsel, who ensured that the legal questions raised would be complex. By the time the Spaniards published their account, the fundamental legal questions of their case against the Mendians had already been raised in the district court of Connecticut. These questions included: (1) whether the people of African descent on the *Amistad* were in fact native Africans or were either born in slavery in Cuba or imported prior to the abolition of the international slave trade by Spain in 1819; and (2) who was in control of the *Amistad* when it was captured by the brig *Washington*, the Mendians or the Spaniards. In addition, public opinion as represented in the newspapers of the northeastern United States supported the release of the Mendians over their return to the Spaniards. Given this situation, the Spaniards' account should be read as responding to both the general attitude of support for the Mendians and the legal questions posed above.

Early in October, the New York *Advertiser and Express* published the Spaniards' account of their ordeal on the *Amistad*, translated from the Spanish paper *Noticioso de Ambos Mundos*. The *Advertiser and Express* characterized the Spaniards as "facing at every moment death with all its terrors and in every form, and contending with thirst against the waves and against the daggers of a lawless horde of Savages" (10/5/39:2,3–5). Like the *Sun*'s account, the Spaniards' emphasizes the violence and brutality of the Mendians, but adds their supposed passion for drinking wine and rum. And like the official report, this account demonizes the Mendians by stating that they performed "superstitious ceremonies" and made "horrible gestures."

Yet this account differs from the *Sun*'s in a couple of important respects. First, it rhetorically erases the African origins of the Mendians by calling them "slaves" and "blacks" but never "Africans." Yet a number of newspapers pointed out that the Spaniards openly called the Mendians "Africans" when they first arrived in port. Whether or not the Mendians were actually natives of Africa proved to be particularly important in the legal battle that decided their fate. This shift from the official account undoubtedly was a response to the inquiries of the court. Related to this renaming was the way in which the Spaniards describe the Mendians' attempt to return to Africa. The account states that the "blacks" ordered them simply to "sail toward the rising of the sun." By denying any connection between the Mendians and Africa, this statement suggests not only that the "blacks" could not master the complexities of navigation, but that they may not have known what was to be found in that direction.

The Spaniards' account also differs from that of the *Sun* in its organization. Their account emphasizes Montez's strategies first to quell the rebellion and then either to be taken by another ship, to escape ashore, or to escape in the boat. Montez appears throughout as the person manipulating a dangerous and uncertain situation to his own advantage, while the "blacks" are presented as mysterious, unpredictable, undirected, and superstitious. The Spaniards' account further connects this characterization to the Mendians' ignorance of navigation. For example, at one point the Mendians told Montez to turn the schooner around because they were sailing toward the Exuma Keys, of which they were afraid. This he did, and it set them going west again toward Havana. When the "blacks" discovered this as the sun began to fall, the account continues, they became quite angry, to which Montez responded that "they themselves had so ordered and they answered that Montez ought to have apprised them of it; he replied that they were very noisy and would not let him do what was best. Then they allowed him to steer towards the East" (10/5/39:2,4). Montez appears as a knowing elder among misbehaving ("noisy") children. What he desired is "what was best," and they eventually recognize his knowledge, if not his authority. By foregrounding Montez's agency and making the efforts of the Mendians appear ineffective if not ridiculous, this account supports the Spaniards' claim that they brought the *Amistad* into port through their own stratagem and challenges the notion that the Mendians were in control of the ship when it was captured by Lieutenant Gedney and the U.S. brig *Washington*. In addition to its limited time-frame, this account restricts intelligent agency to the Spaniards, Montez in particular. These boundaries operate in tandem to construct the Spaniards as the natural superiors of the uncivilized and unintelligent "blacks," who, by virtue of their greater savagery, managed briefly to disrupt the control of the Spaniards, but who did not finally prevail.

Late in October, the *Colored American*, New York's only weekly African American newspaper, reprinted a long description of "Cingues" from the *Herald of Freedom*, not reprinted elsewhere in New York.[29] The description likens "Cingues" to Daniel Webster, the politician from Massachusetts famous for his oratory and antislavery views:

He has Webster's lion aspect—his majestic, quiet, uninterested cast of expression. . . . His eye is deep, heavy—the cloudy iris extending up behind the brow almost inexpressive, and yet as if volcanoes of action might be asleep behind it . . . an unenlightened eye, as Webster's would have looked had he been bred in the desert, among the lions, as Cingues was. . . . The nose and mouth of Cingue are African. . . . He has none of the look of an Indian—nothing of the savage. It is a gentle, magnanimous, generous look, not so much of the warrior as the sage. (Qtd. in *CA* 10/19/39:1,1)

This description strikingly recalls that of the *Sun*, considered above, in its attention to visual detail and cultural comparisons. Like the earlier article, this one figures "Cingue" as royal and wise, but it differs in emphasizing Cingue's Africanness and his difference from indigenous Americans. This description thus unsettles a "hard" racist notion of a hierarchy among races by implying Cingue's higher status than "Indian" "savages" (presumably not the noble sort). Yet it also retains the "soft" racialist sense of unequally evolved cultures, in which environmental difference makes "Cingues" "unenlightened" when compared with the educated Webster. Most interestingly, the description mingles "Cingue"'s wisdom and generosity with the potentially threatening "volcanoes of action . . . asleep behind" them. This image delicately balances, in a way very different from the overtly interpretive material considered later in this chapter, concepts of nature, violence, and righteousness. Combined with "Cingue"'s "unenlightened" condition, the image of the slumbering volcano suggests the avenging force of less-evolved culture that nevertheless has a righteous claim to justice. As we will see later in this study, both Frederick Douglass and Herman Melville also made use of this powerful and complex image.

As part of their strategy to prove that the captives were native Africans and so liberate them both from U.S. jails and from the possibility of delivery to the Spaniards, the *Amistad* Committee engaged a number of specialists to work with them. These included Professor Joshua W. Gibbs, a linguist, and Benjamin Griswold and other "young men" of the Theological Seminary of Yale College. Professor Gibbs produced a study of the Mendians' names that at least four different newspapers published during November 1839.[30] Implicitly arguing for the existence of a Mendian language, which the captives spoke, from an analysis of their names, this study supports the abolitionists' assertion that the Mendians were native Africans recently captured in Africa rather than people native to or long domiciled in Havana. Gibbs argues that the names the Mendians give as their own (as opposed to those given them by the Spaniards) correspond to things in nature and are significant in the Mendi "dialect." He asserts that the Spaniards could not have given them these names because the Spaniards could not pronounce them properly, "[f]or in the Mendi language, rude as it is, there are certain euphonic laws which regulate the formation of words. . . . A foreigner is in constant danger of violating these laws." Thus Gibbs invokes a difficulty in pronunciation associated with unfamiliar phonetic combinations as a sign that the Mendians' origins must be different from that of the Spaniards'. Moving beyond the realm of linguistics, the study declares that the Mendians have no other names, based on the observation that "Singwe has indeed been called Joseph . . . but when asked whether his name is Joseph he rejects it with indignation."[31]

In addition to Professor Gibbs's work with the Mendians, which eventually led to the publication of a Mendi and Gissi vocabulary,[32] a number of "young men connected with Yale College" engaged themselves in daily instruction with the Mendians, teaching them to read the English language and "the plain and important truths of Christianity" (*HAC* 24). One of these young men, Benjamin Griswold, responded to what he called a desire on the part of "Friends of the Africans" for "an article . . . giving an account of the efforts made for their intellectual and moral improvement, and some notice of the manners and customs prevalent in their native country" (*HAC* 25). This ethnographic account reports briefly on the Mendians' form of government, their native apparel, habits of adornment, usual foods, marriage arrangements, funeral customs, and system of religion. Most especially, the account emphasizes their efforts to learn to speak and read English, especially the Bible, their religious instruction, and their affection for their teachers.

Griswold's description of the Mendians' language training begins, "The Mendi language, so far as we have been able to learn, has never been reduced to writing, nor have the natives characters by which they retain and transmit a history of passing events" (*HAC* 28). This preface suggests that, to those who know only Mendi, written language is unknown; with this lack of knowledge, the passage implies, comes a lack of the concept of history. This implication typifies Euroamerican impressionistic representations of African people, which figure the "dark continent" as existing in a timeless prehistoric phase, before religion and civilization. Still, the preface admits a greater specificity in the Mendians' language than the characterization of their speech as a "negro language."

Griswold's account emphasizes the Mendians' intense involvement in the learning process. The Mendians purportedly spent from two to four hours a day receiving instruction, which was difficult at first because "they had been accustomed neither to the requisite effort of mind nor fixedness of attention" (28). Rather than having no mental capacity, a "hard" racist view, Griswold's characterization deploys the "soft" racialist view that the Mendians' cultural environment has not encouraged them to use their minds. Denied altogether is the possibility that the Mendians were accustomed to using their minds in a fashion different from the intellectual work in which the Yale men customarily engaged. Griswold further reports, "Not unfrequently in their desire to retain their teacher through the day, they attempt even to hold him, grasping his hands and clinging to his person, and individuals offer to give him their own dinner on condition of his remaining" (*HAC* 28). Even when the teachers do succeed in leaving, the Mendians "may be found gathered in two or three groups, all reading and aiding each other," and "thus employed will they sit quietly for hours in the most patient, persevering effort to learn 'Merica'" (28). This image of the Mendians as dutiful students supports Tappan's (and others') representations of them as "intelligent and docile" and challenges the initial and official accounts. It disrupts the "hard" racialist logic that figures all Africans and their descendants as innately and immutably inferior to the "Anglo-Saxon" race, especially in terms of their intellectual and moral capabilities. In a country where in most locales it was illegal for enslaved people to learn to read and write, and educational resources for free people of color were extremely limited, this representation of Africans in concerted and successful intellectual effort was not only unusual, but potentially threatening to many.

In addition, the *Amistad* Committee and the Yale men developed the Mendians' learning environment in such a way as to achieve their own agenda. Griswold concludes his account with the following statement, which might be taken as encapsulating that agenda:

These men deserve sympathy—they ought to have protection. Let me ask in their behalf, means to carry on their defense; let me ask the prayers of those who care for them and the perishing millions of Africa, that God will so order events as to deliver them from the bloody grasp of the executioner, and they may return missionaries to their native land to proclaim there the truth of the everlasting Gospel. (31)

Here Griswold calls on his readers to pray for the delivery of the Mendians not so that they might go free, but so that they can become conduits for the abolitionists' religion to the "dark continent." Thus the Mendians were taught to read from the Bible, and literacy was acquired simultaneously with Christianity. This dual acquisition of literacy and Christianity was not itself unusual, as many U.S. Americans learned to read by reading the Bible. But Griswold's conclusion harnesses not just a religious but a specifically missionary agenda to the Mendians' learning process.

Despite this, rather than submission to a "superior" society—the clear if perhaps unwitting message of Griswold's account—the Mendians' effort to learn may be understood as their attempt to gain some kind of control over their hostile environment. Finding themselves in a place where they did not speak the language, did not know the customs or the laws, and were immediately taken into captivity, the Mendians made use of the only tool available to them to gain any degree of voice or authority. By learning the local language, the Mendians were able to speak for themselves rather than through an interpreter (albeit a competent and sympathetic one), or through their abolitionist friends. Although both the language and the situations in which they were allowed to speak largely determined the content of what they said, I want to emphasize their ability to master many of the codes of a hostile environment. Several of them made use of their new abilities by addressing the court, and after their release, by speaking to audiences in overflowing auditoriums.[33] In one of her "Letters from New York," published in the *National Anti-Slavery Standard,* Lydia Maria Child makes a similar observation. Having attended one of the Mendians' farewell meetings, Child commented not only on the skill with which Kinna answered theological questions put to him, but on the Mendians' ability to negotiate the complex situation in which they found themselves: "I thought these honest creatures would be vexatious materials, should any theological drill-sargent try to substitute a routine of catechisms and creeds for the [individual's?] life" (12/2/41:2,2). In addition, in their lectures the Mendians often described their capture, transport, rebellion, and recapture, reproducing what for U.S. Americans was a paradigmatic experience of the "universal" struggle for liberty. In this way the Mendians produced for themselves a position from which to claim their "natural rights." In addition, some learned to write; Ka-le's letter to Mr. Adams (*Anti-Slavery Reporter,* qtd. in *Lib* 4/2/41), written after the Mendians' release, constitutes the only interpretive text they produced (it will be considered in this chapter's next section).

## PART TWO: INTERPRETATIONS

Part Two considers the way in which various factions within the U.S. population argued for particular interpretations of the *Amistad* rebellion by using the discursive strategies of displacement, disruption, and/or insertion. Because the judiciary maintained custody of the Mendians, representatives of President Martin Van Buren's administration were not able simply to turn the Mendians over to the Spanish minister, as he requested, but had to contend with supporters of the Mendians in the district court of Connecticut, the U.S. circuit court for the state of Connecticut, and finally the U.S. Supreme Court. During the time of the trials, the commercial, the penny, and especially the abolitionist presses provided a forum for debate regarding the appropriate fate of the rebel captives.

In the first section below, I examine the compatible strategies of the Spanish minister, representatives of the Van Buren administration, and the newspaper press in the slaveholding states, which figured the rebels as pirates and murderers and interpolated the United States as a slaveholding community. In section two, I analyze how the Mendians' supporters drew upon the simultaneous logics of difference and identification, considered earlier, in order to create an interpretive frame through which U.S. Americans could imagine the Mendians as worthy to claim the trope of revolutionary struggle. I argue that this interpretive frame figured the Mendians as a separate national entity, a distinct people, thereby differentiating them from the enslaved population in the United States.[34] This strategy of insertion, while supporting the captives, also protected the Compact between the States by obscuring the matter of rebellion within the domestic population. The final section considers how the Mendians' lawsuit against their Spanish captors attempted to force the U.S. legal system to grant them protection under the law, and thereby to recognize them truly as persons.

## Slaveholders and the Executive

A little over a week after the schooner *Amistad* and the persons associated with it were captured and brought into port in Connecticut, the Spanish minister to the United States Don Angel Calderon de la Barca, wrote to the U.S. secretary of state, John Forsyth. This correspondence marks the beginning of a relationship between these national entities that grew to involve other members of the Van Buren administration, including attorney generals Felix Grundy and Henry D. Gilpin and district attorney William S. Holabird of Connecticut. This relationship transformed a physical and perhaps ideological conflict between

Africans and their captors into a diplomatic dispute between national entities, thereby replacing a conflict between dark-skinned people and light-skinned men with one between light-skinned men.

Although Spain had signed a treaty with Britain in 1817 abolishing the African slave trade, importation of and trade in natives of Africa occurred almost openly in the Spanish Caribbean. Still, it was important for Spain's relations with Britain for Spanish subjects not to be seen as participating in the African slave trade. In order to assure this appearance, the Spanish government needed to keep U.S. officials from inquiring into the point of origin of the captives.[35] Thus it was in the interests of the Spanish government to deny the jurisdiction of the United States and to procure the immediate return of the captives to Ruiz and Montez.

Calderon de la Barca characterized the *Amistad* case as a dispute between Spanish subjects and their slaves and as a matter to be settled by reference to treaties between nations. While phrasing Lieutenant Gedney's "act of humanity" (*ATA* 7), Calderon de la Barca called for "an observance of the law of nations, and the treaties existing between the United States and Spain" (*ATA* 6), in determining what should be done with the schooner and the "blacks" now in the custody of the district court of Connecticut. The letter demanded the return of the vessel, the return of the "blacks" so that they could be brought to trial by Spanish tribunals, and an acknowledgment that the United States did not have jurisdiction over the dispute. These demands deny the authority of any portion of the U.S. government to participate in determining the fate of any element of the *Amistad* affair.

The minister's letter appeals to both a formal legal agreement between nations and a vaguer notion of common national interests. It invokes Pickney's Treaty of 1795, Articles 8, 9, and 10 of which respectively stipulate that ships driven into port by stress of weather, pirates, or enemies shall be received with humanity, that all property rescued out of the hands of pirates will be returned to its owners, and that vessels wrecked or foundered will receive assistance without cost beyond that to meet expenses. This reference suggests simultaneously and paradoxically that the *Amistad* was driven into port by pirates and that the "blacks" should be returned to the Spaniards as property stolen by pirates. In this schema, the "blacks" are both thieves and stolen property.

This construction of the rebels as pirates replicates that of the initial sightings of the *Amistad* as described in the newspaper press. As I argued earlier, such representations code the rebels as piratical by calling them a "strange crew" and emphasizing the incongruence between their state of dress ("almost or quite naked") and their possessions (a "belt of dollars" and "a gold watch") (NY *Ad & Ex* 8/24/39). Yet what emerged most prominently from my analysis of these reports was not the nature of the rebels but the "common sense" of those reporting having seen them. This "common sense" mirrors the interpretive frame of the minister's letter: both recognize the rebels as pirates because of their racial coding combined with their control of the ship; armed, dark-skinned people make sense only as something outside the law.

Consider for a moment the official definition of a pirate. According to *Wheaton's Elements of International Law*, piracy is defined as "the offense of depredating on the seas without being authorized by any sovereign States, or with commissions from different sovereigns at war with each other" (113; qtd. in *ATA* 60). Pirates are outlaws not only, and perhaps not even primarily, because they attack and plunder ships, but because they do not recognize a (single) national affiliation. Because they are nationless, their acts are not sanctioned by the ideology of a national entity but are performed in the service of their own interests and agendas. Because they do not acknowledge allegiance to any nation, they operate outside of and in opposition to the law of nations. Yet if one recollects the British navy's practice of impressing men into service, the difference between the activities of pirates and navies blurs. Rather than their actions, sailors' (lack of) national coding makes the difference between patriots and pirates.

The Spanish minister was careful to refer to the rebels as "blacks," a racial signifier that has no national connotations. This racial coding discursively erased any national (or ethnic) affiliation of these dark-skinned people and operated as a mark of supposedly natural inferiority. Because they are nationless, the rebels almost automatically qualify as pirates. The law of nations defined not only appropriate national behavior, but what kind of an entity may be recognized as a nation. The minister's reference to treaties implicitly positioned the rebels as outside the community created by the law of nations (i.e., not of the nations of Europe and their descendants). His letter thus combined notions of race and (the lack of a) nation in order implicitly to deny the rebels a position from which to negotiate.

Denying the rebels such a position was a major strategy of containment produced by the minister's displacement of the conflict into the arena of international relations. As property, the rebels had no subjectivity. As pirates, they had no authority. Both cases discursively contained the potential threat to slaveholding societies generated by this incident of slave rebellion. Although the minister does not use the discourse of national identity, his figuring the rebels as property interfaces with the logic of slavery advocates in the United States, who denied the trope of revolutionary struggle to enslaved people.

The minister's letter also appealed to the more ambiguous notion of common national interest, by constructing the national character of the United States as slaveholding. He argues that "the crime in question is one of those which, if permitted to pass unpunished, would endanger the internal tranquillity and the safety of the island of Cuba, where the citizens of the United States not only carry on a considerable trade, but where they possess territorial properties which they cultivate with the labor of African slaves" (*ATA* 9). This passage presents the interests of U.S. citizens in Cuba as a reason for compliance with the minister's requests, but this notion of "endanger[ing] the internal tranquillity" of Cuba also recalls the bloody Haitian revolution of 1799 and raises the specter of slave rebellion more generally. This construction implicitly invokes the aspect of discourses of white supremacy that figured "African slaves" as innately savage, semi-human, and ever ready to massacre their captors.

In further developing the common identity of Spain and the United States as slaveholding societies, the minister's letter mentions people who are "employing all the means which knowledge and wealth can afford for effecting at any price, the emancipation of the slaves" (*ATA* 9). This reference figures abolitionists as the common enemy of all slaveholding societies. Yet the situation in the United States was

complex. Certainly most U.S. Americans were unequivocally interested in the avoidance and suppression of slave rebellion, and many
were against the emancipation of the enslaved population. Most
agreed that support for the Compact between the States required the
protection of slavery. But many abolitionists were also pacifists and
therefore did not support outright rebellion. In addition, as we have
seen, a considerable faction desired the exclusion of blacks *and slavery* from conceptualizations of the United States. Thus, while many
would have supported aspects of the minister's argument, his construction of the national character of the United States as slaveholding was not congruent even with those most powerful in the United
States.

The newspaper press in the slaveholding states reporting on the
*Amistad* affair deployed an interpretive frame similar to that of Calderon de la Barca's letter.[36] For example, the New Orleans *Picayune*
noted the capture of the schooner with, "It is certain . . . that the slaves
have been guilty of piracy and murder and will be dealt with accordingly" (9/7/39:2,2). The same paper framed its much edited version of
the news article from the New York *Sun* as "the whole of the particulars concerning the piracy, mutiny and murder on board the Spanish
Schooner *Amistad*" (9/12/39:2,3). In addition to characterizing the
rebels as pirates, the New York *Evening Star* raised the question of agitation against slavery, as did the minister's letter, calling the *Amistad*
"a God-send to the ultra-abolitionists" (qtd. in *Eman* 9/19/39:81,6).

An article from a Spanish newspaper in New York exemplifies the
ideological assumptions of this interpretive frame. In contrast to the
brief reports in the slaveholding states, the *Noticioso de Ambos Mundos* reported in full the events of the *Amistad* affair, including the account of the Spaniards, and presented arguments very similar to those
of the Spanish minister.[37] In response to the filing of the affidavits of
Fonni, Kimbe, and Cinqué and the subsequent arrest of Ruiz and
Montez, this paper commented: "In what country do we live! . . . where
they say *all* are free—where the constitution of the land says so—where
the slavery of the negro is recognized—where the very Congress has
forbidden the reading within that body of petitions in favor of the
slaves" (emphasis in original).[38] This exclamation of outrage demar-

cates an absolute split between "*all*" who are free and "the negro" who is enslaved. In this schema, the Constitution and the congressional "gag rule" protect those of the community called "*all*," who simultaneously claim the subject-position "all [white] men" and deny any other configuration. Like the Spanish minister's positioning of the rebels as outside the community of lawful citizens, this representation asserts the protection of the rights of slaveholders as the self-evident reason for the "gag rule." Yet again, the "gag rule" was supported by those who perceived the silencing of debate concerning slavery to be part of the Compact between the States. The representation of the U.S. national character as slaveholding, as I will show in my analysis of the *Creole* rebellion, became a site of considerable conflict within the national alliance.

In contrast to the avowedly proslavery agenda of the Spanish minister, the *Noticioso de Ambos Mundos,* and newspapers from the slaveholding states, the goals of Van Buren's administration in this matter are more difficult to determine. In his seminal study of the *Amistad* affair, Howard Jones argues that Van Buren's Democratic Party was an alliance of Northern and Southern forces that would remain intact only so long as the issue of slavery was not a subject of public debate (1987, 53). According to Jones's logic, Van Buren's coalition was dependent upon the same "spirit of compromise" as the alliance formed at the time of the Revolution. Recall that the coalition supporting Van Buren's presidency had been created largely by the politics and presidency of Andrew Jackson, which had refigured the subject-position of the original alliance, "all [landowning] men," to a racially coded notion of masculine subjectivity, "all [white] men." As my argument in the previous chapter also suggests, this refiguring meant that, although competing mythologies of U.S. development emerged in the context of and as a result of the expansion of U.S. Americans into the North American continent, an alliance could be maintained on the basis of a common notion of race. Discussions of slavery therefore could be censored from either a proslavery or a pro-Union position.

The initial behavior of the Van Buren administration supports Jones's assertion that their primary goal was to silence debate on slavery by whatever means. The administration's support of the Spanish minister's requests might be interpreted as a way to keep the moral, ethical, and political issues associated with slavery from being raised in a public forum. But during the course of the *Amistad* lawsuit, the Spanish minister merged the official interests of the United States with those of Spain, and representatives of Van Buren's administration then pursued these combined interests in a legal forum even after the affair could have fallen from public scrutiny. In what follows, I argue that the later actions of the administration indicate a proslavery rather than a pro-Union stance, and I suggest that rather than protecting the national alliance, their goal was to limit the potential of the *Amistad* rebellion to disrupt the increasingly dominant power of slaveholders.

After receiving the Spanish minister's letter, President Van Buren, in consultation with Secretary of State John Forsyth and other members of his cabinet, directed U.S. Attorney General Felix Grundy to write an official opinion supporting the Spanish minister's request for the return of the schooner and the captives (Jones 1987, 58). Grundy's "Opinion" agreed that U.S. courts did not have jurisdiction over the case because the *Amistad* was a Spanish vessel sailing under the Spanish flag and under the control of Spanish subjects. This abdication was founded on Grundy's assertion that international law called for nations to respect each other's laws and official papers. Grundy uses this assertion to argue that the United States cannot question the validity of the *Amistad*'s papers because they are official documents from Cuba. Because the papers are considered valid, the "Opinion" continues, the United States must assume the "blacks" to be the Spaniards' property, unlawfully stolen by pirates. Given this, Article 9 of Pickney's Treaty applies, and the United States is bound to deliver the vessel and its cargo, including the "blacks," to the Spanish minister.

Grundy's "Opinion" thus used the written documentation of the vessel's papers to develop a legal argument supporting the claims of the Spaniards. Written documentation, in a language and form recognized by formal agreements between (European) nations, was the mechanism that authorized the Spaniards' version of events. This evidence was recognized as valid in part because the "blacks" did not have any written documentation to support their counter-claims. Because the papers of the *Amistad* authorized this journey (as did the minister's letter, which began with the sailing of the *Amistad*), Grundy's "Opinion" implicitly supported the narrow time-frame of the Spaniards' account. This narrow time-frame denied that anything relevant to understanding the events of the *Amistad* occurred prior to the ship's sailing, and so denied the rebels' African point of origin, the illegality of their importation into Cuba, and therefore any (legal) motive for their actions.[39] Thus Grundy's validation of the Spaniards' position supported the minister's denial of a position from which the rebels could negotiate.

The unquestioning validation of the *Amistad*'s papers by Grundy's "Opinion" indicates an interpretive frame, sympathetic to slaveholders, that recognized dark-skinned people only as subordinates or slaves. As became clear over the course of the *Amistad* trials, property claims to slaves were a site of considerable conflict among Spanish and British forces in Cuba. While it may have been the intention of Grundy's "Opinion" to keep the U.S. courts from hearing the case of the *Amistad*, the discursive strategy employed by the attorney general to obtain this end nevertheless supported the representation of the national character of the United States as slaveholding.

Two letters written by William S. Holabird, the U.S. district attorney for Connecticut, paralleled the conclusions of Grundy's "Opinion" by urging the secretary of state to seek out some means by which the captives might be removed quickly from the jurisdiction of the judiciary. On September 5, 1839, Holabird wrote to Secretary of State Forsyth regarding the *Amistad*, its cargo, and "41 blacks, supposed to be slaves," stating that "[t]he next term of our circuit court sits on the 17th instant, at which time I *suppose* it will be my duty to bring them to trial, unless they are in some other way disposed of" (*ATA* 39; emphasis in original). He wrote again, four days later, asking "whether there are no treaty stipulations with the Government of Spain that would authorize our Government to deliver them up to the Spanish authorities; and, if so, whether it could be done before our court sits?" (*ATA* 39). Unlike Grundy's "Opinion," these statements do not legally argue for the return of the captives, but rather willingly subvert the judicial process in order to return the captives to the Spaniards (these are only the first in a series of such comments and actions by Van Buren's administration).[40]

Yet the *Amistad* case went to trial. The case was adjourned in the circuit court of Connecticut, then was sent to the district court of the same state, which convened three times, and then a year later went before the Supreme Court, upon the appeal of the district attorney. The arguments presented by lawyers for Ruiz and Montez reproduced the reasoning of the Spanish minister's letter. Relying on the papers of the *Amistad* as *prima facie* and sufficient evidence, they argued that the captives were returnable as property under treaties between Spain and the United States.

During most of the trials, the interests of the national alliance and of slaveholders converged. But once it became clear that the *Amistad* trial would raise substantial questions regarding the legality of slavery, the district attorney, acting upon orders from the administration, announced that "the Spanish minister had 'merged' the claims of Ruiz and Montez with that of the United States [and that h]e as district attorney would present them as one" (qtd. in Jones 1987, 120).[41] From this point on, lawyers of the Van Buren administration represented the Spaniards in court. This "merging" illustrates the compatibility of the minister's and Grundy's interpretive frames, and their common assertion that the dispute should be settled according to formal legal agreements between national entities. Further, this action marked the emergence of the interests of *slaveholders* as the dominant agenda of the administration and the subordination of the interests of the national alliance as a whole. Yet the judiciary's custody of the rebels minimized the potential threat to the national alliance posed by the administration's position. Thus in this case what "the United States" "was" was multifaceted, and the various powerful groups that sought to dominate the nation were able to find representation in the respective branches of government. This prevented a radical disruption in the national alliance.

Despite the important differences among them, these discursive strategies all displaced the conflict between the *Amistad* rebels and the Spaniards into the arena of international relations and recast a conflict between dark-skinned people and light-skinned men as a dispute between light-skinned men. In this arena, a variety of discursive strategies constructed the rebels as without a position from which to negotiate (dark-skinned, nationless, "negro language," without documents). These representations thus operated in a way similar to the two mythologies of U.S. development discussed earlier. Just as these mythologies either discursively erased the presence of slavery and African Americans or represented African Americans only in an enslaved condition, the texts analyzed in this section either discursively erased the presence of the rebels as subjects by asserting their status as property, or figured them as subordinate to and outside of any national community. These discursive strategies of displacement, erasure, and subordination worked in tandem to contain the disruptive potential of this incident of slave rebellion.

## The Captives' Supporters

Immediately following the capture of the *Amistad,* supporters of the captives began to develop strategies for authorizing their actions. The rebels' narrative and their supporters' interpretations challenged the Spaniards and their supporters' version of events. The most powerful and disruptive strategy deployed on behalf of the rebels claimed the trope of revolutionary struggle. The strategies of the rebels' supporters operated like that of revolutionary colonists in that they refigured the social contract to include these native Africans and to exclude the slaveholders' claim to property in persons. This schema represents the actions of slaveholders as equivalent to those of tyrannical monarchs.

The process by which the rebels were made part of the community of "all MEN," by which they are authorized in their acts of rebellion through the discourse of national identity, was complex and paradoxical. Because of the numerous ideological forces that worked to prevent arguments of this kind from being developed, disseminated, and gaining authority, simply asserting that the rebels had a right to resist those who held them in bondage was not persuasive to most U.S. Americans. Supporters of the rebels had to create a means by which U.S. Americans could *imagine* the rebels to have such a right of resistance. The rebels' supporters had to construct an interpretive frame that would position the rebels as part of the community of "all MEN" rather than as part of the enslaved population. Whereas the Spaniards' interpretive frame denied the rebels a position from which to negotiate, that of the rebels' supporters claimed for them a position from which to act according to the discourse of national identity, from which to assert their "natural right" to life and liberty. By giving new ideological import to the notion of natural rights, this claim transformed the pirates into patriots, not of Jackson's America, but of a newly configured nation, one that rejected rather than supported racialized slavery.

In order to gain popular support for the rebels, their defenders further developed simultaneous logics of identification and difference. These logics initially focused on Cinqué as the rebels' leader and patriot extraordinare, but later grew to figure the rebels as a people, a separate national entity. In what follows, I argue that the newly generated ability of many U.S. Americans to imagine the *Amistad* rebels as a people with their own linguistic, political, and cultural specificity (1) meant that they could be imagined to be worthy claimants to the trope of revolutionary struggle; (2) most profoundly disrupted the strategies of containment of the Spanish minister and others; and (3) determined their fate in their district and Supreme Court trials. Further, I show how this process paradoxically both challenged and accommodated the strategies of competing groups to limit to themselves the authority of the trope of revolutionary struggle.

Both newspaper articles and poems by supporters of the *Amistad* captives constructed for the rebels a genealogy of male heroes from the revolutionary period. These genealogies challenged the process of "natal alienation" (Patterson 7) whereby slaves were detached from generations in both ascending and descending directions and so were defined as outside the social realm. Like the strategy of free African American men in their protests against disfranchisement, this construction creates a historical legacy for the rebels that connects them to preceding generations of generally acknowledged patriotic figures. This legacy's logic of identification reconfigures the discourse of national identity as including the rebels.

Those supporters of the *Amistad* captives who were the least concerned about maintaining the national alliance connected the rebels to the founding fathers with no qualifications. Shortly after the capture of the rebels had been reported in New York newspapers, the *Liberator* remarked that "it is a case which calls for the sympathy of all true hearted lovers of liberty, that the brave Cinques and his associates have . . . merely imitated the example of Washington and the heroes of the revolution" (9/6/39:143,6). Just as the proslavery press offered no arguments for their representation of the rebels as pirates, property, and murderers, this unequivocally abolitionist press made no argument for the genealogical equivalence presented here. Rather, the interpretive frame of "all true hearted lovers of liberty" considers this equivalence self-evident or commonsensical. Such an unequivocal assertion was possible for William Lloyd Garrison, editor of the *Liberator*, precisely because he and his supporters regularly argued for a split between North and South, characterized by their slogan "NO UNION WITH SLAVEHOLDERS!"

But because claiming the trope of revolutionary struggle for enslaved people disrupted the Compact between the States, many of the rebels' supporters differentiated the *Amistad* rebels from the enslaved population within the United States. In some news articles, assertions of the rebels' difference were made by avowed nonabolitionists who nevertheless supported the actions of the rebels. In others, implicit logics of difference fundamentally shaped the conceptual frames used to argue on behalf of the rebels. The interaction of differently configured logics of difference and a similar logic of identification produced a number of related but distinct discursive strategies.

In what follows, I focus on these two differently configured logics of difference. The first constructed Cinqué as exceptional and so separated him from his companions and all other black people, while the second differentiated the rebels from the enslaved population in the United States. Although the abolitionist supporters of the rebels did not racialize their descriptions of Cinqué as did the eyewitness account in the New York *Sun*, I argue that these interpretations more profoundly mark the process of differentiation and individualization. This process mirrored black abolitionist discourse by emphasizing Cinqué's masculinity, recasting "all [free] men," and "all [white] men," as "all MEN."

Consider, for example, a letter written to the Boston *Courier*, which quotes these lines: "O'er the glad waters of the dark blue sea, / Our thoughts as boundless and our souls as free," and comments, "Unquestionably the Congolese chieftain has, from his heart of hearts, recognized this sentiment of Lord Byron, and his practical application of it has been an exact copy of our own conduct, to resist unto death, aggression, insult, and an infamous tyranny" (qtd. in *Lib* 9/13/39:146,2). The writer is able to support their actions against "an infamous tyranny" in part because of a long-standing rivalry between Spain, ruled by a Catholic monarch, and the United States, a supposedly secular (but definitely Protestant) republic ruled by "the people." Yet notice, too, the way in which this passage elevates Cinqué to the status of "Congolese chieftain," a status that enables him to recognize "this sentiment of Lord Byron" and separates him from his fellow rebels. Once Cinqué is differentiated and elevated, this passage also equates his actions with those of the community invoked by the "our," that is, "Americans."

This equivalence then serves as the basis of a strong identification: "We must feel the same fire of indignation and ungovernable sense of injustice consuming us, which blazed so fiercely in seventy-six, and heated the hearts of our forefathers red hot" (qtd. in *Lib* 9/13/39:146,2). This call to identify was designed to produce an emotional response in the reader and to revitalize notions of freedom associated with the Revolution. Ironically, this call, as it links Cinqué to the revolutionary "forefathers," also creates an imagined history for many readers, who, given the rate of European immigration during the second quarter of the nineteenth century, would not have had actual "forefathers" who either lived in the United States or fought in the Revolutionary War. This logic of identification thus works not only to authorize Cinqué, but both to socialize European immigrants into a particular story of U.S. national identity, and therefore a particular idea of citizenship, and to produce a specific notion of "American" for all inhabitants. This strategy works similarly to that of African American men who, in the agitation against their disfranchisement, considered in chapter 1, produced a narrative of a biracial nation, based in that case not on rebellion, but on participating in national development, particularly "humbl[ing] the wilderness." In that case as well the strategy produced an imagined history with which many were invited to identify. In this case the letter's progression creates a genealogy for Cinqué that inserts him (and more recently immigrated European men), like a lost son, into the community of "all men." Because of the supposedly transhistorical and transcultural character of natural rights discourse, Cinqué need not have been present during the Revolution to be inserted into its legacy, illustrating the remarkable flexibility and power of this discursive formation.

At least three poems published in the abolitionist press were entitled "Cinquez," whom they represent as the lone and virtuous leader of the *Amistad* rebellion. These poems link these heroic qualities, as in the letter to the *Courier,* with the legacy of the revolutionary fathers. For example, a poem by "R." argues, Thou slayest thine oppressors,—so

> The fathers did of those who see thy woe
> They slew them, and their sons yet proudly tell
> How their father's [*sic*] arms the tyrants fell.
> They fought for liberty:
> In them 'twas *virtue,*—is it less in thee?
>
> . . . . . . . . . . . . .
>
> Who, then, shall censure thee?—ah, only he
> Who is less fit than thou for liberty.
> (Qtd. in *Eman* 10/3/39:92,1)

Yet these lines also create an interesting twist on relations between "Cinquez" and readers. Rather than attempting to persuade readers, this poem asserts that readers will be judged by their response to the actions of "thee"; their membership in the community fit "for liberty" depends upon their recognizing the righteousness of the rebel leader's deed.

Similarly, a poem by "J. D. B." warns,

> Hearts, too indignant to forget,
> Are listening while thy tale is told;
>
> . . . . . . . . . . . . .
>
> This soil would spurn us, should we dare

> To crush thee with a felon's doom;
> Our father's [*sic*] ashes, kindling there
> Would curse us from the tomb.
> (Qtd. in *Eman* 9/26/39:88,1)

Like the letter to the *Courier,* this poem constru[...]
state of indignation as the appropriate response to "Cinquez" 's circumstances, and thereby argues for identification with him. And like
the poem quoted above, this one threatens readers that to ignore the
call to identification is to risk a curse "from [our fathers'] tomb." In
these poems, "Cinquez" not only is more in touch with the ideals of
the founders than readers might be, he has met the requirements for
inclusion by his actions. Now readers are challenged to prove themselves by acknowledging "Cinquez," a man apparently willing to die
for his freedom.

Giving "Cinquez" the masculine features of the revolutionary
republican subject—virtue, bravery, and a desire for liberty—makes
possible, on the one hand, this conceptual call to identification.
These poems masculinize and individuate Cinqué (and give him a
familiar Spanish name), and so position him as a man worthy of
recognition—and protection. This representation of a dark-skinned
rebel as equivalent to the heroes of the Revolution disrupts discourses
of masculine-coded white supremacy and their attachment to the discourse of national identity. But on the other hand, this conceptual call
to identification is set in motion only after a logic of difference has
reduced some forty African people to one special man, "Cinquez."
Thus the very process of hero formation imposes specific limits that
ensure that only this leader will be authorized to rebel. Because of
these limits, the trope of revolutionary struggle may be invoked in
Cinqué's name without sanctioning slave rebellion more generally.

The following equation from the New York *Sunday Morning News*
illustrates the consequences of this logic:

[T]hese blacks nobly resolved to achieve their freedom;—they gained it at the
hazard of their lives. . . . we have no right to take it from them. By the common
opinion of patriots in all times and in all countries, those who make a generous
and successful struggle to throw off the chain of slavery are noble and great,

and entitled to admiration, and we see not why Joseph Cinquez . . . is not as much entitled to the appellation of great, generous and patriotic man, as was William Tell. (9/1/39; qtd. in *Eman* 9/12/39:77,4)

This passage seeks to validate the rebellion by calling upon "common opinion," which it figures as transhistorical and universal. This representation of "common opinion" operates hegemonically by asserting a transcendental acceptance of the trope of revolutionary struggle. At the same time, this representation particularizes the subject of this trope by arguing that only those who make a *"successful* struggle to throw off the chain of slavery are noble and great" (emphasis added).

The rhetorical strategy employed here is complex. By simultaneously asserting the universal authorization of the trope of revolutionary struggle and limiting who will be authorized by this narrative (i.e., only those who rebel successfully), this strategy works simultaneously to validate the rebellion of "Joseph Cinquez" and to invalidate any attempt at rebellion that is not wholly successful, such as that of Gabriel Prossor, Denmark Vesey, or Nat Turner. Given the unlikely prospect of this kind of wholly successful rebellion by enslaved people in the United States, this construction denies to them the trope of revolutionary struggle and the subject-position "all MEN," even as it supports the successful rebellion of "Joseph Cinquez."

The newspaper press continued to represent Cinqué as the heroic leader of the rebels throughout their captivity and even after their return to Africa. But not long after their capture, some of their supporters began to create an identity for the captives as a people, as a separate national entity. The construction of this national identity necessarily differentiated them from the enslaved population in the United States.[42] In addition to constructing a genealogy of U.S. revolutionary fathers, the rebels' supporters developed strategies for inserting them into the community of nations. This process produced a number of conceptual frames and formed the basis of both their legal defense and the civil suit conducted on their behalf.

In one such conceptual frame, both news writers and the Mendians' lawyers argued that the *Amistad* captives should be treated as members of any other nation would be treated if found in similar circumstances. One writer for the *Commercial Advertiser* asserted, "We take it to be the law, now, of all European nations, that no man has more right to hold property in a native of Africa, now or recently residing in the country, than he has to hold property in a native of France or a native of America" (9/14/39:2,2). The Portsmouth *Journal* stated the point even more directly: "They had precisely the same rights that an Englishman or an American would have, placed in a similar situation" (qtd. in *Lib* 9/13/39:146).[43] Both statements argue for the captives' natural right to freedom by equating them with members of nations typically recognized by U.S. Americans and Europeans, and this implicitly constructs them as members of a nation, here erroneously called "Africa."

Yet notice also that both of these statements equate the rights of the captives with those of "Americans," where the community designated by the term "Americans" is assumed to be the free population. The point of origin of the *Amistad* rebels becomes crucial in this reasoning. The rebels can be compared to "Americans" precisely because they are not enslaved people from the United States. Consider this logic deployed by the *Sunday Morning News:*

We are no abolitionists . . . because we believe that the blacks—so long as they remain in this country—are happier and better in a state of subjection. But our government is not bound to protect foreign nations in their slave property. Those blacks, when they left Havana, and were sailing on God's broad, free ocean, were in a state of involuntary durance. . . . they were bound by no parole of honor, they made no compact, and they were morally and by the laws of action usually recognized by Christian nations justified in setting themselves free. (9/1/39; qtd. in *Eman* 9/12/39:77,4)

Although this passage makes use of the racialist logic that figures the enslaved population in the United States as contented, it also draws a clear distinction between that population and "those blacks" of the *Amistad.* This process of separation allows the writer to support the *Amistad* rebellion without disrupting the national alliance. Once this distinction is made, this passage argues that "those blacks," like any other people, have the Lockean right to develop social compacts voluntarily and to rebel against those who hold them against their will.

This paradoxical logic of separation and insertion simultaneously constructs "those blacks" as a people capable of creating a "body politick" and the enslaved population in the United States as "happier and better in a state of subjection."

The language of this passage mirrors that of the enslaved petitioners from Massachusetts who argued for their right to freedom at the time of the Revolution. These petitioners argued that "we are a freeborn Pepel [*sic*] and have never forfeited this Blessing by aney [*sic*] compact or agreement whatever" (Aptheker 1965, 8–9). Both statements rely on the Enlightenment notion that social contracts derive their authority from voluntary agreements made among individuals, agreements to which "those blacks" and the "freeborn [black] Pepel" have not consented. But notice also that this notion of the individual is foundational to that of the social compact, one's membership in a "freeborn" people. Only by positioning either "those blacks," in the *Sunday Morning News* article, or themselves, in the case of the enslaved petitioners, as members of an initially-free population may these writers argue for the right of compact and rebellion. This logic implies that only certain populations are made up of individuals, and only these populations are endowed with natural rights; the Mendians qualified as one of these populations because they were "born free" in Africa.

News writers usually assumed rather than argued that the *Amistad* captives were natives of Africa. They based this assumption on the initial reports of the sightings and capture of the schooner published in the papers. According to a number of articles, Ruiz admitted to Lieutenant Gedney that the rebels had recently been taken from Africa, but he later changed his story to support his property claims.[44] After the Spaniards' supporters began to assert that the rebels were "ladinos," or natives of the Caribbean, rather than "bozales," people recently taken from Africa, the defenders of the rebels gathered evidence and developed arguments to support the rebels' claims that they were native Africans. Evidence and arguments were important, not only to prove that the rebels were from Africa, but to construct a national identity for them; slavery advocates often represented native Africans as savages with no civilized or national qualities.[45] Characterizing the speech of the captives as "the negro language" illustrates the "hard" racialist logic that figured the difference of the captives as biological inferiority.

The fact that the captives spoke languages other than English or Spanish was noted from the first moment of contact with U.S. Americans. A report of the ecstatic first meeting of James Covey, the native Mendian who became the captives' interpreter, and the captives was printed in the papers and referred to numerous times in subsequent news articles.[46] The captives' supporters offered the spontaneous character of this meeting as proof of the captives' preexisting identity as a separate national other—as Mendians. The *Emancipator* argued that the communication afforded by the new interpreter left no room for doubt that these men "had been recently brought from Africa, in defiance of the laws of the civilized world" (10/21/39:102,5). Covey's immediate ability to communicate with the captives granted him authority when he later testified as to the captives' native status. This attention to the linguistic specificity of the captives enabled Euroamericans both to recognize the captives as native Africans and to imagine them as a distinct people.[47]

In contrast to the Spanish minister's and the Spaniards' lawyers' implicit assertions that the "blacks" were nationless, the supporters of the Mendians asserted their status as a people. For example, John Barber compiled and published a catalog of Mendian society, called *History of the Amistad Africans* (1840), which includes illustrations and brief biographical profiles of each of the captives, including the children, and James Covey, their Mendian interpreter. These profiles give information about the specific location and political structures of the communities of the captives, their religious practices, and the status of women vis-à-vis men. Similarly, the New Haven *Herald* printed a list and description of the captives, which included their names, how they counted, and a summary of their tribes and dialects. In these instances, the systematizing logic of Euroamerican culture was used not to assert the cultural inferiority of these dark-skinned people, but to suggest the cultural complexity and specificity of the points of origin of the captives. Although these brief sketches cannot in any sense be considered full descriptions of Mendi life, they should be recognized as attempts by abolitionists to insert the Mendians into the community of nations.

Lawyers for the Mendians focused their arguments similarly. Bahoo, "Cinquez," Grabeau, and Fuliwa testified about their voyages from Africa to Havana and from Havana to the United States. This testimony, like the other Africans' accounts earlier printed in the papers, challenged the limited time-frame of the Spaniards' accounts and asserted the importance of their experience prior to the sailing of the *Amistad.* A number of news writers commented on the way in which the captives demonstrated the position in which they were bound during the middle passage.[48] But the linguistic ability of the three female children was offered as the most compelling evidence. Roger S. Baldwin, the Mendians' chief lawyer, argued that the children were too young to have been brought to Havana prior to the abolition of the African slave trade by Spain, and he offered—and the court accepted—the fact that they spoke only Mendi as irrefutable evidence of their African point of origin (*TAC* 11).

These discursive strategies established the captives as an African people in the minds of many U.S. Americans. A cogent example occurred with Judge Judson at the second session of the captives' district court trial. This judge was the same Judge Judson who had ruled against Prudence Crandall and her school for "young ladies of color" and in favor of the state of Connecticut and its "black laws."[49] Professor Gibbs, the linguistics expert, had been giving his testimony regarding the language of the captives when Judge Judson interrupted him, stating that he "was fully convinced that the men were recently taken from Africa, and it was idle to deny it" (Jones 1987, 122). This affirmative statement by a proudly racist judge indexed the success of the campaign to differentiate the captives from the enslaved population in either Cuba or the United States.

Judson's decision (January 1840), however, did not confirm the Mendians as a people with the status of a nation.[50] Judson ruled that the captives had been taken from Africa recently ("bozales") rather than being born or long domiciled in a slaveholding country ("ladinos"). Because the laws of Spain forbade trade in native Africans, Judson's decision argued that the papers of the *Amistad* were inaccurate, and the Spaniards therefore had no legal property claims to the captives. Finally, Judson ruled that the Act of 1819 prohibiting anyone from bringing natives of Africa into the United States with the intent to enslave them had been violated, and that according to that act, the Africans should be placed under the protection of the president, until such time as he could arrange for a vessel to return them to the coast of Africa. This decision, while offering a different interpretation than the one argued for by the Spanish minister and Van Buren's administration, nevertheless posited agreements between those national entities recognized by the law of nations as the final authority. It argued for the return of the Mendians to Africa on the basis of the unlawful activity of Spain. It did not represent the Mendians as having a right to rebel or a right to self-determination. As such, Judson's decision did not recognize the Mendians as members of the community of nations.

In March 1841, some eighteen months after the capture of the schooner *Amistad*, Justice Joseph Story wrote the Supreme Court decision in the trial of the *Amistad* captives.[51] He ruled that the rebels were clearly African in origin and therefore could not be held legally as slaves by any country that had agreed by treaty to abolish the African slave trade. In contrast to Judson's decision, Story wrote that the Act of 1819 did not apply because the rebels were in possession of themselves when they had been captured, and they had no intention of importing themselves into the United States in order to reduce themselves to slavery. Because the rebels were not slaves, and because they only sought their own liberation, they could not be robbers or pirates. Given this, Pickney's Treaty did not apply, and their return could not be authorized under that agreement. Story's decision thus upheld the right of self-defense by persons illegally held, but it also upheld that property in persons could be instituted by positive law. Story's decision thus confirmed the notion of righteous revolt against an unjust oppressor, stated here in legal language as the right to self-defense by people illegally held. Yet because the decision simultaneously upheld that property in persons was legal in the presence of positive law, it also was a legal restatement of the Compact between the States, in that it combined the sanctioning of rebellion with strict conditions on who may be sanctioned to rebel. It thus reproduced and thereby reconfirmed the way in which the Constitution limited authorized subject-positions to "all [born free] men."

## The Mendians

The only interpretive statement written by the Mendians and published in the popular press appeared after their release from prison, in April 1841.[52] Ka-le, one of the youngest of the freed captives, wrote a letter to John Quincy Adams, thanking him for his help on their case (he had delivered the closing statement before the Supreme Court). Ka-le's letter largely responds to things that had been said about the Mendians—and published in the papers—often using a strategy of inversion to invite U.S. Americans to identify with, rather than against, them:

> We want you to ask the court what we done wrong. What for Americans keep us in prison. Some people say Mendi people crazy: Mendi people dolt because we no talk America language. Merica people no talk Mendi language; Merica people dolt? . . . Dear friend Mr. Adams, you have children; you have friends, you love them, you feel sorry if Mendi people carry them away to Africa. . . . we want you to know how we feel. Mendi people *think, think, think*. Nobody know what we think; teacher we know, we tell him some. Mendi people have souls. . . . All we want is make us free. (*Anti-Slavery Reporter*, qtd. in *Lib* 4/2/31; emphasis in original)

Ka-le challenges any presumed superiority of English and English speakers with a simple linguistic reversal. Why should people from halfway around the world speak your language? he implicitly asks. Ka-le's invitation to imagine friends and family suddenly stolen seeks to overcome the strategies deployed by myriad forces that differentiate absolutely between, for example, Mendians and U.S. Americans, black and white, heathen and religious, barbarous and civilized, slave and free. He asserts not only that "Mendi people *think*," but that what they think is their secret, which they little share. This notion of private knowledge disrupts the assumptions of so many who asserted their ability to describe, represent, and interpret the Mendians and their actions—to *know* them—and hints at an entirely different mode of understanding. Ka-le finishes by claiming the potentially great equalizer, the notion of a common soul, and asserting his and his compatriots' desire for liberty. In so doing, Ka-le, in this letter and in lecture tours throughout the northeastern United States, created a subject-position for himself from which to articulate his oppositional perspective, one that subtly challenged the Mendians' abolitionist supporters as well as directly challenged their overt antagonists. Having learned the operative codes of the culture in which he found himself, Ka-le characterizes the Mendians' desire in terms associated with the discourse of national identity: "All we want is make us free."

After their release, the Mendians spent almost a year lecturing and performing before large audiences in various cities across the northeast. With the help of the *Amistad* Committee, which later founded the American Missionary Association, the Mendians raised enough funds to sponsor their trip home. In December 1841, the Mendians set sail for Sierra Leone, accompanied by two African American missionaries. These missionaries would establish there the first mission in Africa (Beard 8).

"The *Amistad* Affair" illustrates the ways in which rival forces within the U.S. population deployed the discourse of national identity toward differing and typically opposing ends. More significantly, it shows the way in which these forces limited to themselves the trope of revolutionary struggle. Because the *Amistad* captives were native Africans, and by the laws of Spain illegally imported into the Spanish empire, advocates could invoke the trope without endangering the Compact between the States. In the next chapter, we will see the far more limited possibilities granted the rebels of the *Creole*. As Karcher (1992) points out, the illegality of the Spaniards' actions in the *Amistad* affair provided U.S. Americans with a way out of the ethical dilemma of slavery in a republic founded on freedom. But the case of the *Creole* provided no such convenient escape, and in the pages that follow, we will trace a vast array of discursive strategies deployed to diffuse its disruptive potential.

# Chapter Three

# "The Case of the *Creole*" (1841)

## THE SETTING

News of the rebellion on the *Creole* reached New Orleans just two days before the *Amistad* Africans departed for Sierra Leone. Unlike the rebels of the *Amistad*, those on board the *Creole* apparently knew something both of navigation and of the geography of slavery in the Americas. After taking control of the vessel, the rebels demanded to be taken to Nassau in the British Bahamas, where they knew slavery had been abolished and an earlier group of enslaved rebels had achieved their freedom. When the *Creole* reached that port, British magistrates boarded the vessel, took nineteen purported leaders of the rebellion into custody, and allowed everyone else to go where they pleased, most of the former slaves accepting the open welcome of the largely black population of Nassau. Although the U.S. consul in Nassau, and later Secretary of State Daniel Webster and Senator John Calhoun from South Carolina, complained bitterly, the British magistrates refused to send the leaders to the United States for trial, stating that they did not have an extradition agreement; four months later they released them for lack of evidence. At this point the rebels of the *Creole* disappear from the historical record in the United States.

The *Creole* rebels did not become a *cause célèbre*, at least not in the United States. No teeming masses of U.S. onlookers were able to view the insurgents. The case did not go through the U.S. judiciary, but instead was debated in diplomatic relations between President Martin Van Buren's administration and British officials. As with the *Amistad* affair, the initial response of the proslavery press was to shout their outrage against the "pirates" and "murderers" of the *Creole*, while the abolitionist press supported their actions on the basis of natural rights to liberty. Yet both camps changed tactics almost immediately, with slavery advocates challenging the tyrannous acts of their "ancient enemy," Britain, against "American property," while abolitionists, virtually the rebels' only public supporters, abandoned the rebels' cause in favor of critiquing the domestic slave trade. The mercantile, political, and even the sensationalist penny presses of the North, which had covered the *Amistad* so extensively, were notably quiet. As objects of public discourse, produced in the popular press, the *Creole* rebels were displaced from the field of discursive action, their subjectivity and agency obscured by the differently focused agendas of diplomats, politicians, lawyers, and activists. Whereas the *Amistad* rebels provided grist for the culture's meaning mill for over two years, the popular press of every sort shied away from, and sought to mask, the possible meanings of the *Creole* rebellion.[1]

In many ways what happened on board the *Creole* mirrored events on the *Amistad:* a group of enslaved people of African heritage rose up against a slaveholding crew of European heritage, took control of the vessel, and demanded to be taken somewhere where they would be free. Certainly from the point of view of antislavery advocates, and from that of most Africans and African Americans within the United States, more similarities than differences characterized the two incidents. But the case of the *Creole* differed from that of the *Amistad* in one crucial aspect: the *Creole* rebels were from the United States and had been legally held as slaves by the state from which they escaped. Because of this, the ways in which the rebels were represented, and their rebellious acts were interpreted, differed dramatically from reactions to the Mendians in the *Amistad* affair. Their differing status according to U.S. and international law made them into completely different kinds of subjects.

The *Creole* rebellion brought to the fore the struggle for the identity of the United States as slaveholding or free. This struggle had the potential to fracture the Compact between the States along the fault lines between "life, liberty, and estates": slavery advocates used the guarantee of the Constitution against slave rebellion by characterizing their right to property in persons ("estates") as "the spirit of the Revolution" (Rich *En* 1/29/42:4,5); the most radical abolitionists challenged these claims by figuring the acts of the rebels as within the tradition of the founding fathers, as a *"Strike for Liberty!"* (NY *J of C*, qtd. in *Lib* 1/7/42:1,4). Still others sought a geographical limit to slave territory, at which the rebels would acquire the legal right to self-defense. These opposing positions all made use of the trope of revolutionary struggle, which, some twenty years later, would finally lose its meaning under the pressure of the War between the States.

This struggle for the nation's identity took place in a number of arenas, including the Senate and the House of Representatives, the popular press, and diplomatic relations. Secretary of State Webster, Senator Calhoun and other Southern members of Congress, and the slaveholding press called upon Britain to indemnify if not return the "pirates, mutineers, and murderers," and threatened war if they did not comply. Defenders of the *Creole* rebels challenged this position in two ways. At first they inserted the rebels into legal discourse by arguing that their interests as subjects should be taken into account. But perhaps because of the threat this tactic implicitly posed to the Compact between the States, they soon turned to attack the way in which Webster, Calhoun, and the others had conflated the interests of the United States with those of slaveholders, asking "SHALL WE MAKE WAR WITH ENGLAND, TO DEFEND THE AMERICAN SLAVE TRADE?" (Worcester *Spy*, qtd. in *Lib* 3/11/42:1,4). Although this strategy was successful in gathering popular support, it also refigured the rebellion, a conflict between dark-skinned people and light-skinned men over the personal liberty of the people of color, as a power struggle between white men. Thus while addressing one aspect of slavery, this strategy nevertheless deflected the debate away from a conflict among different racial groups within the United States.

### PART ONE: THE PROTEST DELIVERED AT NEW ORLEANS

On December 8, 1841, the New Orleans *Advertiser* published the text of an official "Protest" lodged against the British government by the crew of the brig *Creole*. According to this document, on October 30, 1841, the *Creole* had left Hampton Roads, Virginia, for New Orleans. On the night of November 7, a number of those on board rose up on the crew, killing one person, and took control of the vessel. The rebels demanded to be taken to one of the islands in the Caribbean under the control of the British. The vessel arrived at Nassau on November 9, 1841, at which point British authorities took command of the schooner. Three days later, all but the nineteen who had been identified by the whites on board as perpetrators of the rebellion were allowed to leave.

This "Protest" constitutes the only eyewitness account of the rebellion on board the *Creole* to be published in the popular press.[2] It details the takeover of the ship, a discussion between the rebels and sailors about where to go, the journey to Nassau, and events upon their arrival in that port. Written as proof that "no fault, negligence or mismanagement is or ought to be ascribed to the said appearers," that is, the crew of the *Creole,* this document emphasizes the relatively small number of slaves involved in the "insurrection," the attempts of the crew and other Americans to retake the *Creole* and its "cargo" as they lay at harbor awaiting the orders of the British authorities, and the supposedly illegal interference of the magistrates at Nassau. It was signed by Zephaniah C. Gifford, officer in command, Henry Speck, Blair Curtis, John Silvey, and Francis Foxwell.

The "Protest" deploys a particularizing, gendering logic evident to some extent throughout the *Creole* archive. It repeatedly distinguishes between the nineteen rebels, and especially the "four who took most active part in the fight," and the remainder of the slaves, who supposedly "were quiet and did not associate with the mutineers" and were "kept under as much as the whites." The "Protest" thus allocates all responsibility to the nineteen instigators, giving the names of the most important four as Ben Blacksmith, Madison Washington, Elijah Morris, and D. Ruffin. If only nineteen could be shown to be responsible for the "mutiny and murder," then the economic value of only those nineteen would be lost to their "owners." Assuming that those who were accused of being responsible would be tried either in British or U.S. courts, and that those found guilty would be executed, the fewer found guilty, the smaller the economic loss to their "owners." In addition, this separation supports the "Protest" 's explicit assertion that the rest of the slaves could have been returned to New Orleans had the British authorities not only not allowed them to go ashore, but not encouraged them to leave the ship. Thus the separation provides the basis for an argument for British liability for the loss of most of the "cargo."

The "Protest" also particularizes the actions of the nineteen and so implicitly argues that those actions should not be considered more generally representative of either the actions or the desires of enslaved people. The following passage well illustrates this process: "Madison [Washington] then shouted, 'We have begun and must go through. Rush, boys, rush aft and we have them!' and calling to the slaves below, he said—'If you don't lend a hand, I will kill you all and throw you overboard.'" While Washington is not alone in this struggle, signified by the "we" in "we have begun" and his call to the "boys," this passage distinguishes between the "boys," who seem to be prepared to "rush aft" and further the rebellion, and "the slaves below." The non-gendered beings, whose most important characteristic is their enslaved status, must be coerced into "lend[ing] a hand." This distinction calls on a discourse of gender that associates masculinity with those willing to engage in the struggle for their own liberty, an association central to the trope of revolutionary struggle. Those who supposedly must be coerced into this struggle are marked not by gender, but by their subservient status.

The "Protest" then further emphasizes and extends this separation: "some of the negroes refused to join in the fray, when they were threatened by Washington that they would be killed if they did not join in." The assertion that "some of the negroes refused to join in" echoes the paradigmatic choice between death and liberty, yet here those who "refused to join in" found the idea of death at the hands of the rebels preferable to joining the fight for liberty. Inverting the paradigm positions those who "refused to join in" as outside the community of "all men," as other than free men endowed with natural rights.

A discourse of gender further organizes the independent actions of the male rebels in opposition to the actions of an untold number of mostly nameless women. These women, one of whom is named as Mary, are figured as either actively aiding the white sailors or as the passive objects of masculine agency. For example, during the takeover itself, apparently "female house servants hid Merrit," a passenger who had "superintendence" over the slaves. Afterward, "all the women appeared to be perfectly ignorant of the plan, and from their conduct, could not have known anything about it." Upon arrival in Nassau, British officers "told the women they were free, and persuaded them to remain on the island"; a British officer "told one of the female slaves that he should claim her for his wife." Finally, of those five who reportedly hid on board the vessel in Nassau in order to return to New Orleans, four were female. These details combine to represent the women of the *Creole* as outside the community of those engaged in a violent struggle for their own liberation. This opposition between the actions of men and women further asserts the masculine character of revolutionary action.

The "Protest"'s emphasis on the small number of people who led the rebellion, and their oppression of the others, mirrors the way in which the initial reports named Cinqué as the "ringleader" of the *Amistad* rebellion. This particularizing process draws upon a logic of racial difference, just as the individualizing of Cinqué did. Although the leaders of the *Creole* rebellion are not figured as honorary Caucasians as was Cinqué, if the nineteen rebels, and especially the "four who took most active part in the fight," can be shown to be exceptions, as different from the vast majority, then their acts of rebellion will be subordinated to the "hard" racialist logic that figures Africans and their descendants as without an innate desire for liberty and as rebelling only when encouraged to do so by outside instigators.

Just as Cinqué gave two speeches that echoed the trope of revolutionary struggle, the "Protest" admits, "The 19 said that all they had done was for their freedom." The "Protest" tempers this admission by directly following it with, "The others said nothing about it. They were much afraid of the 19," thus underscoring the notion that *in general* enslaved people lack a desire for liberty. Still, the statement of their goal, that "all they had done was for their freedom," together with their acts of rebellion, indicate their willingness to risk death to achieve their liberation. Thus even as the "Protest" attempts to invalidate the rebellion by arguing that the majority of the enslaved did not participate and were afraid of the rebels, it figures the rebels as claiming their right to liberty. While not as fully articulated as were the appeals of the enslaved petitioners at the time of the Revolution or Walker's *Appeal*, this claim nevertheless recalls those earlier instances.[3]

The "Protest"'s argument that the *Creole* and its "cargo" would have been recaptured had the British magistrates not interfered also denies agency to the majority of black people. At every point after the arrival of the vessel into port, the British authorities are represented as in complete control of the situation. This assertion comes despite the fact that, according to the "Protest," the black population at Nassau outnumbered the white population by more than three to one, that at least fifty boats, "all filled with [black] men from the shore armed with clubs," kept watch on the events on board the *Creole*, and that "thousands were waiting [on shore] to receive" the now formerly enslaved. While the magistrates may have given orders to release all those who had not participated in the rebellion, and those orders were followed, it is also likely that those orders were shaped in part by the presence and concerns of the people of Nassau, who even in this account appear to be active supporters of the fugitives. The "Protest" tacitly acknowledges this when, after Gifford "protested against the boats being allowed to come alongside of the vessel, or that the negroes other than the 19 mutineers should be put on shore," the attorney general replied that Gifford "had better make no objection, but let them go quietly on shore, for if he did there might be bloodshed." The logic of the "Protest" grants authority to the attorney general and figures those in the boats and on shore as supporters of his decision. Yet this statement can just as readily be understood as the attorney general acknowledging that he does not have control over those in the boats and on shore, and that Nassau's black population will act to ensure the liberation of the fugitives.[4]

For several days everyone waited for instructions from the British authorities, and soldiers "mingled with the negroes and told the women they were free, and persuaded them to remain in the island." Upon the delivery of the news that only the nineteen would be held in custody, "A magistrate on the deck of the *Creole* gave the signal for the boats to approach instantly. With a hurrah and a shout, the fleet of boats came alongside of the vessel, and the magistrates directed the men to remain on board of their own boats, and commanded the slaves to leave the brig and go board the boats." Finally, the "Protest" records, "Many of the negroes who were emancipated expressed a desire to go to New Orleans on the *Creole*, but were deterred from it, by means of threats which were made to sink the vessel, if she attempted to carry them away," and it asserts, "Many of the male and nearly all of the female slaves would have remained on board . . . had it not been for the command of the magistrates and interference as before stated." Thus the "Protest" argues that those other than the nineteen were "persuaded," "commanded," and finally "deterred"; the only desire or wish ascribed to them is to return to New Orleans.

Both particularizing the rebels and allocating all authority and responsibility to the British magistrates deny agency to Africans and their descendants. The first strategy figures the majority of the slaves as the passive objects of the agency of first the "mutineers" and then the British magistrates. The second operates similarly by serving the crew's and owners' agenda of proving that the British are responsible for the loss and are therefore liable for reparations for, if not the return of, the fugitives. Together they also diffuse the anxiety of slavery's supporters and other white people in the United States regarding the specter of slave rebellion. Individualizing Cinqué in the *Amistad* case also quelled white anxiety. In the same way, the "Protest" discursively erased the agency, activity, and power of the people of Nassau, and the threat they posed to British authorities had they attempted to produce a different outcome, as well as to the U.S. crew and their supporters. This process makes even more sense when considered in light of white anxiety in the United States regarding the free black populations of the Caribbean, most often evidenced by the supposedly savage and horrific Haitian revolution.

Further supporting its argument that most of the slaves would have been returned to the United States had it not been for the interference of the British magistrates, the "Protest" emphasizes the efforts of proximate U.S. Americans to retake the vessel. Immediately upon arriving in Nassau, Gifford met with the U.S. consul, who requested that a guard be placed on the *Creole* so that no one could escape. After this had been done, and only two or three hours after the brig reached port, the U.S. consul engaged the assistance of Captain Woodside of the *Louisa* and much of the crew of the brig *Congress* to "rescue the brig [*Creole*] from the British officer then in command, and conduct her to Indian Key [near Florida], where there was a United States vessel of war. . . . Frequent interviews were every day had with Captain

Woodside, the consul and the officers of the *Congress,* and the whole plan was arranged." Three days after the *Creole* had arrived at Nassau, and just hours before all but the nineteen were released, the U.S. Americans executed their plan. They sailed out to the *Creole,* with an unspecified number of men and arms, the latter of which were "wrapped in the American flag and concealed in the bottom of the boat," but were prevented from going on board by British soldiers, who had been alerted to the plan. At this moment in the text, the "Protest" reports that the rebels had earlier discarded their weapons before arriving at Nassau and then offers this as evidence to prove that "[i]f there had been no interference of the part of the legal authorities of Nassau, the slaves might all have been safely brought to New Orleans."

Again, in order to allocate determining agency to the U.S. forces, the "Protest" must ignore the people of Nassau. Its description of the approach of the U.S. forces to the *Creole* makes no mention of the "about fifty boats" that supposedly were keeping watch on the *Creole.* In addition, this description manipulates the order of information so as to support the "Protest"'s thesis. By waiting until this moment to reveal that the rebels had discarded their weapons before arriving in Nassau, the "Protest" attempts to limit the use of this piece of information to supporting its assertion that the U.S. forces could have retaken the vessel because those on board were no longer armed. Yet we can also use this information to ask, if the rebels had discarded their weapons, why did the crew not attempt to regain control earlier? If only nineteen of the slaves were in rebellion, and the others wanted to return to New Orleans, as the "Protest" claims, why did not the crew, who were only somewhat fewer in number than the nineteen and who should have been able to count on some support from the supposedly more than one hundred slaves wishing to return to the United States, attempt to retake the vessel? Why indeed?

From a different, but also resistant perspective, the *National Anti-Slavery Standard* astutely recasts the "Protest"'s characterization of the consul's attempt to retake the ship. The *Standard* presents the incident as "the attempt made by the American Consul at Nassau, to wrest this vessel from the British authorities, while in a British port, by force of arms" (1/13/42:126,2). Turning the situation on its head, and thereby making the consul's indignation seem absurd, if not dangerous, the *Standard* asked, what would the American people and the American government think had the British consul done the same thing with a ship in the port of New York?

In both the "Protests"'s and the *Standard*'s critique, prioritizing British interference also displaced the conflict between the rebels and the crew of the *Creole* onto one between the British magistrates and U.S. forces. A struggle between two national entities replaces one between enslaved people and slavery's representatives. Just as the separation of the so-called "mutineers" from the rest of the slaves quells this anxiety, emphasis on a struggle between different national entities masks the reality of violent conflict among factions within the United States.

Thus the "Protest"'s displacing logic operates similarly to that of the discourse of national identity in the context of the Revolution. That earlier formation of the discourse figured compliance or resistance to British authority as an opposition between slavery and freedom. This opposition—paradoxically—masked the presence of the enslaved population in the United States even as it invoked it, and so replaced conflicts between the enslaved population and colonists-turned-patriots with one between the British and the new U.S. Americans. Whereas in the context of the Revolution, a wide variety of people had used the terms "slave" and "free" to describe emerging dominant groups in the United States, in the context of the *Creole* rebellion, those who figure the conflict as between Britain and the United States no longer use those terms. As I will show in the pages that follow, even the existence of living beings called "slaves" was denied as much as possible in favor of the term "property."

PART TWO: INTERPRETATIONS

The United States as Slaveholding

On January 18, 1842, five weeks after the "Protest" was sworn to in New Orleans, John C. Calhoun, senator from South Carolina, proposed a resolution regarding the *Creole* affair.[5] It called for President

Tyler to consider action with regard to "the punishment of the guilty, redress of the wrong done to our citizens, and the insult offered to the American flag."[6] Calhoun was referring to the supposed interference of the British magistrates at Nassau, who had taken "the 19" into custody but had recognized the remaining fugitives only as "Americans." By characterizing the British actions as an insult to the "American flag," Calhoun appropriates the symbol of the national compact for the cause of slaveholders.

Calhoun's resolution precipitated a debate on the Senate floor. Senator Augustus Porter of Michigan objected to the use of the term "slave" in the resolution on the grounds that that word "was not used in the Constitution—that instrument had been so carefully drawn . . . 'persons held to service or labor' was the language, and that was the language of the legislation of Congress." Porter's sole intention may have been to protect the national compact by maintaining the Constitution's strategy of compromise between free and slaveholder. But several senators reacted to Porter's objection as if it were an abolitionist declaration. Amidst the denunciations, Calhoun "regretted that their ancestors had been so fastidious as they were on this subject; they ought to have inserted the word manfully and boldly in the Constitution; and it became them now when they saw so much cause to apprehend danger, to take the manly and upright course." Calhoun feminizes the founders by calling their strategy of compromise mere fastidiousness and characterizes Southern policymakers of his own day as more manly, upright, and bold. Calhoun thus calls upon discourses of gender and masculine sexuality to authorize his rewriting of the Constitution.[7]

The response of Senator William C. Preston from South Carolina made explicit what was at stake in this rewriting; he asserted that the rebels "were slaves and not persons; they were not persons in any signification. . . . The very question was that they were not persons, which Great Britain contends, but slaves, and therefore by surrendering the word in dispute, and using the words in the Constitution, they [the Senate] sacrificed the rights of the South." Preston supports Calhoun's position by asserting that the wording of the Constitution is not compatible with the "rights of the South." Not only is the manliness of Congress at stake in this debate, but the very identity of the nation. For Preston asserts that slaveholders are no longer content to exclude issues raised by slavery for the sake of a national alliance; they now demand unquestioning support from the federal government. As his statement admits, this demand contradicts and overrides the founding document of the republic for the sake of the nation as a slaveholding power. Although Porter continued to insist that "[s]lavery was not known to the federal government [and that] there was great propriety then in avoiding that expression," under pressure he withdrew his amendment and the resolution was adopted as written.

Much to the chagrin of many a Massachusettsian, on January 29, 1842, Secretary of State Daniel Webster dispatched directions to the U.S. ambassador to Great Britain in support of Calhoun's resolutions.[8] Not only did numerous newspapers throughout the country reprint this dispatch, but in the Senate Calhoun moved that one thousand extra copies be printed and distributed, which was granted.[9] In his dispatch, the secretary adopted the position of the *Creole* crew's "Protest" and depositions, which coded the conflict as a property dispute between national powers and discursively erased both the control of the rebels over the vessel and the agency of the people of Nassau.[10] Like the Spaniards and their supporters in the *Amistad* case and the Southern senators quoted above, Webster's dispatch defended the property claims of slaveholders over the rebels' struggle for personal liberty. The dispatch therefore characterized the United States, in its relations with Britain, as a slaveholding power.[11] This approach sought to contain the disruptive potential of the rebellion to the national alliance by refiguring a conflict among "Americans" as a dispute between nations.

As the basis for this strategy of containment, Webster appealed to a notion of international common sense, based on "the comity of Nations," which in his view dictated that it was "the plain and obvious duty of the authorities at Nassau, the port of a friendly power, to assist the American Consul." To support this view, Webster figures the abolition of slavery in the British Empire as "local law," and therefore as irrelevant "in any matter such as this."[12] Webster's dispatch simultaneously characterizes "the comity of Nations" as supportive of slavery and limits the range of free territory. Yet this representation of the status of slavery, as supported by international agreements and legal except where prohibited by positive law, asserted a definitive position on an institution whose status was both changing and ambiguous. By 1842 most—but not all—European and Euroamerican nations had signed treaties with Britain outlawing the international slave trade. Limits on the extension and influence of slavery were an increasingly contested terrain in U.S. politics. Thus Britain's "plain and obvious duty" was not so obvious when viewed in relation to either the internal politics of the United States or then current international agreements.

Webster reinforced his characterization by arguing that "[i]t is in vain that any attempt is made to answer these suggestions [that local law is irrelevant] by appealing to general principles of humanity." This assertion figures natural law as outside the system regulating the interaction of nations.[13] Yet the U.S. Supreme Court had sometimes recognized the supposedly more fundamental laws of nature, specifically those that undergird the trope of revolutionary struggle. In 1797, Chief Justice John Marshall had upheld the right of an impressed seaman to commit homicide during his escape, a right that was later confirmed by Justice Story in the *Amistad* case.[14] The difference in this case, unstated by Webster, was that the *Creole* rebels were legally enslaved by the laws of the Southern states. The logic of Webster's dispatch asserted Southern law as federal law and thus obscured debates between rival factions within the United States on the issue of slavery. It thus operated in tandem with the strategies of dominant groups to deny the trope of revolutionary struggle to the enslaved population.

Writers for the slaveholding press entered the debate over the nation's identity occasioned by the *Creole* rebellion by invoking the trope of revolutionary struggle in the service of their property rights. For example, the Charleston *Mercury* characterized the *Creole* dispute as a "new outrage by British colonial authorities on American property" (qtd. in Rich *En* 12/18/41:3,1). By calling this situation a "new outrage," this characterization recalls those words of the Declaration of Independence that accused the British monarch of a "long line of abuses"; it thereby represents the case of the *Creole* as simply another example of British aggression against "American property." By conflating property concerns at the time of the Revolution with the question of property in persons at this later historical moment, the logic of this article claims authority for its sense of indignation from an earlier period during which dominant groups in the newly formed republic were in alignment in their opposition to Britain. In 1842, invoking the trope of revolutionary struggle, that is, the (property) rights for which one is willing to die, masked the lack of consensus in the United States on the subject of slavery, just as it did at the time of the Revolution. However, this masking has a different meaning at this later historical moment because in 1842 debates over slavery were visible though often suppressed sites of conflict in the public discourse of U.S. Americans.

In addition, the article's logic mirrors that of the discourse of national identity at the time of the Revolution by replacing a conflict among different populations within the nation with a conflict between the United States and what another article called "our ancient enemy" (Rich *En* 1/29/42:4,5), Britain. In representing the conflict as "a new outrage by British colonial authorities on American property," this article, like the "Protest" and Webster's dispatch, allocates all responsibility and authority for events on the *Creole* to British authorities, thereby obscuring the actions of the rebels. Not only this, it subsumes the very existence of the rebels as living beings under the term "property."

The New Orleans *Courier* invoked a similar displacing logic when it called for "punish[ing] the hypocrites [the British], whose end and aim is the destruction of southern prosperity—American liberty and independence" (qtd. in *Lib* 12/24/41:2,2–3).[15] This article equates "southern prosperity," that is, the institution of slavery, with "American liberty and independence," such that the protection or destruction of one is equivalent to the protection or destruction of the other. This scheme makes liberty and independence dependent upon slavery, perhaps even more than they were, as discussed in the introduction, in slaveholders' understanding of the discourse of national identity at the time of the Revolution. Here the paradigmatic choice between liberty and death characterizes a struggle not for personal freedom, but for the right to enslave others.

A scholarly article from the *Southern Quarterly Review*, entitled "The *Creole* Case" (1842), makes visible the racialist assumptions that undergirded slaveholders' claim to the national community. With a logic similar to that of "Domestic Slavery," considered in chapter 1, "The *Creole* Case" argues:

> Nature, not our own act, has thrown a population in the midst of civilized men, whose intelligence is of that low order, and whose moral feelings are so debased, that if left to individual effort, they would become burthens upon society, and outrage every principle which strengthens and preserves it. The control, then exercised over it, through the relation of master and servant, is one demanded by the security of society, and authorized by the justest feelings of benevolence. (57–58)

This passage naturalizes slavery, here euphemistically called "the relation of master and servant," both by denying the European invasion of Africa and the African slave trade, and by asserting the notion of innate (racial) difference. This absolute split based on racial difference supports this text's argument for the right of "civilized men" to self-defense, based on the Lockean notion of property in "liberty, life, or goods" (57). Like Calhoun and his supporters, this article argues that the rights of this class are further secured "by the Constitution of the United States,—by the charters of the States where slavery is recognized,—by the rights of the owners of these slaves as citizens of the United States, as members of society, and as men" (68). Thus this article demarcates absolutely the citizenry from the enslaved, a separation reinforced by the masculine coding of that citizenry, part of the discourse of national identity, and the implicit feminizing of the enslaved population. This writer rises to Calhoun's call "manfully" to assert their rights.

In contrast to those interpretations of the *Creole* rebellion that allocated responsibility to the British magistrates, "The *Creole* Case" emphasizes the rebels' agency. Ironically, this article represents the right of self-defense as the foundation of civil society and the justification for laws that punish violations of the right to property, such as murder and robbery. But because the rebels are positioned as outside the community of citizens, nothing done to them is a violation of law, natural or civil, and they therefore have no right to self-defense. Their act of rebellion can therefore only be interpreted as an act against the natural rights of citizens, as murder of the crew and robbery of the wealth represented by their own persons (59). Thus "The *Creole* Case" appropriates the trope for slaveholders by explicitly racializing "free men," and by figuring as valid only one of many possible subject-positions.

The Washington *Globe* sided with the slaveholding press on the basis of the logic of nation-states. Characterizing the case as an outrage by England against the United States, the *Globe* argued that a vessel carried into the port of another nation by force of mutiny, piracy, or weather "loses none of its attributes of nationality" (2/16/42:3,1). The *Creole* and its crew "were as completely under the protection and legitimate power of the United States, as if lying in the wharf in Richmond. . . . The criminals were in her possession . . . as if manacled in a Virginia jail." Given this, Britain is bound by the law of nations to respect rather than violate that jurisdiction. Thus far this argument replicates that of the "Protest." But the *Globe* further notes that "there is but one qualification to this position [on jurisdiction], and that is a state of war. As the principle of war is to annoy and destroy the enemy, it matters not how he gets within our reach." War transcends regulations provided by the law of nations, rendering irrelevant treaties and comity. The *Globe* includes this note to characterize Britain's actions in the *Creole* case as acts of war. Yet we can also read in it the way in which the logic of nation-states denies to the *Creole* rebels their own declaration of war. This logic seeks to manacle them as if in a Virginia jail, despite the fact that they stood free on deck as a result of their own efforts. As with the Spanish minister's letter regarding the *Amistad* rebels, the *Globe* seeks to invalidate the *Creole* rebels' acts by denying them the authorization of any nation.

In the *Amistad* affair, the judiciary's custody of the rebels minimized the conflict between dominant groups generated by the alignment of the Spanish government and the administration. Those who did not support the actions of the administration could look to the judiciary to protect their interests. But in the case of the *Creole*, the alignment of the secretary of state, Southern senators, and U.S. slaveholders was more powerful because Webster's threat that war might result from Britain's failure to indemnify the "lost cargo" had to be taken seriously. By offering physically to enact the paradigmatic choice between liberty or death in the service of their property interests, this threat positioned slaveholders as the most significant group in the national community. Thus these strategies of containment activated another potential site of disruption.

### Freedom's Limit

Several papers, notably the *Colored American*, initially asserted a connection between the *Creole* and the *Amistad*, calling the second rebellion "Another *Amistad!*"[16] Although parallels abounded, differences emerged immediately. Remember that in the *Amistad* case it had been possible to invoke the tradition of the founders without sanctioning rebellion in the United States (much as those who cheered rebellion in Poland did), and many—abolitionist and nonabolitionists alike—had supported the Mendians in this way. But because the *Creole* rebels were from the United States, no such conceptual division was possible. No instances in the popular press, for example, claim to support the *Creole* rebellion and yet be against abolition. Only the most radical abolitionist writers, who welcomed rather than feared a reformulation of the Compact between the States, applauded the actions of the rebels by creating for them a genealogy of revolutionary heroes.

In one such example, the Massachusetts Anti-Slavery Society offered the following resolution:

That, by all the principles by which we eulogize George Washington and his brave compeers, who delivered their countrymen from the chain of British oppression, we are bound to laud the courage and heroism of the Americans on board the *Creole*, who, rising against their oppressors, secured to themselves, by their own strong arm, the inalienable right of liberty, of which American citizens had most basely robbed them. (Qtd. in *Lib* 2/18/42:4,2)

By calling the rebels "Americans," this resolution challenges any absolute demarcation between the enslaved population and the citizenry of the United States and questions received notions of who can
claim the name "American." Unlike the *Amistad* interpretations, this
strategy of insertion directly focused attention upon conflicts between enslaved people and slaveholders within the United States. As
one writer put it, "at this very moment a *war* of most atrocious character is actually going on throughout the whole slave region" (*Eman &*
*FA* 12/24/41:134,5), and this rebellion is only an expression of it. This
writer implicitly challenges the *Globe*'s logic, which acknowledged
war only among nation-states.

Abolitionist writers further developed this conceptual link by creating a heroic masculine myth for the *Creole* rebels, much as earlier
had been done with Cinqué and the Mendians. This myth employed a
logic of identification that challenged notions of racial hierarchy by
exalting the actions of "the 19" instigators of the rebellion, especially
Madison Washington, "who wore a name unfit for a slave, but finely
expressive for a hero." Washington was particularly attractive to his
supporters not only because his name made an association between
the rebels and the founders seem "natural," but for what they characterized as his "presence of mind and decision of character," and "his
generous leniency toward his prisoners." "The 19" were applauded for
their "complete self-control over their passions, and maintain[ing] un-
interrupted harmony of purpose and action."[17] (Only one of the crew
of the *Creole* had been killed during the uprising, and Washington
reportedly helped dress the wounds of those defeated.) Emphasizing
these qualities of restraint and compassion challenged stereotypical
representations of violent and bestial black men, and thereby tem-
pered the potentially explosive nature of this heroic representation of
the enslaved rebels. This hero-making process was consciously done;
as one writer notes, "In these remarks, our readers will perceive that
we have done little more than to translate, into the appropriate language of freedom, the statements of the Protest, written by their enemies" (qtd. in NASS 12/30/41:118,2). This reference to "the appropriate language of freedom" claims the revolutionary trope for the
cause of personal liberty rather than for property rights, including
property in persons.

Yet the *Creole* rebels' white abolitionist supporters abandoned their heroic representation of the rebellion almost immediately. Apparently they did not consider claiming natural rights for the enslaved rebels to be the most prudent or useful strategy. Many abolitionists[18] had refused to accept Story's decision in the *Amistad* case (which supported slavery where it was instituted by positive law), arguing that slavery violated the natural and unalienable rights of man and therefore could not be made legal under any circumstances.[19] Yet for most Euroamericans—even those who supported abolition—acknowledging that the *Creole* rebels had such a right was far more difficult, if not impossible, because doing so was incompatible with their everyday racialist thinking and practices, be they "hard" or "soft." On another, potentially more explosive level, such an acknowledgment would threaten the national compact by authorizing the rebellion of a subordinated group against a dominant group. Thus defenders of the *Creole* rebels developed an alternative legal argument that admitted limitations on the rebels' right to self-defense. Their efforts centered on the question of state and national jurisdiction and the legal limits of slavery.

Because the *Creole* rebels had, according to the laws of the slaveholding states, been born in bondage, their legal advocates could not convincingly assert that they were a "freeborn Pepel [*sic*]" (Aptheker 1965, 8). William Jay (1842), editor of the New York *American,* inserted the *Creole* rebels into legal discourse by arguing that "the grand mistake of all who have written on the subject is, that they leave entirely out of the question this party, whose interest and right in it are, of all others, the greatest, to wit: the slaves themselves." (This, of course, was the position of the British magistrates and later the House of Lords.)[20] By constructing the rebels as subjects, Jay may assert, as had the *Sunday Morning News* in the *Amistad* case, that "the negroes, slaves, have never given their assent to American law in either [positive or implied] form." Because they had not given their consent, Jay continues, but had been "brought within [the] jurisdiction [of American law] by force, and by force alone . . . when they find themselves or place themselves beyond its jurisdiction, they are no longer subject to that law" (21). Thus Jay modifies Locke's argument regarding the for-

mation of civil society, also used by enslaved petitioners at the time of
the Revolution, by drawing limits on the power of a society to enslave
a non-consenting population.

This formulation supported the conceptual process of hero formation by creating a legal position from which the rebels were authorized
to act. Yet Jay's reasoning sought neither to overturn laws sanctioning
slavery nor to displace the conflict between rebels and slaveholders,
but to demarcate the claims of either side. Supporting Jay's position
and opposing Webster's dispatch, Conway Robinson, a "leading lawyer of Virginia," argued that slavery is a local law and that once slaves
had escaped beyond the jurisdiction of the legislative body instituting
it they were "free agents" capable of acting on their own behalf.[21] Like
Jay's reasoning, Robinson's argument locates a geographical boundary
between slave and free territories as the site of the rebels' transformation from property to persons, from the object of slaveholders' claim to
property rights to subjects of their own narrative of liberation.

While both Jay and Robinson presented sophisticated legal arguments sanctioning the rebels' actions, all negotiations with any direct
effect on the rebels or the question of indemnification took place
within the arenas of diplomatic relations and official congressional
resolutions. Several months after the Senate passed Calhoun's resolution, Joshua Giddings, an antislavery representative from Ohio, used
the opportunity provided by Webster's dispatch to raise the question
of the jurisdiction of slavery in Congress. Southern senators had been
willing to express their outrage against the British in the *Creole* case,
but their construction of the dispute, like that of Webster and the
slaveholding press, had been designed to keep property in persons
from being debated. At that point, no abolitionists had yet been elec-
ted to the Senate. Giddings ventured a potentially explosive series of
resolutions that directly challenged the arguments of Webster, Calhoun, and the slaveholding press.

While acknowledging the authority of positive law, Giddings asserted that slavery violated the natural rights of man and therefore was
"necessarily confined to the territorial jurisdiction of the power creating it." When the *Creole* left the jurisdiction of the state of Virginia the
slave laws of that state ceased to apply and those on board "became

amenable to the laws of the United States," which he argued did not recognize slavery.[22] Thus as Calhoun and Webster tried to push the boundary of slave territory outward under the auspices of the "American flag," Giddings (and Jay and Robinson) tried to arrest that force.

But the most problematic resolution, which earned the series the appellation of a "firebrand course," stated:

That all attempts to exert our national influence in favor of the coastwise trade, or to place this nation in the attitude of maintaining a "commerce in human beings," are subversive of the rights and injurious to the feelings and interests of the free States, and are unauthorized by the Constitution, and prejudicial to our national character.

This resolution draws an absolute distinction, not between the citizenry and the enslaved population as in "The *Creole* Case," but between the interests of the slaveholding states and those of the "free States." Even more, it asserts that something as fundamental to the economy of the South, Virginia in particular, as the domestic slave trade is not compatible with "our [true] national character." Thus not only does it directly challenge Webster, Calhoun, and the slaveholding press's representation of the United States as a slaveholding power, it denies any national recognition or protection of the institution that had come to characterize the South.

While it may have been the intent of the Constitution, as Senator Porter implied, neither openly to sanction nor actively to hinder slavery, this compromise position was becoming increasingly untenable in 1842. Issues involving slavery brought the states' differing interests to the fore, yet "all conflicts with a foreign power," such as the *Creole* rebellion, were also situations in which "it was expressly desirable that," as unionist Henry Clay insisted, "they should present an unbroken phalanx, and that all their party divisions should cease" (*Lib* 1/21/42:2,3).[23] Such a desire for consensus brought into conflict the notion of the United States as a confederation of independent states and that of the United States as a nation within a community of nations. In the debate over Calhoun's resolution, the Senate resolved these conflicts by silencing Porter's objections. The House responded to these conflicts by rejecting Giddings' resolutions and voting 125 to

69 to censor him. (Giddings resigned from the House but was reelected almost immediately by his constituency.) These two acts, together with Webster's dispatch, positioned slaveholders as the most significant group in the federal government.

Although Giddings was censored for a limited sanctioning of slave rebellion, the trope of revolutionary struggle was available *enough* to him that he could invoke it in the service of the *Creole* rebels in a national forum. Apparently no senator was then inclined to use such language; Porter's objection was far less confrontational than Giddings's resolutions. The abolitionist press commented on this fact: "For the fifth time [in relation to resolutions proposed in the Senate], no Northern Senator said a word. Will they ever speak? . . . Are they all scared?" (*Eman & FA* 3/10/42:2,2). Although it would be another nine years before an avowed abolitionist took his seat in the Senate, the press was indignant at the fear, the implicit effeminacy, of Northern senators. Yet despite their support for the *Creole* rebellion, abolitionist writers also changed the terms of the debate by asking, "SHALL WE MAKE WAR WITH ENGLAND, TO DEFEND OUR AMERICAN SLAVE TRADE?" (Worcester *Spy*, qtd. in *Lib* 3/11/42:1,4). By characterizing this question as putting the conflict "in its true light" (*Eman & FA* 3/24/42:2,2), these writers, like Calhoun and Webster, displace the rebellion into the arena of international relations, thereby denying the subjectivity and agency of the rebels and effacing the racial character of the conflict. Yet this displacing logic also gained greater popular support for the abolitionists' position.

Abolitionists were politically savvy enough to recognize where lay the greatest gain. The rebels already had escaped; their fate lay not with U.S. but with British officials. Pursuing their right to rebellion may have seemed a mute point. By marginalizing rebellion and foregrounding the potential for war, they may have been using the case of the *Creole* to their best political advantage. After all, the domestic slave trade deserved attention. In addition, because it did not disrupt so profoundly the national compact, this new emphasis enabled far more people to enter the debate. For example, at this point, the *People's Press*, "a weekly paper published and conducted by two young men of color in New York," took up the question of war with England:

If war be declared, shall we fight with the chains upon our limbs? . . . Shall we shed our blood in defense of the American slave trade? . . . Shall we a third time kiss the foot that crushes us? If so, we deserve our chains. No! let us maintain an organized neutrality until the laws of the Union and of all the States have made us free and equal citizens. (Qtd. in *Eman & FA* 3/31/42:119,1–2)

Clearly the ironic possibility of being drafted to defend slavery was a topic relevant and important enough to these "young men of color" to be debated in a public forum. Yet it is difficult to believe that the *Creole* rebellion itself was not also a topic of importance to these writers.

While the relative lack of extant newspapers edited by African Americans makes conclusions partial at best, I suggest that these writers entered the discussion, initiated by reactions to the *Creole* rebellion but now centering on the role of the United States in international relations, because at this moment it was safe for them to do so. Although the revolutionary trope was available to, if not effective for, white abolitionists, the differently racialized position of these "young men of color" may have made that trope, within the immediate context of the *Creole* rebellion, too dangerous to use. Because many U.S. Americans would have automatically associated the black writers with enslaved people on the basis of race, supporting the *Creole* rebels may have seemed too much like calling for revolution—a dangerous prospect at best. Shifting the debate to the question of war made it possible for "these young men of color" to claim a position from which to express their opinion, at least regarding their own participation in any events resulting from the rebellion. From this position they could assert their perspective by *refusing* to fight, rather than by calling for a fight. Given the daily violence and threat of violence against African Americans, especially those enslaved, this assertion of non-violence may have been a wise rhetorical strategy.

The denial of the rebels' very humanity by their characterization as cargo, on the one hand, and the abolitionists' abandonment of their unequivocal right to liberty on the other, reveals that it was not simply unpopular to authorize slave rebellion by figuring the rebels within a tradition established by the founding fathers—it was *unimag-*

*inable* for many, if not most, U.S. Americans; it was not part of their culture's "common sense." Consider the way in which the particularizing, gendering logic of the "Protest" naturalized racial and gendered stratification. This logic asserted that any rebellion by nonwhite people had to be one not against political tyranny, but against their subordinate place in nature's hierarchy—a riot of savages rather than a rebellion of righteous men. Remember how long and how intensely supporters of the *Amistad* Africans worked to overcome this cultural logic, in the end carefully differentiating them from the enslaved population in the United States. The abolitionists' claim to parity for the *Creole* rebels—"they have simply imitated the example of our fathers"—only made "sense" to U.S. Americans as the fanatical raving of people who wanted to destroy the very fabric of society by going against the dictates of nature. And what is more, the culturally predominant depiction of a desire for liberty as innate and worth dying for created a no-win situation for enslaved men: brutally kept in submission by the very forces that exalted (their own) liberation, they were constructed as suspect not only in their manhood, but in their very humanity. In these myriad ways, powerful forces foreclosed the potential subject-position of "all [enslaved] men."

### International Resolution

Fortunately for the rebels—and it seems they knew this—the House of Lords did not recognize any U.S. laws sanctioning slavery. Britain had abolished slavery in 1833. Given this, British law recognized the rebels as subjects—persons able to act—rather than as property, and the question taken up by the House of Lords was whether or not "the 19" should either be tried in British courts or extradited to the United States for murder. All agreed that Britain did not have jurisdiction, and a debate ensued regarding extradition. Lord Brougham, for example, admitted that "the rights of justice, of social intercourse, and good neighborhood, require" among bordering nations some reciprocal agreement by which nations could "demand and secure gross offenders who had committed crimes in one country and fled for shelter into another." Others agreed in principle, but saw issues such as slavery as posing particularly difficult situations. The earl of Aberdeen noted that the government had gathered legal assistance, all of which concurred that "by the laws of this country there was no machinery, or authority, for bringing those persons to trial for mutiny or murder, and still less for delivering them up."[24] If the rebels had been accused of piracy, which violated international law, then the British magistrates could have handled the case. The U.S. consul had shown no interest in this charge, perhaps because this would have acknowledged the rebels' agency, perhaps because they would have then lost the "cargo" to the gallows. In any event, orders were sent out by the secretary of the colonies, and Nassau's chief justice released them for "lack of evidence." Upon their release, the rebels disappear from the historical record in the United States.

But the *Creole* case did not end there. Over a decade later, while the Spanish minister was also still pursuing compensation in the *Amistad* case,[25] an Anglo-American claims commission in 1855 awarded $110,330 to the former "owners" of the slaves of the *Creole*. This decision vindicated the Southern position, which earlier had been supported by President Tyler's administration. Joshua Bates of Boston ruled that, although slavery was contrary to humanity, the law of nations did not prevent it from being established by positive law. Recognizing only citizens as actors in the case, Bates argued that Nassau officials had violated international law and therefore owed compensation.[26] Bates accepted the "Protest"'s assertion that had British officials not interfered, U.S. forces would have been able to regain control of the vessel. Bates therefore either did not notice or chose to ignore the logical flaw in this reasoning, that the rebels controlled the vessel, which they had *willingly relinquished* to British officials. This ruling makes sense only if Bates takes into consideration the actions of the U.S. consul, Captain Woodside, and the crew of the Congress, *but not* those of the rebels or, perhaps more importantly given their numbers, Nassau's supportive black population. Like Calhoun's resolutions, Bates's ruling erased the agency of the rebels—and Nassau's black population—by figuring the conflict as a struggle between armed national entities. It thereby drew upon, displayed, and supported the logic of nation-states, which not only authorized but only acknowledged the existence of the (white) citizens of recognized nations. Although the *Creole* rebels' supporters were unable convincingly to create an identity for the rebels as citizens or as a separate nation, the rebels were able on their own to manipulate to their own advantage points of friction between Britain and the United States. Despite overwhelming odds, the rebels successfully slipped out from under the immediate control of either nation, leaving the citizens to debate who would pay the bill.

# Chapter Four

## *Benito Cereno* (1855) and

## "The Slumbering Volcano"

The slaveholders are sleeping on slumbering volcanoes, if they did but know it. . . . Those who have trampled upon us for the last two hundred years, who have used their utmost endeavors to . . . destroy our manly aspirations . . . may expect their turn will come one day.   FREDERICK DOUGLASS[1]

There she would be near his own vessel. Upon gaining that vicinity, might not the San Dominick, like a slumbering volcano, suddenly let loose energies now hid?   MELVILLE's Captain Delano

At this point we turn to two literary texts written, published, and first read just about a decade after most of the *Amistad* Africans returned home to Mendiland and the *Creole* rebels disappeared from official sight in Nassau. My primary concern in analyzing these historical fictions, Herman Melville's *Benito Cereno* (1855) and Frederick Douglass's *The Heroic Slave* (1853), lies in the ways in which they entered into then-current debates regarding the place of rebellion and slavery—and slave rebellion—in U.S. national identity. In contrast to myriad studies of Melville's works and most of the increasing amount of scholarship on Douglass's writing, my analysis does not take into consideration these writers' canons, biographies, or intentions. Rather than focusing on the author, my approach centers on what becomes visible in these literary texts when we imbed them in the context of other writings about the same topic produced near the same moment in time. The following chapters differ, therefore, from either older criticism that understood the author to be the definitive maker of meaning, or more recent studies that, while often taking quite seriously the immediate environment in which a text was written and received, nevertheless maintain a primary interest in the specific history, psychology, and/or talent of its author.[2] Instead my project, like the work of Stephen Greenblatt (1988) and Jean Howard (1994) in early modern studies, defamiliarizes these literary texts by situating them in relation to information not traditionally within the province of literary scholars, in this case newspapers accounts and legal, legislative, and diplomatic discourses. In doing so, I bring forth new perspectives on material that, although already cultivated by other critics, still has much to teach us.

In the twentieth century, critics of Melville's canon have written more about *Benito Cereno* than about any other of his shorter fiction, except "Bartleby, the Scrivener" (1853).[3] Prior to the 1950s, critical thought interpreted this story as a struggle between the forces of light and darkness, with the triumph of light in the form of the American Captain Delano, the rescuer of Don Benito Cereno from the clutches of the slave rebels, particularly their leader, Babo. Criticism of the story proliferated after the discovery that Melville had based it upon an event recorded in a historical Captain Delano's memoirs. But most interestingly, interpretations changed dramatically in the wake of the Civil Rights Movement and other liberation movements around the globe. Once associated with darkness, devils, and hell, Babo became for critics a freedom fighter of a nationalist movement. Joseph Schiffman gives Babo a "moral victory," while Charles L. Glicksberg points to his "indomitable spirit." Marvin Fisher erroneously names Babo as the first "militant Negro leader" in "American literature," whose "position is comparable to what are now called Third World views, making Aranda's murder a justifiable and fully rational political act."[4] Eric Sundquist calls him "fearsome and commanding" (1986, 110), while Joshua Leslie and Sterling Stuckey call *Benito Cereno* a "study in the negro as hero" (298). Critics transformed Don Benito Cereno as well, turning a sympathetic victim into a slaveholder getting his just desserts. Most significantly, Captain Delano emerged as the articulator of tropes of racial difference and white supremacy and, though republican, the protector of the peculiar institution.

During this critical revival, numerous critics mentioned both the *Amistad* and *Creole* rebellions in relation to *Benito Cereno*.[5] Yet most did so only in passing or with brief references to John Quincy Adams's defense of the *Amistad* captives or the censure of Joshua Giddings.

These references, usually based on secondary sources, represented the acts of one of these famous men as the most significant feature of the respective rebellion—yet another example of hero formation! Indeed, this approach obscures both the role of the Mendians' principal lawyer, Roger Baldwin, for example, and of the popular press in formulating and articulating public discourse about slave rebellions on ships.[6] Only Carolyn Karcher (1992) has examined in detail similarities between the *Amistad* affair and Melville's story, arguing from the basis of Melville's biography that the *Amistad* affair rather than Delano's *Voyages* would have been Melville's most significant influence. While appreciating Karcher's focus on the *Amistad*, I proceed from a different premise. As I mentioned above, I do not act from knowledge of Melville's biography because I am not working with the author as the organizing principle of my analysis. Rather I structure my critique of *Benito Cereno* primarily with insights gained from my study of the popular press, arguing that these insights enable us to determine how this literary text would have been understood at the historical moment of its publication and reception.

My study of the *Amistad* and *Creole* archives has produced a set of questions for analyzing and evaluating representations of slave revolts on ships. I have argued that the discourse of national identity produced many more potential subject-positions than have been realized, positions that oppositional groups attempted to claim and dominant groups attempted to limit. In particular, I have shown how Euroamericans first joined together by excluding slavery from the nation's founding documents and by denying authorization to slave rebellion, and later drew upon racialist discourses in order to prevent nonwhite people from benefiting from the developing nation. I have also considered how oppositional groups claimed the trope of revolutionary struggle for the enslaved population by asserting nonracialized masculinity over white masculinity, "all MEN" over "all [white] men." This kind of analysis produces the following questions regarding the representations' ideological import at the historical moment of their publication and reception.

Most simply, how are the rebels represented? Is a leader chosen and/or created, and if so, how? What forces amass for or against the enslaved rebels? To what ends are racialist discourses deployed? Most significantly, does the text prohibit or condemn slave rebellion either by figuring slavery as a non-issue or by drawing upon racialist discourses? Does the text support the prohibition either by figuring slavery as a non-issue (as did the Constitution and supporters of the Union), or by drawing upon racialist logics of white supremacy as did slavery advocates? Or does it create an imaginative or legal pathway by which U.S. Americans might identify the rebels as worthy to claim the trope of revolutionary struggle? How do the stories handle the anxiety produced by the specter of slave rebellion? What kind of alliances and identifications are produced and foreclosed, and with what consequences? In addition, how does genre function to make the fiction operate *differently* from the newspaper archives? What cultural work did the stories perform that journalism could or would not? What issues did the fiction writers centralize that were not evident or were marginal in the newspaper press? How did they differently address social conventions and assumptions of hierarchy? Did they expand or contract the inclusionary potential of liberal theory? These questions will be at the heart of my analysis of both *Benito Cereno* and *The Heroic Slave.*

To pursue them, I will also consider *Benito Cereno* in relation to what has traditionally been called its historical source, the eighteenth chapter of Amasa Delano's *A Narrative of Voyages and Travels in the Northern and Southern Hemispheres* (1817); many critics have considered this text crucial to understanding Melville's story.[7] In contrast to the well-known rebellions on the *Amistad* and *Creole,* most scholars predict that Delano's text was little known at the time *Benito Cereno* was published.[8] I consider *Voyages* not for how it influenced the initial reception of *Benito Cereno,* but for how it makes evident some of the choices Melville made in writing the novella. My primary concern is not with Melville's accuracy in representing the rebellion recorded in *Voyages,* or with arguing for or against Melville's status as a racist or progressive writer, but with determining how *Benito Cereno* challenged or normalized masculine white supremacy at the historical moment of its publication and reception.[9]

In the epigraph from *Benito Cereno* that heads this chapter, the

U.S. Captain Amasa Delano apprehensively characterizes the Spanish slave ship, the *San Dominick*, as a "slumbering volcano." Although Delano does not know exactly what he has to fear, he imagines any threat to himself and his authority as an upheaval of the natural order. Although Delano owns no slaves, his common sense stratifies humanity according to race and gender, a dominant mode of understanding shared by many of Melville's contemporaries. Threats from below, volcanic or racial, represent a dangerous force requiring swift repression. From an opposing position, Douglass invokes this avenging volcano as a natural force of "manly aspirations," which one day will erupt against "those who have trampled upon us for the last two hundred years," those like Delano. Douglass figures himself and others who, like him, have lived or continue to live as part of the enslaved volcano upon which the slaveholding empire rests, as contributing to this righteous force. Whereas Melville's Delano fears and hesitantly predicts the loosening of "energies now hid," Douglass calls for "their turn" to "come one day." These divergent responses characterize *Benito Cereno* and *The Heroic Slave*, Melville's and Douglass's respective fictions of slave rebellions on ships, the subject of chapters 4 and 5.

In the little more than a decade between the *Amistad* and *Creole* rebellions and the publication of these two stories, debate over the role of slavery in the United States increased dramatically. Continuing Euroamerican appropriation of native lands and an aggressive war with Mexico further increased the land mass under the control of the U.S. government, repeatedly raising the questions of extending or limiting slave territory and the appropriate position of racialized "others" within the national community. The fugitive-slave provision of the Compromise of 1850, rather than solidifying the Compact between the States, magnified divisions between and among dominant and oppositional groups over the nation's identity as free or slaveholding. Then in 1854 the Kansas-Nebraska Act opened the western territories to slavery through popular sovereignty, overturning the Missouri Compromise (1820) and making civil war almost inevitable.[10]

During these years, Frederick Douglass launched the *North Star* and later *Frederick Douglass' Paper*, which proved to be the most consistently published (and preserved) newspaper edited by an African American in the United States prior to the Civil War. More generally, abolition among African Americans became more militant as formerly enslaved people like Douglass grew to prominence and determined a greater part of the movement's goals (Ripley 23–29). Events such as the *Amistad* and *Creole* rebellions gained greater cultural importance among African American men as they looked for historical examples with which to represent and justify their current projects. During the late 1840s and 1850s, abolitionist lecturers like Henry Highland Garnet and Douglass made into popular heroes leaders of and advocates for slave rebellion, such as Denmark Vesey, Gabriel Prossor, Cinqué, Madison Washington, and David Walker.[11] Douglass's *The Heroic Slave*, an imagined biography of Madison Washington's life, represents an independent (although enslaved) African American man not only achieving physical liberation, but constructing an ideological position from which to authorize his rebellion.

Almost everyone who read *The Heroic Slave* and *Benito Cereno* would have heard about the *Amistad* and *Creole* rebellions. For readers of *The Heroic Slave*, this would certainly have been the case (had they been old enough), because this text was first published in *Frederick Douglass's Paper*, then in *Autographs for Freedom* (1853), both of which had primarily abolitionist audiences, those most likely to have kept track of the rebellions.[12] *Autographs* includes a brief biographical sketch of "Sarah," one of the *Amistad* Africans who had stayed behind to be educated in the United States, an example of the ways in which these two rebellions were tied together and kept alive, at least within abolitionist circles. Given that readers of *Putnam's*, the New York monthly in which *Benito Cereno* first appeared, though progressive, were probably not as consistently abolitionist as those of the *North Star*, my assertion in the case of *Benito Cereno* may not be as obvious. Yet the commercial and penny papers of New York, where the majority of *Putnam's* audience resided, had extensively covered the rebellions, especially the *Amistad*; readers of the local papers would have been familiar with the cases. In addition, several articles that *Putnam's* published within the same year as *Benito Cereno* indicate a tolerant attitude toward African Americans that tended toward antislavery. "About Niggers," for example, concludes: "The nigger is no joke, and no baboon; he is simply a black-man, and I say: Give him fair play and let us see what he will come to" (612). Not long after *Benito Cereno* appeared, the periodical's editor wrote the first platform for the Republican Party, based on an article published in *Putnam's*, thus earning for the publication the appellation "the leading review of the Black Republican Party" from *De Bow's Review*.[13] This editorial tendency would have appealed to antislavery readers, those most likely to have kept track of the *Amistad* and *Creole* rebellions.[14] Although not everyone who read newspapers or discussed the events covered therein also read periodicals, most who read periodicals would have read about or been aware of important events covered in the newspapers. In connecting *Benito Cereno* and *The Heroic Slave* to the *Amistad* and *Creole* rebellions, I emphasize the ways in which these literary texts rely upon the same tropes and rhetorics as legal, legislative, and diplomatic discourses evident in more quotidian and ephemeral texts, such as newspapers.[15]

*Benito Cereno* both parallels and dramatically diverges from the *Amistad* archive. The story opens with Captain Delano and his ship, the *Bachelor's Delight*, anchored at an uninhabited island to collect water, when "a strange sail" came into the bay (46). Because of his "singularly undistrustful good nature" (47), Delano does not perceive this ship as did those who first reported sightings of the *Amistad*, as "a suspicious sail—a pirate" (NY *Ad & Ex* and NY *MH* 8/24/39). Let us remember, though, that according to later reports, several ships earlier had treated[16] with the *Amistad* before it was determined to be— exactly by whom we cannot know—suspicious, "a pirate." It was only *after* this determination was made that the *Amistad* became newsworthy and reports of its movements appeared in the papers. Therefore Delano's initial response to the *San Dominick* perhaps parallels that of those captains who early on treated with the *Amistad*. Not being either suspicious or alarmed, this despite the fact that the ship violated "the custom among peaceful seamen of all nations" (47) by showing no flag, Delano allows his concern that the ship may ground itself upon a sunken reef, apparently unknown to it, to lead him to take his whale-boat in order to offer the ship his assistance. Mists at first obscure Delano's sight of the ship, but upon closer examination,

Delano realizes that the "throngs of black cowls" he mistook for monks "now appear to be" "negro slaves" (48). Like the *Amistad*, the *San Dominick* has "dark festoons of sea-grass slimily" sweeping to and fro (49); but unlike those on the *Amistad*, the Africans on board do not *appear* to be armed. This crucial difference makes possible the suspense of Melville's story. Once sailors sighting the *Amistad* realized that "the strange crew . . . [was] armed with muskets and cutlasses," their sense of normalcy was challenged; accordingly many ships set out in pursuit with the clear intention of capturing it and bringing it into port for salvage.[17] But Delano's inability to perceive, symbolized by the mists, combined with the Africans' acting, obscures from Delano and from Melville's readers the fact that a rebellion has taken place and the Africans actually command the ship. In this way, Melville creates a scenario very different from the *Amistad* affair, one designed to leave readers suspended until the truth bursts forth near the end of the story's first section.

Four parts structure *Benito Cereno*. First, a third-person narrator attached to Delano's perspective recounts Delano's day on the *San Dominick* with Don Benito and his (apparent) servant, Babo; this, the longest section, ends when, as Delano leaves the *San Dominick* to return to his ship, Don Benito's desperate attempt to join him and Babo's attempt to murder Cereno make the Africans' rebellion obvious. Second, an omniscient narrator leaves Delano behind on his ship and follows the crew of the *Bachelor's Delight* as they pursue, board, and eventually recapture the *San Dominick*. (Most critics collapse these two parts into one section told from Delano's point of view. But I think it is crucial, as will become clear below, to recognize when the narrator and Delano split.) Third, the deposition of Benito Cereno, a "document selected, from among many others" (103), recalls the Africans' takeover of the *San Dominick*, their strategies of terror, and their plan to fool Delano and to take his ship as well. Finally, an omniscient narrator comments upon the deposition and why the story has been told in the order given, then concludes the text with a brief narrative section following Cereno and Delano as they sail to Lima, the verdict and sentence against the Africans, and Cereno's eventual death.

Through manipulating the generic conventions of perspective and narrative structure, Melville uses the short story form to do cultural work that journalism could not. In the story's first part, for example, Melville imbeds Delano's perspective inside another perspective critical of it. Although this relation becomes clearest with rereading, even first-time readers often notice the discomfort it produces. The story's narrative structure compounds this effect. Journalism typically first presents the outcome or conclusion of the news it is relating, then fills in the details as space permits. The structure of *Benito Cereno* purposefully suspends sure knowledge of the *San Dominick*'s history, thereby generating an unsure sense of reality, symbolized by the mist shrouding the *San Dominick* or the unbelievably complex Gordian knot. Only by piecing together accounts of antagonists in the *Amistad* affair, as I was able to do because of the richness of its archive, do we even begin to get a similar sense of uncertainty about "what happened." In this way, *Benito Cereno* produces anxiety within its readers, not only about the outcome of the story, but about the reliability of the characters, and ultimately, about their/our own perceptions. This anxiety is simultaneously calmed and increased by the different kinds of material included in the text. Benito Cereno's deposition, at once a legal document, another person's perspective on "what happened," and the background "information" on what happened prior to Delano's arrival, lays claim to objectivity and seems to fill in the missing parts of the story. Yet the narrator's comment, that "If the Deposition have [sic] served as the key to fit into the lock of the complications which precede it, then, as a vault whose door has been flung back, the San Dominick's hull lies open to-day" (114), reminds readers that this text, as well, should not be taken at face value. All of these textual characteristics undermine readers' abilities to trust any of the text, and thereby to settle on an interpretation. In this way, Melville challenges us to suspend our desires for certainty and for knowledge.

Many late twentieth-century critics have responded to the anxiety the text produces by reading it against the grain of Delano's perspective, detailing the way in which we as readers may perceive from the very beginning what Delano does not, that the Africans actually control the vessel and are manipulating white supremacist assumptions to their own advantage. Certainly clues pointing to the limits of Delano's perspective abound. Yet insisting that "the crudest textual criticism . . . reveals Melville had contempt for Delano" obscures the experience of most people's first reading.[18] Such an assertion invalidates the experience of sharing Delano's perspective, which the very structure of the story invites, even compels if not absolutely requires readers to do—at least initially. In the process at least two important aspects of the story are lost: (1) the reader's association with and inhabiting of extreme racialist thought, and (2) the anxiety produced by that association in an environment that implicitly challenges some of its most basic premises. A potential third loss is readers' complicity with Delano's perspective and their confrontation with or elision of information that challenges Delano's—and their own—way of making sense of the situation.[19] With Robert Levine, then, I would "challenge the tendency to read *Benito Cereno* as a transcendingly assured attack on enslavers and racists" (168).

Most critics who assert the limits of Delano's perspective from the beginning do so in order to assert not only the intelligence of the Africans, but the justness of their cause. This criticism functions, then, to alleviate the anxiety produced by *Benito Cereno*'s narrative structure by differentiating critic from Delano and identifying critic with Babo and the rest of the African rebels. Melville deploys racialist discourses to seduce as well as to confuse readers, to seduce them/us into identifying with a perspective that will not only be shown to be partial, but that will also be undermined. Some readers may anticipate that undermining, while some no doubt resist and deny it, and still others feel conflicted and/or confused. For most nineteenth-century U.S. Americans, I would argue, *Benito Cereno* necessarily activated anxieties regarding race, masculinity, and slavery, and as it turned out, slave revolt. Such anxieties could not easily be alleviated. As I argued in chapter 2, supporters of the *Amistad* captives worked long and hard to develop means by which U.S. Americans could identify with the Mendian rebels. In a sense, *Benito Cereno* functions as a test for readers. But it is more complicated than "doing the right thing" by discerning and identifying with a progressive agenda, because even the act of such identifying reveals the construction of that position and suggests that at some point, being inheritors and inhabitants of a racist society, we—particularly but not exclusively for those of us who are white—think and act according to racialist (or racist) logic. The test, then, is not simply to undermine Delano's way of making sense, but to recognize and confront in it connections to our own.

## A MATTER OF PERSPECTIVE

*Benito Cereno* illustrates precisely the problematic of U.S. Americans' inability to imagine slave rebels as righteous rebels. Through Captain Delano, the story investigates strategies of hierarchical differentiation, of making inside/outside, righteous/invalid, white/black, free/slave, all of which served to exclude Africans and African Americans from the national community, while at the same time defining that community as one of free, white men and the women who supported them.

Indeed, Delano embodies the discursive strategies that excluded African Americans from the national community. He constructs his identity and his authority as a white man as always superior to dark-skinned people, regardless of their gender or behavior. In addition, as an effective sea captain, authorized to be a leader among men, even when tyrannical, he occupies a masculine position in relation to the light-skinned but emasculated Spanish captain, Don Benito Cereno. A hierarchy of race and gender organizes the frame of reference by which Delano makes sense of the world, a hierarchy manifested in his desire for orderliness, which he finds sorely wanting on the Spaniards' ship. *Benito Cereno* attaches this racialist logic to Delano's supposedly benevolent, specifically republican nature:

He complied [in supplying water], with republican impartiality as to this republican element, which always seeks one level, serving the oldest white no better than the youngest black. . . . Two of the less wilted pumpkins being reserved for the captain's table, the residue were minced up on the spot for the general regalement. But the soft bread, sugar, and bottled cider, Captain Delano would have given the whites alone. . . . (80)

Delano's desire to serve water equally to all the thirsty on board the *San Dominick*, "the oldest white no better than the youngest black," demonstrates his benevolent republicanism. Delano willingly, even happily and excitedly, provides all with the goods necessary for their subsistence: water and pumpkin. Yet the hierarchical character of his republicanism reserves those foods not needed to stave off starvation, the luxury items of "soft bread, sugar, and bottled cider," for "the whites alone." The specifically racial marker, "whites alone," signals a historical moment closer to that of the text's publication than to the ostensible time period in which the story is set. On board ship, distinctions among captain, officers, and crew were as crucial as those between these groups and enslaved cargo. And the strategies used to maintain the first of these distinctions, particularly that between crew and officers, such as flogging, often replicated those between the enslaved and the rest. Thus Delano's racial distinction obscures other important ones among the "whites," particularly class differences among the Spanish officers and crew and national and religious differences between Delano and the Spanish. This privileging of race over class and nation, as we have seen, characterizes the transformation of the discourse of national identity in the middle of the nineteenth century. Indeed, although the name "Amasa Delano" is not Anglo-Saxon, he may nevertheless comfortably lay claim to Americanness on the basis of his whiteness.

Delano's "best regulated mind" (85) also produces visions of black inferiority and submissiveness. For example, Delano's heart warms at the sight of one of the "negresses" nursing her child: "There's naked nature, now. . . . Unsophisticated as leopardesses; loving as doves" (73). This vision of "naked nature" grows out of and supports the racialist logic that figures dark-skinned people as heathen, uncivilized, and close to nature. At this quiet moment Delano romanticizes the notion of the women's ferocity in the event, for example, of a threat to their children. His racialist thinking splits his bestial characterization of the women into a dualistic form as either dangerous "leopardesses" or nurturing "doves." The Africans' "instinct" for nurturing most attracts Delano when directed toward a supposedly natural superior. In the cuddy, where Delano sits alone with Babo and Don Benito, Babo appears to Delano as having that "docility arising from the unaspiring contentment of a limited mind, and that susceptibility of blind attachment sometimes inhering in indisputable inferiors" (84). Assured, at least momentarily, of Babo's subordinate status, Delano's genial "weakness for negroes" returns (84). When Babo acts the part of a faithful body servant, Delano applauds and feels a homoerotic affection for him; in fact, he seeks to acquire Babo for his own as a man might a wife. His common sense can only comprehend Babo's behavior as adoring and "unaspiring" subservience.

Delano's notion of the Africans' "docility arising from the unaspiring contentment of a limited mind" (84) assumes and asserts that they have no innate desire for liberty. Given this, Delano walks right past the six black men "each with a rusty hatchet in his hand, . . . while between each two was a small stack of hatchets" (50). Unlike the sailors who recognized as dangerous the cutlasses and muskets of the *Amistad*'s "strange crew," Delano does not perceive the hatchets as potential weapons or the men as dangerous. He therefore relieves himself of any anxiety potentially created by *recognizing* black men with weapons. When his suspicions do arise, as when he wonders if, "Upon gaining [the vicinity of his own vessel], might not the San Dominick, like a slumbering volcano, suddenly let loose energies now hid?" (68), Delano focuses not on the "blacks" but on Don Benito. Even then, he "good-naturedly explained away" (69) his anxiety by dismissing the Spanish navigator as a potential source of danger. Even in the face of "extraordinary and repeated incentives" to see a different reality (47), Delano skillfully, if unwittingly, translates the Africans' actions into terms that make him comfortable, that soothe his anxiety, that reassure him of his own superiority—and safety.

Delano's surprise at, then dawning recognition of, the "ferocious piratical revolt" (99) indicates that he was duped, perhaps more by his own perceptions than by the rebels' acting. Numerous critics have pointed to the disparity between Delano's perceptions of "the blacks" prior to this moment and the vision that greets him once the masks are removed.[20] They commonly characterize this disparity as Melville's way of undermining Delano's authority and all that he represents, revealing the "stereotyped faces worn by blacks in our fiction to be masks" (Yellin 224). Few, however, have considered this aspect of *Benito Cereno* in relation to a pattern established by the antebellum slave narratives.[21]

Narratives by William Wells Brown (1849) and Henry Bibb (1849), to name but two, describe an array of deceptive behavior employed by those enslaved in their escapes from bondage. Acknowledging the futility of overt resistance, given the power and pervasiveness of the institution of slavery, Bibb asserts that "the only weapon of self defense that I could use successfully, was that of deception" (17). William L. Andrews points out that the trope of deception in Bibbs's narrative forces readers to "confront the moral problem of how freely a fugitive from injustice could sidestep traditional laws and mores to gain his own advantage" (1988, 17). The effectiveness of such a confrontation resides in the (ex)slave narrator's ability to convince readers of the injustice of the system that compels him or her to act in such a manner and, in so doing, bring the reader to see the ironic justness of the enslaved's deception. This process of persuasion, pioneered by slave narrators and writers of antislavery novels, drawn upon by those who favorably represented the *Amistad* and *Creole* rebels, and used repeatedly by Douglass in *The Heroic Slave*, employs a logic of identification between enslaved peoples and free U.S. Americans, the goal of which was the recognition of a common humanity. But unlike these narratives, *Benito Cereno* does not include or otherwise articulate the perspective of the rebels. Therefore readers are not presented with a black protagonist's explanation for his strategy of deception. What is the effect, then, of realizing these "stereotyped faces" to be masks?

Again, Delano illustrates precisely one of the primary ways in which white U.S. Americans responded to such deception. At the end of the first section, Delano realizes that Benito Cereno is attempting to escape Babo and his cohort, who have taken over the ship: "Captain Delano, now with the scales dropped from his eyes, saw the negroes, not in misrule, not in tumult, . . . but with mask torn away, flourishing hatchets and knives, in ferocious piratical revolt" (99). Delano's racialist perspective must make this vision appear not only as a mutiny— piratical enough—but as a slave revolt as well, as a disruption of the "natural" order that even more loudly calls for suppression. Perhaps Delano perceives all crew members as different from himself and in need of constant control, as Levine suggests, as a gentleman alone in an urban ghetto (204). Yet, as we have seen, Melville's Captain Delano perceives his crew and the Spaniards as members of the same species as himself, as "whites," whatever other class and cultural differences they may have, while he has his doubts about his biological connection to "the blacks" (75).[22] When faced with the undeniable fact of the Africans' rebellion, he switches without apparent discomfort from assumptions of black submissiveness to black savageness. His vision of the now erupting volcano denies to the rebels the paradigmatic choice between liberty and death, ironically not because they fear to fight, but because he can only "make sense" of their actions as a resurgence of savagism, the insurgency of the unfit, the unruly, the untamed, against the better government of a civilized people. His range of responses does not include seeing them as heroic self-liberators. He uses whichever aspect of a racialist discourse he needs to relieve his own anxiety concerning slavery, to relieve himself from responsibility for slavery, and to reinforce his own sense of superiority. To do this he must display inconsistent thinking and behavior because slavery, particularly, as Joyce Adler notes, slavery based on racial distinctions, can only be supported through convoluted and incoherent reasoning. Melville shares with abolitionist writers an understanding of the power dynamics that undergird racialist discourses. But unlike more didactic writers, Melville does not attempt to refute the logics of racialism— which in a sense cannot be done since they are themselves illogical— so much as illustrate how they work.

Thus, realizing that the Africans are in control does not necessarily lead one to identify with them. This realization overturns Delano's most paternalistic racialism, which assumes and asserts not only the Africans' incapacity for intelligent and concerted action, but their natural subordination. But Delano's quick and violent suppression of the revolt indicates that recognizing their control may only make them seem demonic rather than cherubic, with their actions then appearing to overturn the natural order, as a violent volcanic eruption. Righteousness need not be attributed to them once their agency is understood. Remember that "The *Creole* Case," unlike the "Protest," emphasized the *Creole* rebels' violent agency. But because the rebels were positioned as outside the community of citizens, as Babo and the rest clearly are in the worlds dominated by Delanos, nothing done to them can be a violation of law; they therefore have no "natural" right to self-defense. In fact their rebellion, according to this logic, can only be interpreted as acts against the natural rights of citizens, as murder of the Spaniards and robbery of the wealth represented by their own bodies.

Recognizing blacks' capacity for plotting and resistance to enslavement abounds in proslavery reasoning for the repressive measures legislated against those enslaved, particularly prohibitions on assembly, literacy, and mobility. Remember the responses of Southern legislators to Walker's *Appeal*, which was *only a text* that called for resistance. It is a mistake to interpret assertions of black inferiority and submissiveness as coherent beliefs; rather they cover the more profound fear and haunting recognition of their opposites. Racialism, like other discourses, does not operate according to rules of reason and coherence, but rather disperses multiple, often contradictory assertions, thereby becoming increasingly powerful and pervasive.

Identifying with the Africans, seeing their rebellion as righteous, requires another step. To this point *Benito Cereno* does not imagine for us any other vision; it does not provide a means by which *doubting* U.S. Americans—then or now—can imagine the rebels as like themselves. But does the undermining of Delano's perspective create an imaginative space, an interstice, elsewhere in the story? Or perhaps more appropriately given the circumstances of this story, does anything in the text, or in how it interacts within a discursive field of representations of slave rebellion, create a means by which U.S. Americans can imagine the African rebels as members of a nation among a community of nations?

### THE ARCHIVE OF SLAVE REBELLION

To answer these questions, I turn now to the remaining three sections of the story, and consider the ways in which these sections interact with the *Amistad* and *Creole* archives, with *Voyages*, and with *The Heroic Slave*. In this section, I argue that *Benito Cereno* does participate in processes of hero and national identity formation like those employed in the *Amistad* archive, but that its distorted representation of the rebels' savagery complicates and potentially undermines the authorizing aspects of these processes.

Very much shorter than *Benito Cereno*, the relevant chapter of Delano's *Voyages* begins with an excerpt from the ship's log detailing the retaking of the Spanish ship, the *Tryal*. Thus from the beginning Delano's readers know the subject of the chapter to be the quelling of a slave rebellion. Delano tells the rest of chapter himself, beginning with his description of the crew's current condition. Having recently left New Holland, Delano discovered that seventeen men, most of whom had been convicts at Botany Bay, had stowed on board his ship. Fortunately for him, Delano's combination of strict discipline and "good wholesome floggings" enables him to bring them into line, just in time to meet the *Tryal*, an experience in which "no men ever behaved better" (320, 321–22). Delano recounts the way in which he, upon boarding the *Tryal*, promised "to relieve all the wants they had mentioned," as in *Benito Cereno* ordering his men to bring fish, bread, pumpkins, and water (323). Delano recalls his own sympathetic temper, brought on by the obvious appearance of much suffering, a mood he says in the end saved his life. Although briefer than Melville's version, *Voyages* includes several similar incidents, such as the "slave" boys stabbing the Spanish boy, which he calls "rather serious sport" (323); Delano's indignation at what he perceived to be Don Bonito's cool refusal to join him on his ship, the *Perseverance*; Don Bonito's eventual escape by jumping into Delano's whale-boat; and Delano's agreement to stay behind while his men pursued the *Tryal*. In addition, *Voyages* appends not just the declaration of Bonito Cereno, but an array of other documents by Spanish officials, included, no doubt, to support Delano's claim to salvage.[23]

Ironically *Benito Cereno* represents the "blacks" as a people, complete with a symbol (Aranda's skeleton), a motto ("Follow your leader!"), and a mission (journey to a "negro country"). These galvanizing elements, developed from the rebels' common experience of slavery and rebellion, mark the creation of a (national) community from a loose collection of people. Yet this characterization also satirizes abolitionist strategies supporting the *Amistad* captives and asserts the rebels' savagery. In order to refigure the supposedly organic bond between master and slave as bonds among slave rebels, *Benito Cereno* draws upon proslavery tropes of violent disorder, the now erupting "slumbering volcano." Consider the example of cannibalism.

*Benito Cereno* creates an incident of implied cannibalism by the Africans not included—or even hinted at—in *Voyages*. In *Voyages*, the Africans stabbed Captain Aranda in his cabin, brought him on deck while still alive, tied him up, and threw him overboard. All this was done, according to Cereno's recollection of the Africans' motives, in order to "obtain their liberty" (*Voyages* 336). In justifying their acts of violence, the *Creole* rebels similarly stated that "all they had done was for their freedom" ("Protest"). Leslie and Stuckey regard this as a reasonable strategy, for the only way to ensure one's freedom, they argue, is to kill the master (298). This was the reasoning of the Haitian revolutionaries, who so terrified slaveholders in the United States.

But in *Benito Cereno*, after the Africans bring Aranda on board and stab him to death, they take his body below decks, where they remove every bit of his flesh and in three days bring on deck his skeleton, which Babo uses to terrify and subordinate the Spaniards. In this instance, the act of killing the master in order to ensure one's freedom carries not only a sentence of death, but of literally being devoured. The way in which Babo terrorizes the Spanish plays upon their "common sense" fears of Africans as barbaric and brutal. Although Babo brutalizes the whites with their own stereotypes, it is less clear that the text demonizes other Africans' acts of cannibalism. Still, *Benito Cereno* includes a stereotype of African behavior as barbaric and brutal that *Voyages* does not include. Even more, Melville's readers were less likely than he to appreciate the difference between the text's suggestion of cultural relativism and their own "common sense" fears of being eaten. Recall that the "official account" of the capture of the *Amistad* described one of the rebels as "the most horrible creature we ever saw in human shape . . . a cannibal. His teeth projected at almost right angles from his mouth, while his eyes had a most savage and demonic expression." Though published in the penny press, this description was written not by a journalist but by one of the officers of the USS *Washington*. It easily associates ritualistic or decorative practices centered on the mouth with eating human flesh, and interprets his look as "savage" and "demonic." This ludicrous description—anyone with all his teeth at right angles to his mouth would have a difficult time chewing anything, particularly flesh—makes sense only because it relies upon (and perpetuates) irrational fears of racialized otherness. The fear of others' cannibalism seems to have been particularly potent for Christians of European descent, whose own religious practices—symbolically or literally through transfiguration—included consuming the body and blood of their savior. Supporters of the *Amistad* captives had to dispute this description of one of the Africans as a cannibal in order to move forward with their defense. A reporter for the *Commercial Advertiser*, for example, asserted: "The 'cannibal,' or 'man with the tusks,' is a good-tempered fellow, and I venture to say never ate a morsel of man's flesh in his life" (11/1/39:2,2). Because cannibalism signaled heathenish, even demonic, savagery, cannibalizing Aranda's body would have greatly inhibited, if not outright prohibited, identification between the rebels and most U.S. Americans. *Benito Cereno* therefore made questionable—and for many outright undermined—the rebels' right to struggle for liberty, this despite the fact that *Benito Cereno* represents them as violent self-liberators. This representation of barbarity and brutality in turn figures the "blacks" of the *San Dominick* as outside the community of (civilized) nations.[24]

In addition, the absence of any representation of violence by the Spaniards implies that the Africans perpetrated unprovoked violence. In *Benito Cereno*, Melville significantly reduces the violent acts on the part of the Spaniards described in Delano's *Voyages*. Delano states explicitly in his narrative, although his deposition does not include it, that when he and his men returned to the *Tryal* on the morning following the capture, they discovered that all the African men had been secured to the rings in the ship's deck by their hands and feet and that "some of them had parts of their bowels hanging out, and some with half their backs and thighs shaved off" (*Voyages* 328). *Benito Cereno* includes only a single incident in which one sailor attempts to stab one of the Africans, hardly representative of the Spaniards' avenging attitude or their numerous acts of violence. In *Voyages*, the details of

Spanish violence balance Delano's narrative, admitting violence by both parties; as such the violence on the part of the Spanish suggests a motive for the rebellion of the Senegalese, if in retrospect.[25]

In the *Amistad* archive, Ruiz and Montez, the Spanish minister, and Van Buren's administration strategized to obscure any suggestion of violence on the part of the Spanish captain, crew, and passengers. This strategy deployed a limited time-frame that excluded violence done to the Mendians prior to their revolt, including their capture in Africa, their journey on the middle passage, and their treatment on the *Amistad*. Both Delano's *Voyages* and *Benito Cereno* use time-frames similar to that of the Spaniards in the *Amistad* affair. Both narratives begin with the meeting of the two ships, and Benito Cereno's deposition in each text only extends back in time to the sailing of the *Tryal/San Dominick*. Thus the framing devices of each text exclude any information about the rebels prior to the moment when the Spanish ship first set sail.[26] But Delano's *Voyages* includes violent actions by the Spaniards after Delano's crew recaptures the vessel, thereby balancing to some extent the actions of the Senegalese. Melville excludes this information from *Benito Cereno*, a narrative strategy that now appears, given our knowledge of the *Amistad* and *Creole* rebellions, very similar to that of Ruiz, Montez, and their supporters.

Recall also that the "official report" of the capture of the *Amistad* tried to allocate all responsibility for violence to the Africans. It went so far as to claim that the backs of several of the Africans were scarred by Cinqué's beatings. The affidavits of Fonni and Kimbe challenged this interpretation by accusing Ruiz and Montez of whipping them. *Benito Cereno* contains no similar information or point of view to complicate or contest its representation of the Africans' violence. Although the Spanish tribunal at Lima treats the rebels brutally—they are dragged to the gallows, hung, their heads then displayed on pikes—including violence only at this stage displaces responsibility for it from the Spanish crew and slaveholders to the Spanish legal system. And at this point in the narrative this behavior may seem, rather than an integral part of the slave system, like a justifiable if violent response to the Africans' brutality. Given the greater savagery of the rebels in *Benito Cereno*, and the lesser savagery of the Spaniards, at least on board the *San Dominick*, Melville's text creates a clear distinction between brutal Africans and victimized Spaniards that sanitizes and thereby romanticizes the Spaniards rather than romanticizing "slave ability." *Voyages* and the archive of the *Amistad* as a whole, rather than *Benito Cereno*, most fully represent and criticize "transracial savagery" (Levine 221). This distorted view of the rebels and the Spaniards undermines the representation of Babo as hero and the Africans as a national entity deserving inclusion within a community of (civilized) nations.

Differences between *Benito Cereno*'s and *Voyages*'s accounts of the *San Dominick*'s (*Tryal*'s) capture illustrate the way in which *Benito Cereno* further normalizes white supremacy. *Benito Cereno*'s account begins as the whaling boat and yawl leave the *Bachelor's Delight* in pursuit of the *San Dominick*; this section differs from the one before in that the narrative persona separates from Delano (left behind on the *Bachelor's Delight*), becoming a near omniscient perspective that can see all that is visible on board the *San Dominick*. In this brief section, no alternative voice questions the perceptions of the persona, making it oddly like an eyewitness account—but without the accountability of an actual eyewitness. Importantly, the two texts differ considerably as to the number of Africans on board. Cereno's deposition in *Voyages* counts the number of slaves on board the *Tryal* as 72, 9 of whom were "sucking infants," 28 of whom were women of all ages, 20 of whom were males between the ages of twelve and sixteen, and only 14 of whom were full-grown men. Twenty crewmen from the *Perseverance* (Delano's ship) subdued these 72 Africans, a few more than half of whom were adults perhaps, after more than an hour of continual musket fire from the *Perseverance*'s whale-boat and yawl. Armed with a greater quantity of superior weapons, such as knives, cutlasses, and boarding lances as well as muskets, the sailors eventually boarded the ship and overcame the Africans. In *Benito Cereno*, both the narrative and Cereno's deposition set the number of "blacks" at 160, of both sexes, nearly all of whom were still alive at the time of the capture. *Benito Cereno* increases the number of sailors on the *Bachelor's Delight* from the *Perseverance*'s 20, but the eyewitness account makes little of the musket fire from the boats or the sailors' superior weapons more generally. Rather it emphasizes the strategy of the sailors in de-coying the Africans to throw their weapons into the sea and in dis-abling the ship. During the battle, the rebels tire, not the "unflagging sailors": "Their red tongues lolled, wolf-like, from their black mouths. But the pale sailors' teeth were set; not a word was spoken; and, in five minutes more, the ship was won" (102). Thus while the narrative emphasizes the sailors' stamina and determination, it makes little of the vast disparity between the parties in number and technology.

Naturalizing racial difference makes it possible to believe, for ex-ample, that 25 sailors defeated 160 rebels with little trouble, because their natural superiority enabled them to do so. Delano's narrative in *Voyages* makes a point of praising the "skill and intrepidity" of his (ad-mittedly criminal) crew in retaking the *Tryal*, "with only twenty men to board and carry a ship, containing so many slaves, made desperate by their situation" (322). Despite his assumed superiority, Delano re-alizes how very dangerous the situation was for his men. How much more so the takeover of the *San Dominick*, with two and a half times as many Africans, "made desperate by their situation," on board. *The Heroic Slave* provides another useful point of reference for analyzing *Benito Cereno* in this regard. In the last scene of *The Heroic Slave*, a man, Williams, addresses the former first mate of the *Creole*, arguing that any "resolute white man" could have subdued with only a whip the rebelling slaves of the *Creole*. Williams thus gives voice to a gen-eral white supremacist assumption that white men can easily subor-dinate any number of "blacks" because of their "natural" ability to intimidate (61–62). Yet the former first mate responds with a central lesson of Douglass's story, that white sailors cannot so easily over-come determined rebels because on a ship they do not have an entire social, political, legal, and military system to support their repressive practices. By asserting the ease with which the crew of the *Bachelor's Delight* overcame the rebels of the *San Dominick*, *Benito Cereno* both undermines the power of the rebels as a whole and supports racialist discourses that made such a victory seem natural and inevitable.

In addition, Melville's transformation of Babo from *Voyages* to *Be-nito Cereno* individualizes Babo in a process related to that by which popular press accounts and interpretations made Cinqué and Madison

Washington into heroic rebel leaders.[27] Although Cereno's deposition from Delano's *Voyages* at one point calls Babo "the ring leader" (335), Babo acts as part of the community that includes his son Mure, Atufal, and at least ten other Senegalese men, as well as Francisco, a mulatto native of Buenos Aires, Joaquin, "a smart negro," and twenty-eight women of all ages (334).[28] In Cereno's deposition, the consistent use of the pronoun "they" when referring to the agent of the rebellion and the Spaniards' subjugation illustrates this communal activity. The deposition also names Mure as both the one who kept watch on Benito Cereno and, somewhat contradictorily (to the description of Babo as "ring leader"), as "captain and commander of them" (341). In contrast, in *Benito Cereno* Babo masterminds the rebellion, a composite figure of both Babo and Mure in *Voyages*. Cereno's deposition in *Benito Cereno* refers to the agent of the plot against the Spaniards as "he" rather than "they." The transformation of *Voyages* into *Benito Cereno* distinguishes Babo from his companions by making him into an intelligent individual, as the *Amistad* archive had fashioned Cinqué. For example, *Benito Cereno* gives Babo credit for the plot against Delano, whereas in *Voyages* Cereno presents the idea. This difference between the two texts makes the Babo of *Benito Cereno* more ingenious (through being the sole leader and creator of the plot), elevating him to the status of creator, "a Nubian sculptor" (87), thereby questioning the white supremacist assumption of black stupidity.[29]

This process mirrors that by which Madison Washington and Cinqué were made into heroic rebel leaders. A letter to the New York *Evangelist* proudly "translated" the words of the "Protest" into the "appropriate language of freedom" (qtd. in *NASS* 12/30/41:118,2). This letter transformed Madison Washington into the sole leader of the rebellion by marginalizing the actions of the other three principal rebels, in addition to the remaining "18," presumably because he "wore a name unfit for a slave, but finely expressive of a hero." Douglass's *The Heroic Slave* further exaggerates this process by creating a life history for Madison Washington from the "traces" left by him (26) and leaving entirely aside the efforts of others. In the *Amistad* archive, Cinqué from beginning to end was consistently singled out as the Mendians' leader. Yet over time other of the Africans emerged from the initially faceless mass of slaves: Fonni and Kimbe filed affidavits; Grambeau testified in court; Ka-le learned to read and write, and wrote to the papers; Kinna displayed his knowledge of Christian doctrine before large crowds; one of the young girls took a Christian name, Sarah, and decided to stay in the United States. John Barber's *History of the Amistad Captives* included sketches of each of the captives' faces and details of their lives. Thus while Cinqué remained their undisputed leader—according to their own preferences, apparently, as well as by popular construction—over time he became one of a more complexly represented and understood group.

*Benito Cereno*'s representation of Babo most closely mimics the *Amistad* archive in this respect. Though the undisputed leader, and though less one of the group than his counterpart in *Voyages*, Melville's Babo still works within a community that includes the oakum pickers, hatchet polishers, Atufal, and the "Ashantee negresses" (92), indeed to some extent the entire population of the formerly enslaved. His plan depends—far more than did Madison Washington's, for example, in either the *Creole* archive or *The Heroic Slave*—upon not only the cooperation but the help of virtually everyone. Certain other characters are individuated as well, such as Francesco (as the mulatto's name is spelled in Melville's text) and Atufal, the latter of whom, rather than Babo, is an African chieftain. In this way, *Benito Cereno* imbeds Babo within a community, thereby making their status as a people more plausible, even as Babo orchestrates their actions.

Those making Cinqué or Madison Washington into heroes in the *Amistad* and *Creole* archives and in *The Heroic Slave* identified male rebel leaders with heroes of the U.S. Revolution so that either they could invoke the trope of revolutionary struggle for them, or so they could claim and assert it themselves. What is the function of hero formation in *Benito Cereno*? Are Babo's words and acts "translated into the appropriate language of freedom"? Does Babo's individuation and intelligence set in motion a logic of identification?

*Benito Cereno* does not present any emancipatory possibilities for the rebels, who eventually are executed or remanded to slavery. Neither does it create for them either a position from which to articulate their oppositional agenda or a sympathetic narrative perspective to interpret their words and acts. *Benito Cereno* does not give the rebels of the *San Dominick* the opportunity to record or otherwise fashion their experience so it would be accessible to others after their capture, in court testimony, for example, as did the Mendians of the *Amistad*. Once captured, Babo "uttered no sound, and could not be forced to. His aspect seemed to say, since I cannot do deeds, I will not speak words" (116). Even more provocatively, the story ends with the picture of Babo's head, "that hive of subtlety, fixed on a pole in the Plaza, [which] met, unabashedly, the gaze of the whites" (116). Melville constructs an image dominated by the unknown power of Babo's mind, an intelligence far greater than accounted for by any racialist discourses, one that readily uses deception as well as violence in the service of its own agenda. Thus *Benito Cereno* does the cultural work of representing one central anxiety driving the silencing of slave rebellion, the unspoken, suppressed, and unacknowledged fear that "they" may be as intelligent as—or more so than—"we." Yet *Benito Cereno* gapes wide where the rebels' perspective might have spoken. Where Frederick Douglass used the occasion of the *Creole* rebellion to imagine a life story and to create a subject-position for Madison Washington, Melville made no such attempt on behalf of Babo and the other rebels.

A number of critics have pointed to this absence. For instance, Jean Fagan Yellin remarks, "Although he did not attempt to render the black man's living face or to sound the tones of his authentic voice, Melville's tale . . . dramatized the perception that his voice had not been heard" (224). Karcher argues similarly that "Melville's many interpolations add up to a consistent pattern: an unmistakable effort to reconstruct the slaves' side of the story and to accord it with as much visibility as possible within the framework of a narrative faithful to the fact that the slaves' 'tyrants have been their historians'" (1992, 219).

Yet given the numerous materials representing the opinions of African Americans, including the Mendians' accounts (as mediated as they are) in the *Amistad* archive, Walker's *Appeal* and Garnet's "Address," the New York *Colored American*, the emergence of the *North Star* and *Frederick Douglass' Paper*, the proliferation of slave narratives, and the emergence of African American fiction with William Wells Brown's *Clotel* and Douglass's *The Heroic Slave*, the perception of their silence cannot be justified. Representing Babo as silent, as unable or unwilling to speak, does not have the same effect as having him speak, as Nat Turner did, or as George does in *Clotel*, and then having the legal system disregard what he says.[30] At the historical moment at which *Benito Cereno* was published and received, African Americans, as I have shown, were speaking and writing in many arenas; they were contesting the institutional structures that excluded them and the rhetorical strategies that represented them as unfit for membership in the national community. To dramatize "the perception that [the black man's voice] had not been heard" ironically also reinforces that erroneous perception, giving it imaginative weight and validity.

*Benito Cereno* most skillfully represents the anxieties of Euroamericans regarding race and slavery, both showing the ways assumptions of white supremacy worked to calm those anxieties and demarcating the limits of this mode of understanding. This representation was far more likely to heighten than to temper anxiety regarding slave revolt. Melville shows a sensitivity to his subject greatly appreciated from the safe distance of the late twentieth century—and no doubt by those of his contemporary readers who already were predisposed to interpret favorably the rebellious acts of enslaved Africans. Yet many of his contemporaries evidently did not share this view. The reviewer for the New York *Sun*, which had so extensively covered the capture of the *Amistad*, called *Benito Cereno* "a strangely conceived story." Another stated that "we became nervously anxious for the solution of the mystery it involves" (*Knickerbocker*).[31] Given the way in which slave rebellion was popularly represented at the time of *Benito Cereno*'s publication and reception, a reading that identifies Babo with U.S. Americans, and thereby challenges the prohibition on slave rebellion, was not available to most U.S. Americans.

If the abolitionist supporters of the *Amistad* captives attempted to create a means by which U.S. Americans could imagine the Mendians to be members of a community of nations, and Douglass's *The Heroic Slave* created a similar means for imagining Madison Washington to be a heroic claimant of the trope of revolutionary struggle, *Benito Cereno* denies that imagining except to the most determined readers against the grain. Some twentieth-century critics have done this, Leslie and Stuckey in their characterization of Babo as Brer Rabbit most brilliantly (294–97). No doubt some of Melville's readers did as well; certainly Douglass would have had he read the story. Yet given the discursive field at the historical moment in which the text was published and received, and the pervasiveness of explicit racialist logics, I would have to agree with Sidney Kaplan, that *the text itself* does not provide a means by which to do this (20).

# Chapter Five

## *The Heroic Slave* (1853)

### BEYOND POLITICAL ABOLITION

In 1853, Frederick Douglass took up the subject of the *Creole* rebellion in his only piece of fiction, *The Heroic Slave*, imagining a life history and creating a subject-position for the rebel leader, Madison Washington. Douglass's revision of the popular press coverage of the *Creole* rebellion challenged U.S. Americans to imagine the action of the *Creole* rebels, especially Madison Washington, as like that of the founding fathers. Upon the decks of the brig *Creole*, at the end of the novella, Washington proclaims,

"You call me a *black murderer.* I am not a murderer. God is my witness that LIBERTY, not *malice,* is the motive for this night's work. I have done no more to those dead men yonder, than they would have done to me in like circumstances. We have struck for our freedom, and if a true man's heart be in you, you will honor us for the deed. We have done that which you applaud your fathers for doing, and if we are murderers, *so were they.*" (66; emphasis in original)

Washington seeks to justify the rebels' actions by setting up an equivalence first between himself and the crew of the slave vessel: "I have done no more to those dead men yonder, than they would have done to me in like circumstances"; then between the rebels and patriots of the U.S. Revolution: "We have done that which you applaud your fathers for doing, and if we are murderers, *so were they.*" Washington challenges his listener, the *Creole*'s first mate, as the text does Douglass's readers, to recognize this equivalence, arguing that any "true man" "will [do so by] honor[ing] us for the deed."

For Douglass to talk about rebellion in these terms was radical, indeed explosive, not because he was invoking the memory of the Revolution—as we have seen, many writers and orators of the 1840s and 1850s, proslavery, free soil, unionist and abolitionist alike, did so as authorization for their causes—but because he was a former slave using that memory to justify slave rebellion. Recall that various discursive strategies of containment, earlier considered in my analysis of the *Creole* rebellion, displaced the conflict between rebels and slaveholders and their helpers into the arena of international relations. This displacement refigured a "racial" conflict as a "national" one. These strategies mirrored the divergent yet compatible mythologies of U.S. development, considered in chapter 1, in that all depended upon and supported discourses of racial difference and white supremacy, either erasing the presence of Africans and their descendants in North America or figuring them as naturally subordinate "servants" to Euroamericans. The discursive field created by these strategies of containment and mythologies of development foreclosed for the *Creole* rebels—and African Americans more generally—any position from which to articulate their necessarily oppositional version of events. Daniel Webster's dispatch and articles published by the slaveholding press not only excluded the rebels from negotiations, but by figuring them as "cargo" also entirely denied them their subjectivity. Douglass's story specifically challenged the myriad forces marshaled to deny to enslaved people the right to rebellion.

In addition, as I have shown in previous chapters, the abolition of slavery was never certain. The sure sense that slavery would end, that "a house divided cannot stand," today makes "common sense" because it was made part of U.S. America's official story, first by Abraham Lincoln and later by Woodrow Wilson and other politicians and historians of the twentieth century. But in 1853, three years after "slavery ha[d] been nationalized in its most horrible and revolting form" by the Fugitive Slave Law, and "the power to hold, hunt, and sell men, women and children, as slaves, remains no longer a mere state institution but is now an institution of the whole United States," abolition seemed—and was—far from inevitable.[1]

Douglass's argument in *The Heroic Slave* moves beyond the goal of political abolition—the legal end of slavery—to assert the inherent equality of enslaved African American men with the patriots of the U.S. Revolution.[2] Although the original platforms of the New England

and American Anti-Slavery Societies, written in the 1830s, included in their goals "secur[ing] to the colored population of the United States, all the rights and privileges which belong to them as men, and as Americans," by the 1850s the abolitionist movement had split into several factions, most of which did not actively pursue equal rights for African Americans. In particular, *political* abolition, which emerged in the late 1840s under the leadership of Richard Chase, was primarily concerned with the way in which the dignity of white working men was supposedly degraded by having to compete with enslaved labor. After a decade of working toward abolition through moral suasion, Douglass in the early 1850s became interested in the strategies of political abolition, despite its racialist overtones. Political abolitionists, including most significantly for Douglass, Gerrit Smith, asserted that the Constitution did not support slavery and called for using the political process to bring about the end of slavery. Prior to the 1840s most people agreed that the Constitution protected slavery. Even the black abolitionists who converted William Lloyd Garrison to anti-colonization thought of the Constitution as protecting slavery. Chase was among the first to argue that slavery violated the Constitution, a new interpretation based on the Declaration of Independence's address to "all men." Like Chase's argument, Douglass's later political theory recast the Revolution as an arrested movement for general emancipation. But Douglass's theory also moved beyond Chase's goal of a legal end to slavery to assert the inherent equality of African American men with the patriots of the U.S. Revolution. In this he combined the platform of equal rights for "all men," which black (and some white) abolitionists had always supported, with an interpretation of the Constitution as antislavery and a strategy of using the political process to promote reform.

As we have seen, at the historical moment at which Douglass's novella was written, published, and received, slave rebellion was virtually unrepresentable in national forums, and further, the righteousness of such an act was unimaginable to most U.S. Americans. My interpretation questions contemporary critical discussions that judge past efforts by what might be considered appropriate today.[3] Judging with almost a century and a half of hindsight makes it extremely

difficult fo[...]ppreciate—why a particular strategy seemed [...] ctive at an earlier historical moment. Clai[...]unding fathers may not hold the
promise it [...] bent upon us, it seems to me, to
discern why [...]ve—and effective—strategy.[4]

Although not the first, Frederick Douglass was among the few African American men to write openly in support of slave rebellion in
terms echoing the U.S. Revolution. As I discussed in chapter 1, David
Walker's *Appeal to the Coloured Citizens of the World* (1829) quoted
the opening of the Declaration of Independence, emphasizing that
"ALL men are created EQUAL!!" (114). Walker called out to his "coloured brethren," asking "had you not rather be killed than to be a slave
to a tyrant, who takes the life of your mother, wife and children" (64),
and "when shall we arise from this death-like apathy?—And be men!!"
(100). Walker's deeply masculine appropriation of revolutionary rhetoric, distributed from his Boston tavern in pamphlets hidden in sailors' clothing, was considered incendiary. Within a year Southern
planters had placed a price on his head, and he died mysteriously,
perhaps of poisoning.[5]

In 1843, Henry Highland Garnet delivered "An Address to the
Slaves of the United States of America" at the black national convention in Buffalo, a speech so controversial that white abolitionists uni-
versally condemned it; it was only published five years later with the
financial support of John Brown (Ripley 407). Like Walker, Garnet
represented masculinity, defined in part by the ability to defend one's
female family members, as an essential feature denied enslaved people, challenging his projected audience: "you tamely submit . . . while
[your wives] are defiled before your eyes. In the name of God we ask,
are you men?" He not only asserted the equivalence of the struggle of
the enslaved and that of the Revolution, stating "the heroes of the
American Revolution were never put upon harder fare" than his audience. He also delineated a history of rebel leaders that included
Denmark Vesey, "the patriotic Nathaniel Turner," and "that bright
star of freedom," Madison Washington. Garnet challenged the widespread condemnation of Turner's insurrection, including that of pacifist abolitionist leader William Lloyd Garrison, by reconceptualizing

Turner as "noble and brave." While he counseled, "Let your motto be RESISTANCE," he also cautioned against "revolution with the sword, because it would be IN EXPEDIENT," calling instead for a general strike. Garnet's "Address" is one of the earliest extant examples of an increasingly militant position among black male abolitionist leaders that claimed the oppositional nature of revolutionary rhetoric in order to challenge the predominant cultural logic of masculine white supremacy.[7] He was perhaps the first African American orator/writer to applaud Madison Washington publicly as the leader of the "[n]ineteen [who] struck for Liberty or death" on board the *Creole.*

In 1853, the same year that Douglass published *The Heroic Slave,* William Wells Brown's *Clotel; or, The President's Daughter* similarly drew upon statements associated with the discourse of national identity. Like David Walker, Brown quotes from the Declaration of Independence to make an explicit comparison between the plight of the enslaved and the British colonists (204). Mrs. Carlton, a young slaveholder seeking a way to emancipate her slaves, inserts enslaved workers into a narrative of national development as did Walker and those at the New York State Convention of Colored Citizens (1840), considered in chapter 1 above. She responds to her husband's suggestion that they send their slaves to Liberia with, "Is not this their native land? What right have we, more than the negro, to the soil here, or to style ourselves native Americans? . . . The negro has cleared up the lands, built towns, and enriched the soil with his blood and tears . . . and throughout the struggles for liberty in this country, the negroes have contributed their share" (206). Like Douglass with Madison Washington, Brown even more forcefully connects through his name one of his central characters, George, with the founding fathers, claiming that he "could boast that his father was an American statesman" (261). In contrast to the way in which Melville structured *Benito Cereno,* Brown creates an opportunity for George to assert his motives for participating in Nat Turner's rebellion. In an admittedly contrived courtroom scene, George is allowed to say whatever he wants because he earlier rendered a valuable service to the town. George gives the lie to the British colonists-turned-patriots' characterization of their status as slavery, arguing that "your fathers were never bought and sold like cattle, never shut out from the light of knowledge and religion, never subjected to the lash of brutal task-masters" (264). Having clarified their respective positions, George, like Madison Washington, compares their struggles once again, "You say your fathers fought for freedom—so did we," only to assert that success or failure is the only difference that matters: "Had we succeeded we would have been patriots too" (264). Here Brown hints at the very reason Cinqué and Madison Washington so captivated the imaginations of those committed to antislavery: not only were their rebellions successful, but the rebels got away. Though limited in their implications for reform in the United States by the very facts that made their successes possible, these two rebel leaders nevertheless proved that freedom through violent struggle was obtainable for enslaved men.

Although Brown points to success rather than race or reasoning as the factor finally determining one's status, his argument is undercut by his representation of George. Not only the son of a statesman, George "was as white as most white persons. No one would suppose that any African blood coursed through his veins. His hair was straight, soft, fine and light; his eyes blue, nose prominent, and he was often taken for a free white person" (262). Even whiter than George Harris in *Uncle Tom's Cabin* (1852), Brown's George illustrates the unjustness of slavery for men who are indistinguishable from those already in power, but he hardly makes a case for visibly African American men. Of course one of the strategies of abolition was to question any absolute difference between the races and to assert instead a racial continuum among those enslaved and between enslaved and free. Yet in an environment in which notions of innate and immutable racial differences were normative, even among most antislavery advocates, having one who is so light-skinned and European-looking assert the equivalence of the founders' struggle with those enslaved necessarily undercuts the radical potential of the assertion. *Clotel* shares with *Uncle Tom's Cabin* a racial hierarchy that grants the trope of revolutionary struggle only to enslaved men who are virtually white.[8]

In the 1840s, Douglass began including Madison Washington in his speeches for a range of purposes, most especially to illustrate "the spirit that is in the black man" (1979, II, 154).[9] While still in England,

Douglass in 1845 told Washington's story to illustrate the contradiction that has been the focus of our investigation: "It was considered no crime for America, as a nation, to rise up and assert her freedom from the fields of fight; but when the poor African made a stroke for his liberty it was declared to be a crime" (1979, I, 245). Three years later, in the speech from which I take my title, Douglass presented Washington's rebellion on the *Creole* as an example of the danger enslaved people posed to slaveholders, arguing that "the slaveholders are sleeping on slumbering volcanoes, if they did but know it" (1975, II, 151). Douglass's repeated use of Washington as a heroic—and threatening—figure demonstrates both the significance of and tension produced by evocations of rebel slave leaders. In these speeches, Douglass made a point of Washington's Africanness or his blackness, in either case contesting the racialist assumption, evident even in *Clotel*, that the spirit of liberty inheres in white rather than black blood.

In "Slavery: The Slumbering Volcano," which includes the longest version of Washington's story, Douglass describes Washington as he emerges from the ship's hold as "a black man, with woolly head, high cheek bones, protruding lip, distended nostril, and retreating forehead" (1975, II, 155).[10] Although Douglass uses what even he admits to be the most stereotypical features to characterize Washington,[11] just as Brown did with his description of George in the passage quoted above, he makes his point against racialist assumptions that "there is no fight in us" (1975, II, 154). *The Heroic Slave* adds another dimension to this approach. Though not as stereotypically African as in "The Slumbering Volcano," Washington nevertheless is explicitly described as " 'black, but comely.' His eye, lit with emotion, kept guard under a brow as dark and as glossy as the raven's wing . . . there was nothing savage or forbidding in his aspect" (28). While making sure that readers identify Washington not as a virtual white man, but as one of African heritage, Douglass also emphasizes as more significant than the racial character of his features their keys to his personality. Washington's voice, "that unfailing index of his soul, though full and melodious, had that in it which could terrify as well as charm." And "his broad mouth and nose speak only of good nature and kindness" (28). In his most thoroughly revised description of Washington, Douglass addresses the racial politics within abolitionist writing, by white and African American writers alike, not simply by inverting the descriptions (African for European), but by also emphasizing character in addition to color.

Like Walker, Garnet, Brown, and Stowe, in *The Heroic Slave* Douglass asserts the equivalence of the struggle of the enslaved with that of revolutionary republicans. Yet he does not simply figure Madison Washington and his fellow rebels as within a tradition established by the founders in order to suggest that African American men desire mere inclusion in the community of the nation. Nor does he obscure racial differences between his protagonists and the founders. Rather he recasts the legacy of the Revolution from an oppositional perspective, arguing that the national community needs to be reconceptualized in order not only to include, but to serve African American men, enslaved and free. By not depicting the violence of the rebellion, Douglass tempers the incendiary potential of his topic, focusing instead on its more significant ideological implications. To illustrate the oppressive, immoral nature of the institution, he uses a strategy developed within abolitionist literature of representing slavery from the position of those enslaved. Douglass draws upon but also extends the slave narrative genre, generating his critique from the point of view of a specific individual, while at the same time writing a new version of U.S. history. This shift in perspective and agenda reconceptualized slavery—rather than slave rebellion—as a threat to national identity. By voicing such a deeply disruptive notion, Douglass did not need to represent actual violence for his argument to be explosive.[12]

## A NARRATIVE OF GENDERED DEVELOPMENT

To make his argument convincing, Douglass creates a personal history for Madison Washington, extending abolitionist strategies supporting the *Amistad* and *Creole* rebels.[13] Indeed, in writing Washington's life, Douglass answers a call sent out by the *Liberator* for someone in Nassau to find Madison Washington and record his story (*Lib* 6/10/42:93,5). The *Amistad* archive includes several accounts by the captive rebels that recorded events in their lives prior to their rebellion (their capture in Africa, their journey to Havana, and their treatment by the Spaniards on board the *Amistad*). These accounts shift the frame of reference for the rebellion back in time, thereby constructing a narrative structure that justifies the captives' rebellious—and violent—actions. Although the *Creole* archive does not contain testimony from any of the rebels, it does include an article from the *Friend of Man*, republished in the *National Anti-Slavery Standard* on April 4, 1842, just weeks after the rebels were released from jail in Nassau. This article claimed,

> About eighteen months since, Madison was in Canada. . . . He staid a while in the family of Hiram Wilson, who describes him, like the *Creole* protest, as a very *large* and *strong* slave. Madison had been some time in Canada—long enough to love and rejoice in British liberty. But he loved his wife who was left a slave in Virginia still more. At length Madison resolved on rescuing her from slavery. Although strongly dissuaded by his friends from making the attempt in person, he would not listen, but crossed the line into this State. . . . So strong was Madison's determination, that at this time he assured his friends he would have his wife or lose his life. (emphasis in original)

This article shifts the time-frame of the *Creole* rebellion into Washington's past, positing there his motivation not for escape from slavery, but for his return into its very jaws. In contrast to all other evidence in the *Amistad* and *Creole* archives, this article suggests that an individual's freedom depends upon the freedom of loved ones. Although perpetuating the gendered structure that defines manhood through the possession of female family members, with its corollary of feminine dependency (we have only to remember the gender of the most famous conductor of the underground railroad to see the assumptions at work here), this set of relations nevertheless admits the significance of family bonds *for the individual.* These bonds are so important that they recast the paradigmatic choice between liberty and death as a choice between having "his wife or los[ing] his life."

Douglass draws upon this article for the skeleton of his story, shifting the story back in time even before Washington's escape to Canada. Douglass thereby constructs a frame of reference and set of criteria different from most of the *Creole* archive with which to understand the rebellion.[14] Although Douglass includes in his story the romantic relation between Washington and his wife, he does not grant it the same significance as Washington's gendered development from slave to man. Douglass thus contests certain confining aspects of the *Creole* archive and liberal political theory more generally, particularly those regarding law and race, while acceding to its gendered structure. Washington not only tells the story of his life, for example, he interprets it as well, and most important, he claims the revolutionary demand for personal liberty—not property rights—with which to authorize his acts. By attaching the paradigmatic choice between liberty and death to his oppositional agenda, Douglass gives it new ideological import. When read against the newspaper reports of the *Creole* rebellion, Douglass's Madison Washington emerges from the faceless mass of slave cargo—and from the silent and sketchy rebel leader rendered by abolitionists—as a carefully drawn, articulate, and charismatic figure. *The Heroic Slave* constitutes Douglass's attempt to create an imaginative pathway by which doubting U.S. Americans could recognize Madison Washington as a righteous, masculine rebel.

To create this pathway, the novella develops two interrelated themes: Madison Washington's gendered development from slave to man, and the reconfiguration of power relations called for by slavery's threat to the health of the nation. In doing so *The Heroic Slave* marginalizes both the legal debates regarding the *Creole* rebellion, the primary concern of the House and Senate, and diplomatic correspondence. Indeed, Douglass makes irrelevant the legal questions by ending the story with Madison Washington not going to jail to await the decision of nation-states, but disembarking victorious "amidst the deafening cheers of a multitude of sympathizing spectators" (69). Instead the story represents as central the process through which the protagonist comes to recognize and overcome his inner sense of enslavement, derived from both larger cultural proscriptions about black inferiority and his lived experience as a slave. *The Heroic Slave* thereby recasts as psychological what in the *Creole* archive was the legal boundary between freedom and slavery. While Walker and Garnet also thought it was important to overcome internalized oppression, *The Heroic Slave* complicates their call for manly resistance, offering illustrations of why an enslaved man may not appear to be manly to people who have not had to live his life.[15]

Washington's psychic journey begins in the Virginia forest, where he comes to assert his desire and willingness to struggle for his liberty and explores possibilities for future action. He first compares himself to birds and reptiles, which he calls "my superiors," because they are "freer and better off" than he is (27). Even more vexing, when threatened by Washington a snake turns to "give [him] battle. [Washington] dare[s] not do as much as that." Worse than the beating he has recently received, is "the *galling* consciousness of cowardice and indecision." Washington then rejects his internalized sense of worthlessness, reminding himself of the bravery he displayed by earlier risking his life to save a drowning boy. He resolves, "*Liberty* I will have, or die in the attempt to gain it" (27; emphasis in original). Thus Washington articulates the revolutionary trope of liberty-or-death and claims "the inalienable birth-right of every man, precious and priceless" (27–28).

This progression, from conceiving of oneself as inferior to reconceptualizing oneself as worthy to be free, models for African American, especially formerly enslaved, readers a psychic journey to liberation. The narrator's comment that "at that moment he was free, at least in spirit . . . his fetters lay broken at his feet" (28) confirms Washington's mental act of self-liberation. Washington shouts his outrage at the way he has been treated, "this working that others may live in idleness!" (27), and yet he remains eminently rational, the narrative emphasizing that "there was nothing savage or forbidding in his aspect" (28). Thus this scene contests those racialist discourses that figured dark-skinned people as either contented in their subordination or savage and raging in their resistance. Weighing his options, Washington determines that he will most likely be killed or sold if he openly resists; running away appears to be the most promising possibility: because he knows that "Tom escaped" (27), he will try that road as well.

Washington first makes a solitary journey to freedom, typical of many protagonists of male-authored slave narratives—and of the mythic young man who heads west. His psychic development continues when he realizes that, although he has physically escaped to Canada, "with [his wife, Susan] in slavery, my body, not my spirit, was free" (51). He returns to Virginia for her, but they are surprised as they escape; she is shot and he is recaptured as he stands guard over her dead body. His bond to Susan revises the earlier scene in which his fetters are broken by his determination to be free; this attachment asserts that the continuing slavery of loved ones compromises individual liberty—and that only a heterosexual union makes one fully a man. Although this formulation problematically represents Susan as entirely without agency, it nevertheless rejects a solitary masculinity in favor of a patriarchal model of manhood similar to that called for by Walker and Garnet. This revision marks the first step in Washington's movement toward greater commitment to the liberation of African American people more generally.

The final increment of Washington's psychic journey comes on the deck of the *Creole*, "where every breeze speaks of courage and liberty" (62). Recall that in the *Creole* archive Joshua Giddings, William Jay, and Conway Robinson all argued that at the geographical limit of the state of Virginia's jurisdiction those enslaved on the *Creole* acquired the natural right to revolt. Because only the slave states and not the federal government recognized the legality of slavery, they argued, once outside a state's legal limits those enslaved were transformed from property to persons, from objects to subjects.[16] In *The Heroic Slave*, Douglass refuses to acknowledge the validity of such legal definitions, admitting only that at sea, the rebels are now far from the "physical force of government, State and national" (62). In this romantic, natural setting, Washington throws off the survival strategies of deception and submissiveness and asserts the equivalence with which I began this chapter:

"I am not a murderer. God is my witness that LIBERTY, not *malice*, is the motive for this night's work. I have done no more to those dead men yonder, than they would have done to me in like circumstances. We have struck for our freedom, and if a true man's heart be in you, you will honor us for the deed. We have done that which you applaud your fathers for doing, and if we are murderers, *so were they*." (66; emphasis in original)

Washington not only leads an entire ship of people to freedom, but justifies without qualification their actions by claiming the "American" notion that the cause of liberty justifies rebellion. This transformation worked to convince Douglass's resisting readers that whatever negative connotations they may have associated with Washington's "blackness" insignificantly compare with his bravery, eloquence, willingness to die for liberty, moral restraint, and rationality. I suggest that the principal factor determining whether or not they heard his implicit call for abolition, and accepted his assertion that "we have done that which you applaud your fathers for doing," depended upon whether or not they found his display of masculinity compelling.[17]

In order to grasp why masculinity was so important, we need to recall that the most obvious, yet the most fundamental feature of the revolutionary republican subject was masculine gender. At the time of the Revolution, this subject did not have an explicit class or racial marking, although material conditions and social, political, and economic practices determined that typically elite men of European descent were authorized by what Locke called "Political Power." Class and slavery were masked by the apparently universal address to "all men," and race had not yet come to play the central ideological role that it would in the nineteenth century. Douglass appropriated a late-eighteenth-century notion of manhood, of republican male virtue, characterized by bravery, eloquence, moral restraint, concern for the common good, and a willingness to die for liberty, and transported it into a different historical context, a different social and political field in which racial difference had become one of the most salient ways of signifying relations of power. Like other political orators and writers of his own time, Douglass chose for his heroic model not nineteenth-century nation-builders like Andrew Jackson and Zachary Taylor, or unionists like Daniel Webster and Henry Clay, but republican revolutionaries. Antebellum political rhetoric instead favored Patrick Henry, Thomas Jefferson, and George Washington. But by connecting their known history with the activities of an enslaved man, the opening paragraph of *The Heroic Slave* challenges the legal, social, and economic strategies of dominant groups that defined the national political community—the inheritors and rightful claimants of the rhet-

oric of the Revolution—as free, white, and male. This definition denied authorization to slave rebellion, as Douglass points out:

> The state of Virginia is famous in American annals for the multitudinous array
> of her statesmen and heroes. . . . History has not been sparing in recording their
> names, or in blazoning their deeds. . . . By some strange neglect, one of the
> truest, manliest, and bravest of her children . . . a man who loved liberty as well
> as did Patrick Henry,—who deserved it as much as Thomas Jefferson,—and
> who fought for it with a valor as high, an arm as strong, and against odds as
> great, as he who led all the armies of the American colonies through the great
> war for freedom and independence, lives now only in the chattel records of his
> native State. (25)

In creating this connection, this passage asserts that the revolutionary
alliance was inherently contradictory because it did not include enslaved people from the Southern colonies, and it suggests a newly
configured alliance.

Rather than a founding father in blackface, Douglass's Madison
Washington constituted a new position based on masculine gender,
which asserted as more fundamental than racial difference or differences in class or status, gender solidarity among men.[18] From this
position, Douglass asserted a new meaning for revolutionary rhetoric,
not simply the abolition of U.S. slavery, but the *equivalence* of the
struggle of enslaved men with that of the republic's masculine founders. Like other political abolitionists, this meaning recast the Revolution as an arrested struggle for general emancipation. But this interpretation also challenged those paternalistic white abolitionists who
recognized slavery as evil and anti-Christian, but who did not imagine
slaves or African Americans more generally as equal members of the
national community.

This challenge presents the possibility of a new national alliance,
based on a common masculinity, one that includes the founders and
those slave rebels who have broken their fetters and claimed their
freedom.[19] This alliance does not "accurately" portray the founders, in
that although many of them were aware of a theoretical contradiction
between their fight for their own liberty and their status as slaveholders, most did little during their lifetimes actually either to bring

about abolition or to emancipate their own slaves. Rather Douglass's (re)vision centralizes what enslaved people and abolitionists considered most valuable and laudable in the Revolution, and marginalizes those acts of the founders that they considered worthless. This rhetorical strategy reimagines the history of the Revolution in the service of a radical agenda, one that projects not just freedom for British colonists, but equality for enslaved men as the goal of the original fight for liberty.

*The Heroic Slave* develops this argument by asserting that the Virginia of 1841, now an immoral and deteriorating society, differs dramatically from the Virginia of the founders. At the beginning of part 3, the narrator describes the following scene:

Just upon the edge of the great road from Petersburg, Virginia, to Richmond, . . . there stands a somewhat ancient and famous public tavern, quite notorious in its better days. . . . Its fine old portico looks well at a distance, and gives the building an air of grandeur. A nearer view, however, does little to sustain this impression. . . . The gloomy mantle of ruin is, already, out-spread to envelop it, and its remains, even but now remind one of a human skull, after the flesh has mingled with the earth. (47)

The "fine old portico," with its "air of grandeur," actually decays at the core, no more than a covering for a fleshless skull. This condition results, one learns several pages later, from a change in the state's economic interest, since "almost all other business in Virginia [has been] dropped to engage in [the slave trade]" (50). By juxtaposing past and present, this image undercuts the authority of those present-day sons of Virginia who trade in human flesh, while simultaneously renovating the memory of the revolutionary fathers. This description metaphorically represents the festering contradiction at the heart of the republic, the result of slavery in a supposedly free society.

Although Douglass self-consciously characterizes *The Heroic Slave* as created from "marks, traces, possibles, and probabilities" (25–26)—all that the *Creole* archive provides him with—he also presents the story told here as more trustworthy than the annals of history because it more accurately mirrors the text's notion of the founders' true ideals. The text describes the tavern's inhabitants, for example, as "hangers-on" and "corrupt tongues" whose stories are not recorded because they only tell "of quarrels, fights, *recontes,* and duels," and are full of "vulgarity and dark profanity" (52). The text's reference to these unrecorded stories asserts simultaneously the irrelevance of the tavern's inhabitants' stories and the greater significance of the one the text tells. Rather than a reason to question the validity of the narrative presented, this self-consciousness indicts dominant systems of record keeping and history making, thereby undermining systems of evaluation that separate Madison Washington from James Madison and George Washington. Taken altogether, the tavern passages and the references to the scarcity of historical data represent Madison Washington as a more rightful heir of the legacy of Old Virginia than those currently in power; the demise of the tavern and its inhabitants makes space for, even calls for, the emergence of a new order.

## A NEW NATIONAL ALLIANCE

Formal elements of *The Heroic Slave* represent the appropriate power relations of a new national alliance. In each part, a white man plays a crucial but not central role. In parts 1, 2, and 3, Mr. Listwell plays the part of a western farmer traveling in Virginia who first listens to Washington sympathetically but anonymously, and twice later aids him in his escapes. In part 4, Tom Grant, the first mate of the brig *Creole,* narrates events on board the *Creole.* These characters' important, yet secondary and supportive, positions suggest that their principal purpose in the text is to illustrate the process of change necessary in Euroamerican attitudes if a new alliance may have a chance to develop. Washington does not depend upon Listwell's help and Grant's storytelling, so much as Listwell and Grant depend upon Washington for the vision to transform the national community. Listwell and Grant therefore function as exemplars for white readers.

In part 1, Listwell happens upon Washington in a forest in Virginia, where Washington delivers a soliloquy. Listwell, as Robert Stepto notes, "listens well" to this solitary speech (1984, 182), which Listwell characterizes this way: "Goaded almost to madness by the sense of the injustice done to him, he resorts hither to give vent to his pent up feelings, and to debate with himself the feasibility of plans, plans of *his own invention*, for his own deliverance" (30; emphasis added). This description asserts that Washington, like Babo in *Benito Cereno*, creates his own analysis and method of escape, thereby challenging those gendered, racialist discourses that figured enslaved people as emasculated subjects who rebel only when encouraged or coerced into doing so by outside—typically white—agitators. This text reverses that formulation, for upon hearing of Washington's plans, Listwell declares, " 'From this hour I am an abolitionist' " (30). In this schema, Washington's resolve and vision, rather than white abolitionist prodding, produce the catalysts for progressive change.

In parts 2 and 3 Washington and Listwell meet, first at the Listwells' home in Ohio and then in Virginia after Washington has been recaptured and is traveling in a slave coffle on his way "down river." Initially Listwell forges an alliance with Washington when he and his wife not only provide Washington with shelter for the night and a means to get to Canada, but listen attentively to what has happened to him since Mr. Listwell first heard him speak in the forest. Listwell's willingness to risk his farm in order to help Washington reach Canada (44) acknowledges a connection more fundamental than physical property between himself and Washington and his "ill-starred race" (30).[20] Although Listwell does not declare his willingness to die for Washington's liberty, his system of ethical and moral evaluation now explicitly privileges personal and communal liberty for "all men" over his own material prosperity. This unusual willingness to aid an enslaved man constitutes an important step in recasting the authorized community of the United States.

Circumstance further tests Listwell when he meets Washington again, as the coffle is taking Washington to Richmond in order to be "shipped" to New Orleans: it requires one thing to aid a fugitive in one's own "nominally free" territory, and quite another to aid someone in bondage in the heart of Old Virginia.[21] But by this time in the story, Listwell has already visited the decaying Virginia tavern and experienced there the destructive influence of the domestic slave trade on the tavern's inhabitants. At Richmond, he meets the challenge by purchasing a set of files and smuggling them to Washington as he boards the *Creole*. In doing so, Listwell uses his greater material and social resources to enable the rebellion of a group of enslaved people. He does not lead the struggle, nor determine its shape or outcome; he simply lends what aid his more privileged position enables him to lend. Listwell provides a means but not a motive or a method.[22]

In addition to playing an emotionally and materially supportive role in relation to Washington, Listwell's character functions as a bridge for free people, especially Euroamericans, over to the perspective of enslaved people. By risking his farm, and perhaps his liberty or life in Virginia, Listwell chooses to enter into some of the daily dangers in enslaved people's lives, forcing him to employ their strategies of survival and resistance. For example, although he earlier resolved always to be outspoken against slavery, when in Virginia Listwell does not mention his abolitionist sentiments. Virtually hiding in his room in the decaying tavern, Listwell concludes, "it was wiser to trust the mercy of God for his soul, than the humanity of slave-traders for his body" (53). His decision constitutes the first step in a strategy of deception and protection used by oppositional and emergent groups to learn about those more powerful than they while hiding their own intentions. This teaches Listwell and Douglass's readers that the "submissiveness" of enslaved people may be a conscious strategy rather than a sign of "natural" inferiority. As it turns out, Listwell's silence at this point allows him later to take on the role of "nigger-buyer" (50), which in turn enables him to follow Washington and the rest of the coffle to Richmond and there to aid them. In taking on this role, Listwell assumes a false identity, as did Babo and the other African rebels of the *San Dominick*, a strategy of deception commonly used by escaping slaves. By participating in this fashion, Listwell not only aids Washington and provides a model for abolitionist action, but his experience also supports Washington's earlier argument for the necessity of such strategies, be they deceptive or illegal.[23]

Through Listwell, *The Heroic Slave* reverses the relation between abolitionists and rebels evident in the *Amistad* and especially the *Creole* archives, in which white abolitionists primarily created and interpreted the rebels' stories. These abolitionists had access to literacy and print culture that, in the case of the *Amistad*, the Africans only slowly and partially acquired, and in the case of the *Creole*, was unknown, unavailable to, or undesired by the rebels themselves. As I mentioned earlier, during the years between the *Creole* rebellion (1842) and the publication of *The Heroic Slave* (1853), orators such as Douglass and Garnet spoke of Cinqué and Madison Washington as heroic, exemplary figures.[24] *The Heroic Slave* extends this process of *African American* hero formation: Douglass's Washington, already articulate in the official language of Euroamerican culture, does not need anyone to speak for him, except in his absence, and he takes on the role of speaking for his people. Washington himself analyzes and interprets his actions, which the white abolitionist obligingly and contentedly follows. Thus the vision of African American men and the material and social resources of white male abolitionists found the new national alliance.

Part 4 takes place in a Virginia coffee house, several months after the *Creole* rebellion. The less sympathetic Tom Grant, former first mate of the *Creole*, replaces Listwell, and he is deep in conversation with another sailor, Jack Williams, regarding events on the *Creole*. Where Listwell had eagerly listened to and aided Washington, Grant has been forced to do his will. His character functions not as a model for appropriate (white) abolitionist action, but as an example of a slavery advocate's and white working man's reform.

Like Listwell, Grant comes to appreciate that enslaved people employ strategies of deception for their own protection. As the scene opens, Williams accuses Grant of "ignorance," and seeks to humiliate him by casting into doubt his [white] manliness. "With half a dozen *resolute* white men," Williams brags, "I could have had the rascals in irons in ten minutes. . . . All that is needed in dealing with a set of rebellious *darkies*, is to show that yer not afraid of 'em" (61; emphasis in original). Williams's assertion relies on a racialist logic that denies both manhood and personhood to "*darkies*" by characterizing them as similar to dogs. It simply takes a strong hand to handle them. Now that Grant has had firsthand experience with a revolt at sea, he takes a more complex view of the situation and warns Williams against applying the same rule in all circumstances: "It is quite easy to talk of flogging niggers here on land, where you have . . . the whole physical force of the government, State and national, at your command. . . . for the negro to act cowardly on shore, may be to act wisely" (61–62). Recognizing the power structure supporting the geography of slavery, Grant asserts that it is "quite another thing to quell an insurrection on the lonely billows of the Atlantic, where every breeze speaks of courage and liberty" (62). Grant's awareness challenges Williams's "common sense," which, like that of Amasa Delano, assures him of his own masculine, racial superiority. What Williams takes to be an aspect of the natural world, that is, racial difference and emasculated black subservience, Grant characterizes as a survival strategy, as "act[ing] wisely." By juxtaposing the disparity between their points of view, Douglass throws into relief the way in which Grant's experience on the *Creole* has forced him to reconsider his received notions of masculine white supremacy.

Grant's conversion goes so far that he admits to having found Washington irresistible after hearing him justify his actions by invoking the trope of revolutionary struggle: " 'I forgot his blackness in the dignity of his manner, and the eloquence of his speech. It seemed as if the souls of both the great dead (whose name he bore) had entered him' " (66). Grant's recognition of Washington's manliness, evident in his dignity, eloquence, and similarity to the founders, challenges his assumptions to the degree that he decides to leave the slave trade (63). Yet Grant also registers his discomfort with this recognition, simultaneously acknowledging the righteousness of the principles Washington espouses, while still concluding that "I could not bring myself to recognize their application to one whom I deemed my inferior" (68). Although the connection between Grant and Washington is tenuous, and Grant scorns the abolitionist label—responding to Williams's suggestion that he is as "good an abolitionist as Garrison himself" with *"That man does not live who shall offer me an insult with impunity"* (63; emphasis in original)—abolitionists would have counted as a victory his decision to leave the trade.

Together Listwell and Grant span a range of appropriate processes of development in Euroamerican men. Listwell, who might have been a free-soil man, proclaiming "no blacks" as well as "no slavery," be-

comes an abolitionist concerned primarily with the liberty of enslaved people rather than the protection of his material property.
Grant, who once not only supported but helped to operate the domestic slave trade, becomes willing to argue against it in public, calling it
a "disgrace and scandal to Old Virginia" (63), and willing to entertain
new ideas regarding African Americans. Through their contact with
Madison Washington, both characters gain the vision to move toward
a new awareness; Listwell helps create a new alliance while Grant
leaves an old one.

Grant's paradoxical thinking illustrates precisely the difficulty
writers like Douglass faced: how to claim the trope of revolutionary
struggle in a way that convincingly disrupted racialist logics, and
thereby "made sense" to resisting readers. While Grant recognizes
Washington's ability: " 'The leader of the mutiny in question was just
as shrewd a fellow as ever I met in my life, and was as well fitted to
lead in a dangerous enterprise as any one white man in ten thousand' "
(65), he cannot accept his ideological claim: " 'It was not that his principles were wrong in the abstract; for they are the principles of 1776.
But I could not bring myself to recognize their application to one
whom I deemed my inferior' " (68). Grant's attitude, like John Adams's
dismissal of all claims to liberty but those of his fellows, presents
exactly the way in which social convention operating on a different
register worked to foreclose the inclusionary potential of natural
rights theory and the discourse of national identity. By not representing the violence necessary for the *Creole* rebellion (Grant lay uncon-
scious during the fight), Douglass disarms gendered, racialist discourses that would figure Washington as a "black murderer" or raging
savage. In the *Creole* archive, only proslavery papers and pamphlets
represented violence after the initial reports of the rebellion. Supporters of the *Creole* rebels instead focused on reasons for and interpretations of the rebellion. In a similar fashion, *The Heroic Slave*'s discursive erasure of violence not only calms readers' potential fears,
but asserts that explanations for such acts are more significant than
the acts themselves. In addition, Washington's nonviolent behavior firmly establishes his masculinity in comfortable, middle-class
terms. And although Grant repeats Washington's words for the record,

Washington interprets his acts; the text gives final word to Washington's ideological claim. *The Heroic Slave* thus emphasizes the presence and importance of an authorizing discourse, which figures Washington not as an unthinking "black murderer," but as a patriot of a reimagined national alliance.

Unlike *Benito Cereno*, which does not grant the rebels a position from which to speak, or a sympathetic character to represent them, the structure of *The Heroic Slave* gives readers sufficient information regarding Washington's development and motives to read this scene against the grain of Grant's perspective. Whether or not they chose to do so tests white readers. Means of identification have already been established such that readers can imagine, as Grant *almost* does, Washington as a member of the community of "all men," worthy to claim the trope of revolutionary struggle. Just as Listwell and Grant have tasks to perform and processes of development to undergo in the story, the text now challenges its intended audience to do their part, to recognize Washington as the "embodiment of expressive, forceful self-determination" that he has already shown himself to be.[25]

Washington's restrained actions on the *Creole* exemplify a new moral order, the best hope for a now-decaying Virginia. Unlike Babo in *Benito Cereno*, Washington prevents the vengeful execution of the white sailors because he considers such an act unnecessary for the rebels' victory, and because he recognizes a solidarity among men. Acknowledging the natural rights of his male opponents, regardless of their race, tempers his bravery, physical prowess, and ability to fight for his freedom.[26] This heroic model disrupts racial hierarchies by asserting the importance of similar gender characteristics, implicitly critiquing pervasive representations of Anglo-Saxon manhood that exalted an unrestrained aggressiveness toward peoples of color, such as those that arose in the late 1840s in connection with the war with Mexico.[27] Washington thus emerges as an agent and prophet of a new, masculine moral order, galvanized by the festering contradiction at the heart of the republic. His appropriation of the trope of revolutionary struggle resolves that contradiction by making not only abolition, but *equal rights for African American men* part of a new narrative of national identity. When read against the *Creole* archive, Douglass's

Washington appears as an uncompromising version of abolitionist strategies to gain recognition and authority for the enslaved rebels, as part of a new politics of masculine solidarity.

Since the Civil War, historians, politicians, literary critics, and other cultural workers, such as the adopters of the national anthem and the pledge of allegiance, have appropriated and masked the agenda of political abolition. Douglass's version of political abolition recast the Revolution as an arrested struggle for general emancipation. This interpretation of the mission of the Revolution has subsequently been characterized as a crucial stage in the teleological development of the United States toward ever greater liberation. But between the Revolution and the Civil War, the mission of the Revolution was not typically interpreted in this way. Political abolition arose in the context of what we have seen in previous chapters to be the increasing power of slaveholders in the federal government. Its interpretation of the Constitution ran counter to contemporary political thought and the predominant cultural logic of masculine, white supremacy. Although others, such as free-soil advocates, also promoted the notion of teleological development, this notion typically did not include the abolition of slavery or, even more important, the equal rights of peoples of color. In order to transcend racial difference and enslaved status, Douglass's later political theory based citizenship on masculine gender. A central goal of mine has been to rematerialize the context in which political abolition, and particularly Douglass's more radical version of it, deeply disrupted not only proslavery ideology, which it was created in direct opposition to, but then-predominant formulations of U.S. national identity more generally.

In a cultural and social context in which the commensurate humanity of dark-skinned people was a matter of public debate, and righteous slave rebellion was unimaginable for most U.S. Americans, Douglass's exemplary hero, not only the equal but the obvious superior of the white male characters, asserted the ability of African American men. Yet Madison Washington's very perfection also replicated the questionable logics of individuation and particularization deployed in the *Amistad* and *Creole* archives, thereby limiting the usefulness of Douglass's representational strategy. The structures of

Locke's individualism haunted Douglass's and others' efforts to challenge limits placed on the inclusionary potential of liberal political theory. Remember that Locke's "body politick" defined individuals *as not* "children, servants, wives, or slaves." The predominant cultural logics of the antebellum United States represented only white men as capable of perpetual advancement; individually determined capacities were granted to them alone, while all others were defined as forever limited by their race and gender. Because the culture typically recognized only white men as potentially infinitely capable individuals, racially marked heroes—in addition to the process of being separated from others like them—almost necessarily appeared exceptional rather than representative. In the 1850s, Locke's individualism and racialist discourse reinforced each other and gave shape to dominant formulations of the character of the national community.

Today we also tend to see Douglass's appropriation of republican masculinity as limited by the way in which it marginalized black women in promoting "the race."[28] He does the same later in debates surrounding the Fifteenth Amendment in 1877. He was consistent in doing so throughout his life, despite his lifelong, public, and apparently deeply felt support for women's rights.[29] Yet we may best understand this position, and the representational limitations of *The Heroic Slave*, I think, not as an *individual's* lack of insight, but as one man's response to and manipulation of a much larger, extremely complex, and overly determined discursive formation. I hope to have shown just how successful *The Heroic Slave* was in creating an imaginative pathway for righteous rebel slaves and in radically contesting white supremacy, even as it also served to reproduce masculine individualism. This work has enabled me, as a white feminist, to understand better why manhood has often been the terrain upon which Anglo-African relations in the United States have been played out.

During the Revolution, the most economically and politically powerful Euroamericans were able to come together because they excluded racial slavery from their revolutionary agenda. When black activists claimed the trope of revolutionary struggle either for the enslaved population or for themselves, they not only challenged the dominance of slaveholders, they disrupted a fundamental principle of the Compact between the States, the tacit agreement to keep slavery a state rather than a federal issue. By claiming the authorizing ideology of the Union, these activists sought not simply the same rights as those supposedly already enjoyed by white U.S. Americans, but a reconfiguration of the political, economic, and social structures of the United States.

Although abolitionist supporters of the *Amistad* captives provided the Mendians with forums in which to tell their story, none of the popular press reports of their activities, including the *Colored American*'s articles on their "lecture" tours, record their interpretations of what happened to them. Except for Ka-le's brief letter, white abolitionists created and published the public interpretations of their acts. Even less was published regarding the *Creole* rebels, who apparently disappeared once they were released from Nassau's prison.

In the speeches in which he invoked the memory of Madison Washington, Frederick Douglass acts the part of historian, retelling the rebel leader's story and interpreting its significance for his audience. But in *The Heroic Slave*, Washington not only recounts his experiences, he claims the trope of revolutionary struggle to authorize his actions. Yet he does so only after having distinguished the life and perspective of an enslaved man from one born free. This distinction transforms the meaning of the trope, not by calling for the same rights as free men, but by challenging the very basis of that notion of freedom, that is, the quiet continuation of racial slavery.

When one imagines the national identity of the United States in the period between the Revolution and the Civil War as either without slavery, or as opposed to slavery, one loses the radically disruptive character of this proposition. Such imagining appropriates the agenda of political abolition—the end of slavery, and Douglass's more radical version of it, an end to race oppression—and recasts it as part of the initial mission of the republic and the nation. In rethinking the trope of revolutionary struggle *together with* the popular press's responses to slave rebellion, I have hoped to make visible the central but masked role of slavery and other forms of race oppression in the formation of national identity in the United States.

# Afterword

It may seem perverse to return to the inclusionary potential of liberal political theory and the discourse of national identity at the end of a text that so extensively documents the ways in which various forces placed limits on that potential. Yet I think we must return to it if we want to understand the project of Frederick Douglass and so many other African Americans, particularly but not exclusively men, who turned to the theory of natural rights in an attempt to carve out a place for themselves in a hostile environment.

A return to this point need not imply a reinstatement of the unified liberal subject as the subject of history and action. Rather it recognizes liberal theory as a complex discursive system that produced particular kinds of subject-positions that could be manipulated and transformed by historical agents, who may or may not have recognized themselves as liberal subjects, but who nevertheless laid claim to the authority that subject-position granted them. Discerning the difference between manipulating and claiming the authority of liberal theory and positing the free-willed individual as the subject of history brings us back to the difference between discourse and ideology. Throughout this study, I have shown that conceptualizing liberal theory as a discursive formation enables us to understand the ways in which words, phrases, and subject-positions associated with that formation were given *different* ideological import by competing and unequally empowered groups. In this endeavor may lie our very ability to appreciate not only the projects of resistance launched by so many in the nineteenth century, but the distance between their historical moment and our own.

The historical work I have engaged in requires that we not simply read back into the past our current understandings of liberal theory—or liberalism, which in the twentieth century has come to mean something quite different—or our sense of its efficacy in our own historical moment. We need not now imagine liberalism as a viable political option, although in the face of the rising power of the religious right that position may have new *political* import. Nor does it mean that we have to jettison our understandings of and belief in the importance of difference, which as feminists we have worked so hard to obtain. Indeed, recognizing the saliency of difference first led me to question the monolithic rejection of liberal theory as middle-class ideology. It led me instead to take seriously the claims of historical figures in the past—particularly those distant from the centers of power and their efforts to create for themselves not only positions from which to speak, but interpretive modes that addressed their concerns—without simply reading, interpreting, judging their actions with contemporary hindsight.

Foucault's brilliant analyses of the production, distribution, and dissemination of discursive forms associated with the liberal state, particularly those means by which rationality created the deviant forms of madness, perversion, criminality, and so forth, display incredible and disturbing insight, but also marked twentieth-century hindsight. The very power of his vision comes from its breadth and depth, its ability to illuminate interconnections among tremendously complex systems. I have used Foucault's theory of discourse with a different intent and emphasis. I have been primarily concerned with analyzing carefully—even minutely—the ways in which certain historical agents deployed, manipulated, sometimes attempted to extend, but more often attempted to limit, a relatively limited discursive form, the discourse of U.S. national identity. I have tried to illuminate some of the resistances to the liberal state generated by those excluded from it, resistances that made use of, yet transformed, the very logic of their exclusion not only by reversing the relation between subject and object, but by undermining the very production of persons *as* objects. By creating subject-positions from which to speak and write the discourse of national identity, these agents did not so much achieve the liberation and equality promised by liberal theory, as resist the charges of unfitness deployed against them. My intention thus far has been to understand not so much the limits of their efforts, as the challenge posed by them to the limits of their own time.

This study has documented one particular way in which certain members of a disenfranchised population used liberal theory in order to challenge their exclusion. As we have seen, these efforts took the form of challenging racialist discourses of white supremacy, which had limited the application of the discourse of national identity to "all [white] men." Limits on the inclusionary potential of liberal theory may be built into the theory, as Uday Mehta suggests. Yet these limits need not only be those conventional or residual notions of hierarchy, inherited from an earlier age, but may also be newly produced, or given new emphasis, such as with white supremacy in the nineteenth-century United States. Does liberal theory then necessarily exclude some group or groups? Certainly the way in which an enslaved population gave meaning to the notion of freedom, and the way in which an emasculated blackness gave meaning to masculine white supremacy, suggests that the process of inclusion and exclusion helps to constitute the formation of identity/ies. But if convention can be changed, either through the creation of new norms or through resorting to residual aspects of traditional cultures, then why can convention not be transformed to be more rather than less inclusive? The so-called extension of the elective franchise completed by Jacksonian democracy challenged many traditional hierarchies, if only to institutionalize a new one.

So many have returned to the notion that all are born free and equal because this notion has the power to contest so powerfully conventional limits on political, social, and cultural participation. Our "common sense" notions of who may be included and who has to be excluded can and has changed. Liberal theory was the discursive terrain upon which determinations of inside and outside were made through various definitions of "all": all men, all white men, all MEN, all Anglo-American men, all educated men, all white people, all educated people, all Americans. Its very malleability and inclusive potential—which we must remember in the wake of the Revolution and on a world scale brought about a remarkable shift in power relations, if not the equality of all people—made it possible for disenfranchised groups to mobilize liberal theory's inclusive logic in opposition to the agenda and interests of those more powerful than themselves, those who initially asserted the logic in the service of their own concerns. This needs to be grasped in order to take fuller account of the ability of subaltern groups to mobilize the inclusive potential of liberal theory against the historical and conventional exclusions associated with it. Rather than being fixed, the ideological import of the theory changed depending upon the particular circumstances, the interactions of specific agents and agendas pursued.

Yet this study also suggests that masculine individualism was more fundamental to liberal theory than white supremacy, which, as we have seen, became attached to the discourse of national identity in the nineteenth century. Analyzing the efforts of African American men to use liberal theory, we can see that they were caught in recognizing the struggle for liberty as paradigmatically masculine and largely individual. This position led them rhetorically to marginalize black women, for example, by basing their arguments for inclusion on their rights "as men"—which included the possession of female family members—and more subtly by not publicly appreciating the efforts those women took to maintain life, particularly under slavery, to love and nurture children and other loved ones. Their efforts, as I have shown, radically contested white supremacy, but also reproduced masculine individualism.

The masculine character of the individual, posited by Locke and reproduced largely without contest in the United States, perhaps explains why so few women articulated their concerns in the terms of this discourse. In the nineteenth century, women far more often chose fictional narratives and expository discussions about woman's proper role in national culture as the means by which to express themselves in written forms. And no wonder; the eighteenth-century founder of liberal feminism, Mary Wollstonecraft, was demonized in her own Britain and castigated also in the United States, her personal life held up for public scrutiny and censure. Still, several important examples of women calling upon the notion of natural rights, if not precisely characterizing their struggle as that between liberty and death, spring immediately to mind.

Women as diverse as Maria W. Stewart, Lucretia Mott and Elizabeth Cady Stanton, Frances Watkins Harper, and Harriet Jacobs drew upon aspects of liberal political theory, and more particularly the discourse of national identity, in order to assert the concerns of women. In the 1830s, for example, Maria W. Stewart, a follower of David Walker and the first woman to speak publicly and leave copies of her speeches, challenged the masculine bias of then emerging African American political discourse by figuring women as central to the cause of racial uplift and to modeling appropriate behavior. She proclaimed, "Oh ye daughters of Africa, awake! Awake! Arise! No longer sleep nor slumber, but distinguish yourselves. . . . What have ye done to immortalize your names beyond the grave? What examples have ye set before the rising generation? What foundation have ye laid for generations yet unborn?" (30). Her writing was more ambivalent when it came to claiming the discourse of national identity. In addressing Euroamericans, Stewart included women when she asserted that "our souls are fired with the same love of liberty and independence which fires your soul." Yet in calling upon the same narrative of national development articulated by David Walker and the New York State Negro Convention (1840), she derives "our" claim to liberty and independence from the fact that "the blood of our *fathers,* and the tears of our *brethren* . . . have enriched your soils" (40; emphasis added). Perhaps because black abolitionist discourse was only just emerging, or perhaps because Stewart was the first woman to speak publicly and refigure this discourse, she too asserted that "the Constitution of these United States . . . hath made *all men* free and equal" (29; emphasis added). Even so, on the whole her writing indicates not so much an acceptance of masculine supremacy, as the powerful force of gender in shaping and determining the potential subject-positions of the discourse of national identity. Significantly, Stewart's lecturing was not well received even in the relatively radical enclave of Boston, and she not only discontinued her lectures after only three years, she actually left the area.

Some fifteen years later, Elizabeth Cady Stanton and Lucretia Mott wrote and proposed the Declaration of Sentiments (1848), which was adopted at the first woman's rights convention at Seneca Falls, New York. Like Walker's *Appeal,* and the platforms of myriad other liberation movements in Europe and its colonies, this document echoed and revised the Declaration of Independence. Written by Euroamerican abolitionist women in response, in part, to their exclusion from the World's Anti-Slavery Convention in London and from speaking publicly against slavery, the Declaration of Sentiments recast the subject authorized by the Declaration of Independence as "all men and women." The document condemns men for their tyrannical treatment of women, including not only disfranchisement and taxation without representation, but also civil death under marriage, the absolute power of a husband during marriage and over the children after divorce, the closing of economic and religious opportunities to women, and the destruction of women's self-confidence and self-respect. It proposes resolutions, grounded in natural law, "binding over all the globe, in all countries and at all times" (80), for women's equality with men in regard to law, intelligence, morality, and sphere of action, all "result[ing] necessarily from the fact of the identity of the race in capacities and responsibilities" (82).

Mott and Stanton not only claimed familiar but limited aspects of the discourse of national identity, such as the franchise and political representation. They also imagined for women a civil identity that precisely challenged the institution of marriage as they knew it, and more generally challenged discourses of gender that specifically subordinated women.[1] Their strategy remarkably echoed that of the African American men considered in this study, in their use of the very logic of liberal theory in order to challenge limits placed on its inclusionary potential by residual convention, in this case masculine supremacy. Yet it also differed significantly in not limiting the grounds upon which they made their claim, for example, as they might have, and as many later did, as *white* women. Although subsequent woman's rights conventions and their rhetoric first shied away from abolition, and later claimed their rights as educated, native-born, Euroamerican women, at this historical moment Mott and Stanton asserted the hopeful and radically inclusive "fact of the identity of the [human] race in capacities and responsibilities." Their document became the acknowledged manifesto of many woman's rights conventions in the years to come.[2]

Writing in the next decade and a half, Frances Watkins Harper (1853) and Harriet Jacobs (1861) represented African American women as heroic protagonists involved in communal struggles for liberty. Unlike the orations of Maria Stewart, and the expository Declaration of Sentiments—both explicitly political forms—Harper and Jacobs integrated notions of natural rights into the consciousness of female characters portrayed in the popular genres of poetry and slave narratives. For example, Harper's poem "Eliza Harris" revises a familiar figure from Harriet Beecher Stowe's *Uncle Tom's Cabin* (1852). Like Stowe's novel, Harper's poem presents the mother's difficult flight as support for the child's: "For she is a mother—her child is a slave." Yet unlike Stowe's merely charismatic heroine, Harper grants Eliza the paradigmatic choice between liberty and death: "And she'll give him his freedom, or find him a grave!" Moreover, Harper's Eliza is specifically heroic: "Oh! poverty, danger and death she can brave,/For the child of her heart is no longer a slave!" While Harper's poem does not cast Eliza as claiming her own right to liberty, she does share the values of the Revolution in her desire and willingness to struggle for her son's liberation. Furthermore, that "she can brave" "poverty, danger and death" figures her as a historical agent. This representation of Eliza thereby offers an alternative to stereotypes of passive womanhood—such as Susan in *The Heroic Slave*—and it further contests negative associations of feminization with passive acceptance or non-resistance. It thus problematizes gender in two important respects: in the way it disrupts both disempowering characteristics assigned to women, and in the gender coding of dominant representations of African Americans.

Harriet Jacobs's *Incidents in the Life of a Slave Girl* complicated the claim of her pseudonymous protagonist, Linda Brent, to personal freedom with her responsibility and connection to others. Narrating the story in first person, Brent claims and revises the trope of revolutionary struggle when she describes the years she spent eluding the lecherous advances of her aged master and the jealous punishments of his much younger wife. Her master's claims to her body— "He told me I was his property; that I must obey him in all things" (27)—echo the aggressive and acquisitive logic of masculine white supremacy, evident in "The Course of Civilization," which defined the invasion of North America as the Manifest Destiny of the republic.[3]

Brent challenges these claims with the paradigmatic choice between liberty and death; she states soon after beginning her seven years of concealment: "When I started this undertaking, I had resolved that, come what would, there should be no turning back. 'Give me liberty, or give me death,' was my motto" (99). While Cinqué, Madison Washington, Babo, Douglass's Washington, and Patrick Henry all made their "strikes for liberty" in traditionally masculine ways—in violent and public confrontations—Jacobs presents a new vision of heroism as Brent wages a primarily rhetorical and emotional battle for the liberty of her children and herself from the attic of her grandmother's home. Through her letter writing, Brent manages the sale of her children to their father, thereby challenging the masculine assumption that physical battle characterizes heroism.

Yet Jacobs consistently represents Brent's psychic if not physical freedom, like that of Harper's Eliza, as tied to the condition of her children. Her motivation to escape at a particular moment comes when Dr. Flint threatens to bring her son and daughter to the plantation where she has been working in order for them all to be "broke in" (94). And when she finally succeeds in manipulating her master into selling her children into apparent freedom, she remarks: "The darkest cloud that hung over my life had rolled away. Whatever slavery might do to me, it could not shackle my children" (109). Where Douglass's patriarchal Madison Washington combined the typically masculine qualities of physical prowess with the more feminine qualities of moral restraint, Harper's and Jacobs's heroic models combine the typically masculine choice between liberty and death with the more feminine feature of responsibility and connection to others.

Harper's and Jacobs's work critiqued not only the conventionally masculine form of the trope of revolutionary struggle, but its association with individualism. Not only their concern for children, but their acknowledgment of the assistance of other members of their community, disrupts the process of hero formation, which we have seen in *every* one of the four instances of slave rebellion considered in this study, that individualizes, particularizes, separates, and elevates. Less explicitly, but no less profoundly than the Declaration of Sentiments, Harper and Jacobs offer new discursive and conceptual possibilities by recasting the subject-positions "all [white] men" and "all MEN" as "all women and children."[4]

Important though they were, these efforts are few when compared with what we have seen in this study to be the daily debate among men, particularly white men, regarding the legacy of the Revolution and the appropriate application of liberal political theory. Far more often women writers, African American and Euroamerican alike, chose to explore other subjects, such as the abolition of slavery and woman's appropriate sphere, than to challenge directly the masculine coding of the discourse of national identity. Interestingly, in her two antislavery novels, *Uncle Tom's Cabin* and *Dred* (1856), Stowe drew upon the discourse of national identity in the service of slave rebellion—but only for her male characters.

George Harris in *Uncle Tom's Cabin*, the enslaved man so nearly white he has to dye his brown hair black and his yellow skin brown to pass for a Spaniard, in at least two passages compares his own plight with that of the founders. Ironically, though, Stowe imbeds George's claim to fight for liberty until death within his disavowal of the United States. Recalling the story in which his mother, once the favored but enslaved mistress of his slaveholding father, was sold and separated from each of her children after her master's death, each of his sisters being passed to the markets in New Orleans, George expresses his disgust of laws that sanction such behavior, exclaiming, " 'Do you call these the laws of *my* country?' " (167; emphasis in original). Noting his twinned disinheritance from nation and family, " 'I haven't any country anymore than I have any father,' " he asserts his plan to adopt Canada as his home, and threatens, " 'if any man try to stop me, let him take care, for I am desperate. I'll fight for my liberty to the last breath I breathe. You say your fathers did it; if it was right for them, it is right for me!' " (167). A few chapters later George reiterates his position as he, now with wife and child (and a helpful Quaker), turns to fight the slavecatchers on their heels. In his own "declaration of independence" (253), George disputes the jurisdiction of U.S. law over those not protected by them, arguing, " 'We don't own your laws; we don't own your country; we stand here as free, under God's sky, as you are; and . . . we'll fight for our liberty till we die' " (253). George

implicitly asserts the natural and religious chara[...] [...]
revolutionary struggle, calling upon it to justify hi[...] [...]
than his inclusion in the national community. S[...] [...]
edges on one level George's right to liberty. But [...]
Stepto notes, "sends [him] packing" because she h[...]
how this "miscegenated hothead" would actually fit into U.S. society
(1986, 142).[5] Although Eliza earlier managed a miraculous escape over
the Ohio with her son, Harry, once she is reunited with George, Stowe
subordinates her story to his. Appropriately possessed and protected
by her husband, Eliza falls silent, their mutual struggle for liberation
characterized by "his declaration of independence."

In *Dred,* her more forceful critique of slavery in a republic based
on freedom, Stowe also reproduces the masculine gender coding of
the discourse of national identity. In contrast with George Harris,
Dred, the definitively dark-skinned—and admittedly wild and other-
worldly—son of the slave rebel leader Denmark Vesey, leaves enslavement not for Canada but for the neighboring dismal swamp. Modeled
on Nat Turner, Dred both prophesies the end of slavery with the coming of judgment day, and plans rebellion with Harry, a light-skinned
fugitive from slavery, and others still living under slavery on nearby
plantations. Dred and Harry explicitly lay claim to the Declaration of
Independence, which they read aloud to others. (Elsewhere Stowe
points to the contradictions of Southerners reading the Declaration
aloud on the Fourth of July so that those enslaved may hear, though
they are not supposed to consider the words as applying to them.) But
though Stowe clearly supports these men's claim to natural rights
theory, she also questions the righteousness of a violent struggle, even
to obtain liberty.

Stowe not only suggests that passions once released may turn
vengeful, but asserts that judgment rests with God. While planning
their rebellion, one man proclaims: " 'We will reward them as they
have rewarded us! In the cup that they have filled to us we will mea-
sure to them again!' " This threat of revenge in kind horrifies Dred,
who replies, " 'God forbid . . . that the elect of the Lord should do
that! . . . We will not torment them with the scourge and fire, nor defile
their women, as they have done with ours! But we will slay them

utterly, and consume them from off the face of the earth!' " (II, 232). But even more significantly, at this moment Milly enters what up until this point has been a conversation among men who have named their oppression as exclusion from law and knowledge, and as assaults upon "their" women, injustice figured as attacks upon their manliness. Milly challenges not *their* claim to natural rights discourse, but *anyone's* attempt to rectify the evils of the world directly through violence: " 'If dere must come a day of vengence, pray not to be in it! It's de Lord's strange work. O, brethren, is we de fust dat's been took to de judgment-seat? dat's been scourged, and died in torments? . . . Didn't He hang bleeding three hours when dey mocked Him, and gave Him vinegar. . . . O, brethren, pray de Lord to give 'em repentence! Leave the vengeance to him' " (II, 233–34). Milly's feminine approach counsels against direct confrontation in favor of emulation of Christ's sacrifice on the Cross. She calls for submission, not to the tyranny of slaveholders and their lackeys, but to God's will, to God who alone will decide the fate of humankind. Milly's position implicitly critiques, then, the actions of British colonial revolutionaries as much as rebellious slaves, for both groups sought or seek to use human means to challenge injustice on earth. Her plea tempers the crowd's anger: "the key-note of another harmony had been struck." Dred admits, " 'Woman, thy prayers have prevailed for this time! . . . The hour has not yet struck' " (II, 234).

Although Milly's position most closely resembles Stowe's own— feminine, antiviolence, and focused on the agency and justice of God rather than of men—still this novel much more fully articulates than did *Uncle Tom's Cabin* the position of African American men who claimed not only natural rights discourse, but the trope of revolutionary struggle. In many places throughout *Dred* black men invoke language explicitly derived from the U.S. Revolution. Not only this, Stowe characterizes Denmark Vesey as one of those "grave, thoughtful, energetic men, with their ears and eyes open, and their minds constantly awake to compare and reason," who had developed "a good degree of intelligence and manliness" (I, 247) in the comparatively lenient early years of South Carolina's history. She quotes extensively from records of his trial, concluding that "none of us may deny that, wild and hopeless as this scheme was, it was still the same in kind with the more successful one which purchased for our fathers a national existence" (I, 257). Stowe's repeated connections between the acts of rebellion that founded the nation and those contemplated and acted out by enslaved men signals simultaneously three points: the equivalence of these struggles, their masculine character, and their questionable righteousness in the eyes of God. The amount of textual space she provides to the expression of enslaved men's claim to a heritage of rebellion as well as liberty, far more than she devotes to Milly's challenge, acknowledges and even asserts its significance.

The much more rebellious character of *Dred*, when compared with *Uncle Tom's Cabin*, written four years earlier, appears obviously influenced by the (written) activism of African American men. In the intervening years, both *Clotel* and *The Heroic Slave*, in addition to published speeches such as Douglass's "The Meaning of July Fourth for the Negro," claimed, analyzed, and recast the legacy of the founders for African Americans, particularly those enslaved, and particularly men. Stowe moves from her ambivalent support for the rebellious George Harris and her much stronger support for the more religious pacifist Uncle Tom, to a much stronger representation of the righteousness of rebellion not only for Harry, but for all of the enslaved in *Dred*. Though Stowe refuses actually to imagine a rebellion, I would argue that she does so because of her underlying belief that finally such a rebellion, in an environment in which the rebels, as she saw it, could not hope to win, would degrade its agents by drowning them in blood. Like her contemporaries, including Brown, Douglass, and Martin Delany, author of *Blake*, Stowe cannot imagine successful rebellion within the confines of the United States, and therefore sends off to Canada (or Europe or the Caribbean) her surviving protagonists.[6]

The only female writer I know to have written about the *Amistad* and *Creole* rebels during this period was, like Stowe, concerned with the violence inherent not only in the rebellions, but in the discourse of national identity. Furthermore, each clearly associated this violence with a masculine rejection of religion. During her tenure (1841–43) as editor of the *National Anti-Slavery Standard*, Lydia Maria Child published two editorials discussing the *Amistad* and *Creole* incidents.[7]

One of her "Letters from New York" (#12, 12/2/41:2,2) reported on "farewell meetings of the Mendians" at Zion's church, where she heard them "for the first and last time." Child reports having been disturbed by remarks made by one of the Africans' teachers, Mr. A. T. Williams, who apparently wanted to clarify that the Mendians had rebelled "in consequence of being tormented by the cook, who told them they would be cut up and salted for sale, as soon as they arrived in port." As we have seen, this statement coincides with those purportedly made by the Mendians at the time of their capture. Child, however, admits that this motive, presented in such

unheroic form . . . knocked in the head all of my *romantic* associations with Cinquez, as a brave soul, preferring death to slavery. . . . when it was explained, as if in apology, that they did not rise against their masters, I felt disturbed. I was strongly moved to ask "By what standard are these strangers to be tried? By the gospel standard, of which they had then never heard? Or by the same standard that the world judges of Washington . . . and William Tell? The latter was the standard not *professed* merely, (like the gospel) but *practically* acknowledged by nearly all of every American audience. Why, then should an assembly with such sentiments be assured, in tones of apology, that Cinquez had not done what Washington . . . would assuredly have done under similar circumstances?" If any people on earth have a right to fight in self-defense, the captured and enslaved negro has most peculiarly that right; and the advocates of defensive war are neither consistent nor magnanimous in refusing to make this admission. (emphasis in original)

Child begins by acknowledging her susceptibility to the press's romanticizing of Cinqué, but then she immediately turns to challenge those who would deny to the Mendians the authorization of revolutionary rhetoric. Thus Child recognizes the way in which romantic hero-making has very real effects. Interestingly, although Child so forcefully asserts the connection between Cinqué and Washington, and asserts the peculiar right of "the captured and enslaved negro" to self-defense, she ends the above passage with this comment: "I, of course, cannot [admit to the negro's right to self-defense]; because I believe all war to be a violation of the gospel." In a fashion similar to Stowe over a decade later, then, Child at once gives voice and credence to the equivalence of the struggle for freedom of British colonists and enslaved African Americans, while at the same time registering her disapproval of violence. Articulated here as a difference in religious and political standards, Child's distinction regarding appropriate behavior, I would argue, is gendered as well, with the violent struggle either for liberation or for self-defense being "peculiarly" masculine.

Several months later, in her editorial regarding the case of the *Creole*, "The Iron Shroud," Child mediates her discomfort with the rebels' violence by granting causality to God. Child's editorial begins by asserting that slavery's power was waning in the face of abolitionist organizing and God's will, claiming that "I speak reverently, when I say God has himself visibly entered the lists against" slavery (3/3/42:2,6). She then goes on to connect the *Creole* with the *Amistad* rebellion:

But of all the events having an important bearing on our cause, there is none so remarkable as the case of the Amistad. That those Africans should have been cast upon our shores, of all the shores of this wide earth; that they should have entered a *northern*, instead of a southern port . . . truly these things are wonderful . . . Not less wonderful is the fact, that the Amistad case should have prepared the way for the Creole. A few years ago, Madison Washington would have been dismissed by the press of the free States, as a "base wretch," . . . now the press of the free States, with few exceptions, utters no condemnation, while very many pour forth expressions of sympathy. (3/3/42:3,1; emphasis in original)

Child figures the *Amistad* as divinely directed to Long Island, and as serving the divine purpose of abolition, "prepar[ing] the way for the Creole." Child presents the press as almost unanimously supportive of the *Creole* rebels, a representation that supports her overall argument regarding slavery's demise. As we have seen, my argument differently characterizes the (in)action of the Northern press, acknowledging on the one hand that few outwardly condemned the rebels, but also asserting on the other that their refusal to take a position on the story, and even among the abolitionist presses to turn the focus away from the rebels to the domestic slave trade, hardly indicates full-fledged support. Child's reading makes sense as an acknowledgment of change and action in difficult times. Yet notice, too, that Child grants agency first to God, then to the press of the free states, and says very little about the action of the rebels themselves. In this way she avoids having to support the violence inherent in the rebellions. Although in her "Letter No. 12" quoted above Child was willing to give voice if not unconditional support for the Mendians' acts of self-defense, here she obscures that aspect of the incident altogether. As the female editor of one of the nation's leading abolitionist papers, she refused to use, because of her (gendered) interpretation of the gospel, what I have come to see, in this incarnation, as a near-exclusively masculine discourse.[8]

I have argued that the discourse of national identity was a particular incarnation of liberal political theory that used certain elements of Locke's notions of natural rights while discarding others, transforming all in the process. Recent research has begun to explore another incarnation of the notion of natural rights, one located historically prior to Locke's treatises and geographically distant in the Americas, particularly in what is now the northeastern United States. This research not only opens out a new angle on the component elements of Lockean theory, but suggestively displaces Locke and other European philosophers from their position as primogenitors of the notion of individual liberty. It argues that individual liberty and democracy characterized the social and political interaction of many groups indigenous to the Americas long before Columbus's famous landfall.

Analyzing textual evidence from European sources, several studies trace the influence of observations of the New World by European explorers on European thinking. William Brandon (1986) argues, for example, that "our current idea of liberty developed much of its modern sense in Europe and America in the three centuries following European contact with the New World," and that these observations "headlined notions of liberty, a popular liberty involving elements of equality and masterlessness, that may really have been in a fairly literal sense new notions for Europe" (3–4). Arthur Slavin (1976) asserts that "it is simple to make a long list of treatises on politics written after the Discovery which show no trace of American influence. . . . But the most startling and fruitful work in England took America into account from the outset" (139). German Arciniegas (1986) suggests that "from America have emerged the cornerstones of political philosophy that has transformed the world" (3). To illustrate this influence, Brandon and Arciniegas have amassed impressive collections of eyewitness accounts, including those of French missionaries, members of the Virginia Company, and Spanish sailors, that, while admitting the sometimes "brutish" behavior of the natives, also revel in their relative ease and freedom in relation to European life.[9] Among those many who, like Samuel Purchas, wrote about the Americas based on such accounts, scholars point in particular to Thomas More's *Utopia* (1516), set in the South Atlantic somewhere in the New World, as "opening up the idea of freedom, politically, ethically, and economically" (Slavin 143). Unlike Locke's *Treatises*, *Utopia* exhibits what Brandon identifies as one of the most salient general differences between New World and Old, the practice of holding property collectively rather than individually.

Certainly eyewitness accounts, as we have seen, reveal as much about the cultural assumptions of the observer as about the behavior of the observed. Speaking generally, these European observations identified in American cultures the absence of the political forms with which they were familiar, and in many cases they read this absence as both freedom from the coercive and repressive practices common among European cultures, and the absence of *all* political forms. (Certainly this was not the case with those who encountered the imperial nations of the Incas and Aztecs, whose political and social organizations, while different, could hardly have been missed!) European assumptions about what constituted political and social hierarchies inhibited European adventurers from recognizing the political and social forms of indigenous Americans, and instead they erroneously homogenized and universalized many of those forms as the laws and precepts of nature. Though perhaps not its original intent, characterizing American peoples as living in a state of nature enabled Europeans to imagine that way of life as one to which all peoples—particularly themselves—would have equal claim. In the generations following contact, Europeans, particularly British and French philosophers and political theorists, succeeded in appropriating certain aspects of New World cultures by characterizing them as the appropriate condition of all human beings when in a state of nature. This characterization meant that these Europeans did not have to recognize or confront the intricate, well-balanced, and long-developed political and social systems of indigenous Americans, thereby making it easier to erase the American influence on European political theory. Ironically, but also appropriately, it was in America rather than in Europe that liberal political theory first was used as the basis of a new society.

Scholars in American Indian studies now are contesting the erasure of America's influence on European thought by mapping connections between indigenous American political forms, particularly that of the Iroquois Confederacy, the longest continually operating democracy in what is now the United States, and European political theory and the democratic governmental forms of the United States. Donald Grinde, in an important collection of essays written by scholars in American Indian studies, *Exiled in the Land of the Free* (ed. Lyons et al., 1992), asserts that the common sense of many Indian peoples recognizes individual liberty and democracy as the normative values of many native tribes, values that served as a "democratic blueprint for the creation of Western democracies" (228). Jack Weatherford (1988) argues in a similar vein that modern pow-wows illustrate such principles of individual liberty, with leaders attempting to persuade, calling for, even exhorting—but never coercing—participants to assemble and act. Grinde, along with other contributors to *Exiled*, such as Oren Lyons, John Mohawk, and Vine Deloria, argues that contact between European colonists and indigenous peoples in the Americas acted with far greater influence on the thoughts of the colonists than did references to classical Greece or Rome. Such references may have been significant to Continental philosophers, but for those actually making a life for themselves in America, they argue, the native tribes provided much closer and more relevant examples. Bruce Johansen (1982) has documented extensive contact between Benjamin Franklin most notably, but also other colonists such as Caldwaller Colden and Thomas Paine, and Iroquois sachems who, particularly before the end of the Revolutionary War, negotiated with both British and colonial officials as representatives of a sovereign nation. Johansen argues that Franklin admired the Iroquois and their confederacy, and offered it as early as 1740 as a model for an alliance among the colonies. And more recently Grinde and Johansen have collaborated on *Exemplar of Liberty* (1991), which combines historical indigenous and Euroamerican views of cultural interaction between the Iroquois and British colonists–turned–American patriots. Although many Americanists continue to link U.S. political theory and governmental forms solely to European traditions, typically ones based on antiquity, this research, particularly the newly available information on indigenous political and cultural traditions, offers exciting new avenues for investigation.

Indeed, this new research challenges us to rethink the primacy of Lockean political theory in conceptions of not only natural rights and personal liberty, but in contracts that construct human beings as social beings. Unlike Thomas More's vision in *Utopia*, Locke based liberty and the social contract on personal property. Indeed, Locke's schema presents as axiomatic the notion that before the organization of society, all men are in "a *State of perfect Freedom*," which is "a *State* also *of Equality*" (II, 4), a state in which individual and masculinized human entities ("Man") have property in their "Lives, Liberties, and Estates." Locke's version of the prepolitical state, the natural world, already depends upon the possession of property; further, his conception of the political state is brought into being by the need to protect and enjoy that property. Thus Locke's notions of rights, liberty, and civil society, largely adopted by colonial policymakers in British America, were imbedded by them in U.S. governmental forms. And as we have seen, in the nineteenth century the notion of property, particularly property in persons, complicated the conceptualization and implementation of freedom and emancipation. Virtually every conflict analyzed in this study centers on opposing connections between and definitions of liberty and property. The new research into indigenous America may enable us, particularly those of us not a part of it, to imagine a different kind of liberty, one not tied to the property concerns of the liberal state, and yet still connected to notions, for example, of democratic participation. Challenging the primacy of property may also help displace the masculine coding of liberty by disrupting the supposedly independent/dependent relation of "Man" to his "children, servants, wives, and slaves," relations based on an uneven distribution of property. Iroquois political theory posits a different relation between men and women, with men responsible for speaking, negotiating, and persuading, and women responsible for choosing which men will speak, negotiate, and persuade. I am not advocating a nostalgic return to pre-Columbian America, or the romanticizing of indigenous political forms. Rather I find in this work inspiration to conceptualize liberty and gender relations in forms different from Lockean, liberal liberty, with its relations of (in)dependence. As we head into the twenty-first century, we need ideas and inspiration to help us resist the limits of our own historical moment.

# Notes

## INTRODUCTION: REBELLION AND THE LEGACY OF THE REVOLUTION

1. The minutes of the Continental Congress differ from this account in giving June 25 rather than June 28 as the date of this vote, and in recording the vote as eight nays and three ayes. More significantly, this vote took place in the context of a series of proposed revisions to the Articles of Confederation, made by most of the states, virtually none of which passed. My sense from the minutes is that the various delegates were reluctant to agree to changes unconsidered by their constituencies and did not want to appear to accede to others' concerns while not being able to guarantee their own amendments. Thus the committee may be reading too much *intentionality* into the Congress's vote, although the *result* was an opening for the legal citizenship of people of color.

South Carolina's delegation, which proposed the insertion of the word "white," similarly proposed inserting, after the words "the several states" quoted in the text, the phrase "according to the law of such states respectively, for the government of their own free white inhabitants." This also was voted down. Yet it indicates this state's discomfort—and that of the two other unnamed states that voted with it—with acknowledging the authority of other states to grant citizenship, particularly to people of color. *Journals of the Continental Congress*, 11, 652–53.

2. David Roediger cites Shane White's research (1988) in stating that "37.8 percent of male free black heads of household held artisanal jobs in 1800, a proportion that was to decline by a fourth within the next decade" (25). By the 1850s, 87% of blacks in New York held menial jobs (Takaki 1979, 111–16).

3. I take this phrase from the title of David Roediger's book, *The Wages of Whiteness* (1991). Roediger argues that although industrialization negatively impacted the material conditions of many white male workers, the emergent working class gained a different kind of pay through assertions of the natural superiority of their whiteness, which he terms, following W. E. B. DuBois, "the wages of whiteness."

4. Certainly some scholars earlier produced understandings of slavery and the experiences of African Americans that emphasized their survival strategies, re-

sistance to oppression, and achievements. Herbert Aptheker (1943, 1945, 1948), Benjamin Brawley (1921), John Hope Franklin (1947), Bella Gross (1932), J. Saunders Redding (1950), Harvey Wish (1937), Carter G. Woodson (1926), and of course William C. Nell (1855) and W. E. B. DuBois (1903), immediately come to mind. Nevertheless, the 1960s and 1970s witnessed a sea-change in all sorts of writing about African American history, fictional, poetic, and economic as well as purely historical.

5. See Frances Smith Foster's introduction to *Minnie's Sacrifice; Sowing and Reaping; Trial and Triumph: Three Rediscovered Novels by Frances E. W. Harper* (1994) for a brilliantly illuminating discussion of black literacy prior to the twentieth century.

6. I draw the term *"together with"* from Edward Said's "Representing the Colonized" (1989), in which he argues that, "[d]espite its bitterness and violence, the whole point of [Frantz] Fanon's work is to force the European metropolis to think its history *together with* the history of the colonies awakening from the cruel stupor and abused immobility of imperial domination" (233). "The whole point" is to force a new reading of European history that is shaped by the context of imperialism and the colonies' "emerging counternarrative." The counternarrative is then no longer alternative, sitting ineffectually alongside its older and more authoritative predecessor, but a powerful factor in a new, world-scale dialectic.

The historian Nathan Huggins (1991) similarly asserts in the context of the United States that "there can be no white history or black history, nor can there be an integrated history that does not begin to comprehend that slavery and freedom, white and black, are joined at the hip" (xliv). Following Edmund Morgan's famous thesis (1972), Huggins usefully argues for a fundamental connection between the concepts and the material conditions of slavery. Huggins's argument is limited, in my view, in that it does not sufficiently account for differences within the colonial population, and in that it also creates a white/black binarism that masks the presence of other peoples of color.

Within recent years, literary (and increasingly interdisciplinary) scholars of the United States, commonly called the New Americanists, have begun to map myriad interconnections among the productions of African American and Euroamerican cultural workers. The work of the following scholars similarly seeks to imbed African American literature and history firmly within conceptualizations of U.S. America: Russ Castronovo (1995); Carolyn Karcher (1980); Eric Lott (1993); Dana Nelson (1992); Karen Sánchez-Eppler (1988); Eric Sundquist (1985; 1993); Priscilla Wald (1995); Robyn Wiegman (1995). I also see my study as analyzing a canonical text, Herman Melville's *Benito Cereno*, based on criteria developed from my analysis of a newly important text, Frederick Douglass's *The Heroic Slave*. This critical strategy not only asserts the significance of Douglass's work, it also makes Melville's less familiar by entreating us to think in the terms that Douglass set, terms that were primarily concerned with the ideological import produced by a text at the original moment of its reception. This approach not only includes, but situates as central, the expressed concerns of one of the most important African American orators, writers, and activists of the nineteenth century.

7. I use the term "nation" to denote those whose concerns and interests policymakers, legal theorists, newspaper editors, religious leaders, and other cultural workers address, serve, and protect. I use the term "national identity" to describe a new discourse that proposed a notion of "the people" upon which first a loose set of state governments and then a federal government were founded. As will become clear over the course of this chapter, this discourse did not produce a unified notion of "the people," but rather a range of possibilities that acquired or lost saliency and authority at different historical moments. The ways in which various historical actors participated in changing such significances is the subject of this book.

In these usages I differ from many students of nationalism. I do not, for example, understand the nation in this context in terms of ethnicity, or as a kind of structural coherence that binds people together in a common mode of temporal and spatial imagining. See, for example, Ernest Gellner (1983) and Benedict Anderson (1991).

8. I use the term "subject-position" to describe positions that are authorized to speak, write, and act by the rules of a given discursive formation. Such positions simultaneously enable and limit speech, writing, and acts by granting the agent using, manipulating, or caught in them certain kinds of authority regarding particular issues. The specific limits and possibilities of any given subject-position, as I will explore in this book, need to be determined within specific historical circumstances. The term "subject-position" makes no claim as to the sense of self of any historical agent, or even the degree to which a given agent actually believes the statements he or she is authorized to speak from a given position. Rather "subject-position" highlights the *strategic* character of discursive interaction. This notion will be developed more fully later in this chapter.

9. Frederick Douglass uses this term in one of his speeches, "Slavery: The Slumbering Volcano" (1849), as does Herman Melville in *Benito Cereno* (68).

10. Donald A. Grinde (1992) lists this as one of many incidents in which colonists dressed as Indians in order "to assert a new identity that was emerging as the colonists became more restive under British rule" (248). Grinde also records many other ways in which colonists imitated and absorbed Indian behavior—and values.

11. Conditions worsened in three historical sequences: the first from the earliest

moments of forced importation of captives from Africa through the early eighteenth century; the second from the Revolution through the Civil War; and a third from general emancipation and Reconstruction through the development of Jim Crow, circa 1900.

12. See in particular chap. 3 of Bercovitch's study.

13. I also want to distinguish liberal political theory from liberalism, which in the twentieth century has been criticized as a paternalistic system designed to assuage middle-class white guilt for racism and poverty, and as presenting a false pluralism that simply masks unequal relations of power. Liberalism is a particular political ideology that arose in the context of the Depression and the New Deal, and bears a complicated relation to Locke's theory.

14. For the past two and a half decades historians of the revolutionary period have debated the meaning and historical antecedents of republicanism. Beginning with Bernard Bailyn, continued by his student Gordon S. Wood, and also argued from a different direction by J. G. A. Pocock, historians have asserted republicanism, not created during the Enlightenment but derived from ancient times, to be the predominant mode of thinking of the revolutionary generation. Most recently historians have started to rethink this argument, questioning both the predominance of any particular ideology during the revolutionary period and clear demarcations between the genealogies of republicanism and liberal political theory.

Joyce Appleby rightfully values the way in which the new emphasis on republicanism undermined the liberal notion of free-willed individuals picking and choosing from an array of ideas, which had underlain historiography until the 1960s. The shift to an emphasis on the determining influence of ideological systems, Appleby notes, enabled a new way to understand the interaction of language and group formation: "ideas exerted influence as parts of a whole . . . and then only because the whole illuminated reality. Those who share a paradigm form a community. . . . For each group a common language made coherent social action possible" (467). Yet these republican revisionists too strongly stress, Appleby argues, the predominance of republicanism as a pervasive paradigm that controlled what it was possible to think and do. Rather, in eighteenth-century British America in particular, with its lack of censorship from the state, the availability of the press, and the relatively high rate of literacy, there was no ideological consensus, but rather a complex ideological terrain in which different idea-systems competed, prominent among them being liberal theory as well as republicanism. See Appleby's introduction to the special issue on republicanism of *American Quarterly* (1985). For more on the historical debate regarding republicanism see, for example, Robert E. Shalhope (1982); the exchange between Lance Banning and Joyce Appleby (1986); and the special issue of *American Antiquarian Society* 102 (Summer 1992).

15. The emphases in all quotations from the *Second Treatise* are in the original. The roman numeral of the in-text notation, "II," designates the *Second Treatise*, and the arabic numeral designates the *section* rather than the *page* number.

16. Roediger takes the quotation from Okoye 14–15 (emphasis in original).

17. Although the explicit explanations of this interdependent relation were not developed until the nineteenth-century, Morgan locates the origins of this paradox in the Virginia Bay Colony. Being the site of the earliest Southern colonies, Virginia may be considered formative of the Southern stance on slavery more generally. Morgan suggests that colonial elites would have enslaved indentured British immigrants, who usually had been defined as paupers, vagrants, and criminals in Britain, had their charters made that legally possible. Because of the enormous tracts of land granted the elite and the virtually all-male character of immigration, opportunities for advancement and for marriage were extremely limited for indentured servants; these conditions led "the wild bachelors" to revolt in 1687, but they did not develop a program for reform. In order to increase the economic stake of these servants once they became freedmen, landowning elites decreased the number of indentured servants allowed (or forced) to immigrate from Britain and increased the number of enslaved Africans imported. This shift meant that indentured servants, as freedmen, could eventually become at least small property-owners, and therefore participate in the social contract in the Lockean sense.

Thus historically in Virginia, the rights of male British immigrants were preserved, indeed restored, at the cost of the rights and an increase in the degradation of both female and male Africans. These male Euroamerican landowners, large and small, built a new society that masked their class differences by emphasizing their common freedom, which had meaning precisely because of the presence of an enslaved population. Morgan posits slavery as the single most important factor that enabled Virginians to develop the notion of republican government in a plantation society, and he concludes that "[t]he very institution that was to divide North and South after the Revolution may have made possible their union in a republican government" (29).

18. This is from a leaflet marked "Boston, April 20th, 1773," which originated in the town of Thompson: "Sir, the efforts made by the legislative [*sic*] of this province in their last sessions to free themselves from slavery, gave us, who are in that deplorable state, a high degree of satisfaction. We cannot but wish and hope, Sir, that you will have that same grand object, we mean civil and religious liberty, in view in your next session . . . *as men*, we have a natural right to [equity and justice]" (Aptheker 1965, 7; emphasis in original).

See also Frances Smith Foster (1993) on the petition of Belinda, an enslaved woman who sued for part of her deceased master's estate, which Foster characterizes as her "attempt to hold the new government to its avowed recognition of the individual's right to life, liberty, and the pursuit of happiness" (44).

19. See the first chapter of my "The Slumbering Volcano" (1992); and "The Masculine Borders of the Republic" (1993). The petitions are reprinted in Aptheker (1965).

20. Ironically the masculinity of the revolutionary republican subject influenced the gendered configuration of African American political organizations. Most such organizations were run by men and were concerned primarily with the racial politics that excluded them from participation in mainstream politics. See Horton (1986) on the gender conventions of African American politics and the ways in which they sought to silence women when their concerns ran counter to those of men.

21. On this point I disagree with William Andrews (1988), who sees the use of revolutionary rhetoric by African Americans as backfiring. Andrews argues that Douglass's efforts are undermined from the outset by his adherence to the "authorizing mythology of an oppressive culture" (187). In the pages that follow, my disagreement about conceiving of revolutionary rhetoric as ideology will become clear.

22. See Foucault's *Archeology of Power*, 21–70.

23. Recent scholarship has begun to pursue connections between liberal theory and Enlightenment thought more generally and political theory and cultures indigenous to the Americas. See, for example, Brandon (1986) and Lyons et al. (1992). I will discuss this more extensively in the afterword.

24. Foucault describes dispersion as the foundation of discursive formations in the following way: "What one finds are rather various strategic possibilities that permit the activation of incompatible themes, or, again, the establishment of the same theme in different groups of statement. Hence the idea of describing these dispersions themselves; of discovering whether . . . one cannot discern a regularity: an order of their successive appearance, correlations of their similarity, assignable positions in a common space. . . . Whenever one can describe, between a number of statements, such a system of dispersion, whenever, between objects, types of statement, concept, or thematic choices, one can define a regularity . . . we will say . . . that we are dealing with a *discursive formation*. . . . The conditions to which the elements of this division (objects, mode of statement, concepts, thematic choices) are subjected we shall call the *rules of formation*. The rules of formation are conditions of existence (but also of coexistence, maintenance, modification, and disappearance) in a given discursive formation" (37–38; emphasis in original).

25. Raymond Williams (1983) also identifies a third, more popular usage of ideology, that of "abstract, impractical, or fanatical theory" (154). On the etymology of

ideology see Williams 1983, 153–57. For a thorough discussion of some of the limitations of the term, see Williams 1977, esp. 55–71.

26. I am indebted to Ann Laura Stoler for this reference to Mehta's article.

27. The terms "residual," "dominant," and "emergent" are Raymond Williams's. The residual "has been effectively formed in the past, but it is still active in the cultural process, not only and often not at all as an element of the past, but as an effective element of the present." "Emergent" refers to new meanings and values, but particularly those that are "substantially alternative or oppositional" rather than "some new phase of the dominant culture." Since "the dominant culture has effectively seized . . . the ruling definition of the social," emergent formations contest such appropriations and assert new oppositional—not merely alternative— definitions. See in particular Williams 1977, 121–27.

28. It is worth noting that the meaning and application of "natural rights" differed greatly for different colonial-turned-patriot policymakers. In Massachusetts slavery was abolished by judicial decree, which interpreted the state constitution's claim that "all men are created equal" to be in conflict with chattel slavery. In Virginia virtually the same wording in the state constitution was not interpreted to have any bearing on chattel slavery (Saxton 29).

29. This is not to suggest that all claims by excluded or, in Antonio Gramsci's terms, subaltern groups are oppositional or counter-hegemonic. Rather, I want to emphasize the continual *possibility* of oppositional appropriations, and to stress that in order to determine the particular meaning of any claim or appropriation we need to attend carefully to the specific context in which it is made. I have been particularly influenced on this point by Lisa Lowe. See her more thorough exploration of this (1991), esp. 1–29.

## CHAPTER ONE 1839: RHETORICS OF NATION, RACE, AND MASCULINITY

1. Qtd. in Dumond 215 (emphasis in original).

2. See in particular 98–115 and 139–57.

3. Coming out of Saxton's work on blackface minstrelsy, Eric Lott's "White Like Me" (1993) slices at a different angle the topic I am investigating. Lott argues provocatively that white masculinity incorporated within itself, thus partly defining itself according to, white ideologies of black masculinity as they were performed in blackface minstrelsy. This thesis complements from another perspective my argument, like that of many others, that the racial constructs of whiteness and blackness have meaning only in relation to one another. In contrast to Lott, I

am much more concerned with how these constructs were deployed both in the formal political process and in formulations of national identity.

4. I thank Angelia Zito for bringing this to my attention.

5. I bracket the term "white" not to indicate an assumption of whiteness—in fact I am arguing for the active construction and assertion of the category "white" at this historical moment—but as a way to indicate the *insertion* of "white" into that founding text's, the Declaration of Independence's, address to "all men."

6. I thank Priscilla Wald, in both conversations and *Constituting Americans* (1995), for her insights on this topic.

7. Land Acts in 1800, 1804, and 1820 each reduced the amount of land that had to be bought at one time and the cost per acre, thus increasingly lowering the cost of a claim. In addition, the proliferation of state banks made it easier for those without cash to obtain loans to purchase land. Blum et al. 162, 189.

8. The enslaved population increased in the following way between 1820 and 1850: in Alabama, from 40,000 to 340,000; in Louisiana, from 70,000 to 245,000; in Mississippi, from 32,000 to 310,000. In the late 1830s, some 70,000 Choctaws, Creeks, Cherokees, Seminoles, and Chickasaws were forced on the "Trail of Tears" from the southeastern part of North America to what later became the state of Oklahoma. Takaki 1979, 78.

9. Not all groups from any region favored expansion; some called for limited or controlled growth. But whether for or against expansion, all dominant groups assumed white racial superiority. See Frederickson 130–64 and Horsman 229–48.

10. It is not my intention to suggest that the Democratic Party as a whole supported the doctrine of free soil at the time this article was published. Rather, the mythology developed in this article is representative of one faction within the party, and its publication in the *Democratic Review* indicates that faction's importance. In fact, a split in the party over the question of the extension of slavery eventually led to the demise of the party. See Foner, esp. chaps. 2 and 5.

11. I use the term "mythology" to denote an ideology of origins. See Williams 1983, 210–12.

12. The Missouri Compromise admitted Missouri as a slave state, and Maine as a free state, and divided the Louisiana Purchase along 36°32' north latitude, north of which slavery was to be "forever prohibited." It was later overturned by the Compromise of 1850 and especially the Kansas-Nebraska Act, which opened the territories to slavery by the principle of popular sovereignty.

13. That laws were enacted against interracial marriage indicates the existence of sexual relations among people of different races apart from slavery. Mixed-race people, often called mulattos or octoroons depending upon the number of black people in their immediate family history, became an increasingly important topic

of abolitionist literature because of the critique their very existence gave to this argument. Richard Hildreth's *The Slave, or Memoirs of Archy Moore* (1836), later expanded and reprinted as *Archy Moore, the White Slave; or Memoirs of a Fugitive* (1856), was the first antislavery novel; it chronicled the story of a white-skinned slave. The figure of the tragic mulatta/o later became an important convention of antislavery and abolitionist discourse, whose paradoxical purpose was to create solidarity among different racial groups and to assert the fact of forced miscegenation. See Carby 89–91 and Foster 1979, 128–30.

14. And descends from the Virginia Bay Colony, as Morgan describes it (see note 15 of my introduction).

15. See, for example, "Is Man One or Many?" *Putnam's Monthly* 4 (1854): 1–14; "Are All Men Descended from Adam?" *Putnam's* 5 (1855): 79–88; "Is the Human Race One or Many?" *Harper's New Monthly Magazine* 9 (1854): 548–51; "Are We One or Many?" *Harper's* 9 (1854): 687–91. Horsman has documented this phenomenon particularly well; see especially chaps. 8 and 9.

16. During the 1850s, 87% of blacks employed in New York held menial jobs; the figure was 90% in New Haven, Connecticut. The skilled/unskilled stratification of the labor market had a caste pattern. Takaki 1979, 111–16. Takaki does not offer a breakdown by gender.

17. Blum et al. argue that so-called common men were not strictly separated from property owners anyway (206).

18. See David Brion Davis 1970, 360–66 and 1975, 85.

19. This information is based on Sterling, particularly 104–19.

20. Qtd. in *Walker's Appeal*, 82.

21. See also James Stewart (1976).

22. See also Staudenraus, esp. 12–187.

23. Thanks go to Judith Weisenfeld for apprising me of this connection.

24. See Dann on the black press, and Dick and Bell on the "negro" convention movement.

25. See Ripley for an informative, if male-centered, discussion of black abolitionist discourse.

26. Henry Highland Garnet (1843), in his sketch of Walker's life, writes, "It was the opinion of many that he was hurried out of life by the means of poison, but whether this was the case or not, the writer is not prepared to affirm" (vii). Given that Southerners had placed a price on Walker's head, murder seems likely.

27. Charles Wiltse suggests that Walker would plant his pamphlet into the pockets of clothes he sold to sailors going south, where the garments would be bartered for food and drink, and thereby fall into the hands of Negro dealers who would know how to distribute them. Wiltse qtd. in Richardson 7.

28. See Stuckey (1987) for a powerful analysis of Walker's *Appeal* particularly in relation to Southern slave culture.

29. For discussions of resistance, see, for example, Aptheker (1943), Angela Davis (1971), and *Slave Insurrections* (1822).

## CHAPTER TWO "THE *AMISTAD* AFFAIR" (1839)

1. Paul Gilroy's important study, *Black Atlantic*, uses "the image of the ship—a living, micro-cultural, micro-political system in motion . . . [to] immediately focus attention on the middle passage, on the various projects for redemptive return to an African homeland, on the circulation of ideas and activists as well as the movement of key cultural and political artefacts: tracts, books, gramophone records, and choirs" (4). He focuses on the intercultural mingling both among people kidnapped from Africa and thrown together as "blacks," in the belly of slaveships and as sailors, and Europeans and Euroamericans throughout the Atlantic world. My study differs from his in examining the ways in which legal, nationalist, and racialist discourses produced categories by which populations were simultaneously combined and divided as "black," "American," "enslaved," "Mendian." My study analyzes those discourses that obscured the intercultural minglings that his study brings to the fore.

2. Mendi was most likely part of present-day Mali.

3. For an excellent analysis of the court case between the *Amistad* captives and Ruiz and Montez, see Jones (1987). The most readily available and useful contemporary material includes *The Amistad Case* (*AC*); Barber, *History of the Amistad Captives* (*HAC*); *Trial of the Prisoners of the Amistad* (*TPA*); and Peters (1841).

4. This notation system should be read as follows: *abbreviated title of newspaper* month/day/year:page,column. Full titles for these nineteenth-century newspapers are supplied at the head of the selected bibliography, below.

5. The best previous scholarly study of the *Creole* case is Jones (1975). See also Jervey and Huber, and Hicks.

6. Other well-known rebellions include those of Gabriel Prossor and Denmark Vesey, which were discovered before they could be fully implemented. Perhaps the most famous rebellion was that of Nat Turner, in which some sixty white people were killed, and countless African Americans, slave and free, were harassed and/or killed by Euroamericans in retaliation. See Gray. The revolution in Haiti (1799) was the largest and most successful rebellion in proximity to the United States. Throughout the first half of the nineteenth century, slavery advocates responded to suggestions of general emancipation by invoking the Haitian rebels' violent acts

toward their former masters. See, for example, "The First Fruits of Abolition," NO *Picayune* 9/17/39.

7. Calhoun's argument thus restated the first article of the *Second Treatise*, in which Locke excludes children, women, servants, and slaves from the "body politick" (see introduction). See Aptheker 1989, 23–25, on Calhoun and the "gag rule" and on the censorship of antislavery materials more generally.

8. News coverage of the "*Amistad* Affair" was copious in newspapers of the northeastern United States, New York City and New Haven, Connecticut, in particular. Abolitionist presses, not surprisingly, present the greatest detail on the legal debates that arose in conjunction with the *Amistad*, often quoting selections from newspapers from a wide area, including the slaveholding states. The *Emancipator* and the *Liberator* provided coverage of events relating to the *Amistad* and extensive interpretations of those events. In addition to the newspapers, the abolitionist press published at least five pamphlets and books on the subject of the *Amistad* captives: *Argument of John Quincy Adams; Argument of Roger S. Baldwin;* John Barber, *A History of the Amistad Captives* (*HAC*); *Trial of the Prisoners of the Amistad* (*TPA*); and U.S. Congress House of Representatives, *Africans Taken in the Amistad* (*ATA*). Two kinds of papers with a wider distribution than the abolitionist presses also covered the *Amistad* story, the penny press and the commercial papers. The New York *Sun*, a penny press, was the first to publish the official account of the rebellion, together with a sensational report of a visit to the *Amistad*. Commercial papers, such as the *Commercial Advertiser, Journal of Commerce,* and the *Advertiser and Express*, consistently covered the trials and judicial decisions. Some Southern commercial papers, such as the New Orleans *Picayune*, did no more than note the capture of the "piratical vessel" and publish the official account of the rebellion. Others, such as the Richmond *Enquirer*, also commented on the trials and judicial decisions, but generally refused to print the particulars of debates raging in the North.

9. With respect to the *Amistad*, several histories (popular and scholarly) and many novels provide versions of "what happened" on board the schooner and in the court trials that followed. See, for example, Cable, Martin, and Owens. Information about the *Amistad* is available from a variety of sources, most of which discuss the trial in relation to one of the more famous white men involved in it, that is, John Quincy Adams or Lewis Tappan (see Able and Klinsberg, eds.). Barbara Chase-Riboud's *Echo of Lions*, which she calls a "non-fiction novel," focuses on and imagines a subjectivity for the captives, and so offers a very different view of "what happened" than that provided by Jones's legal history (see note 3, above). See also Strother for the role of the *Amistad* affair in developing the underground railroad. In addition, the rebellion on the *Creole* has proven to be an important

event for African American writers, including William Wells Brown, Pauline Hopkins, and Frederick Douglass, whose novella, *The Heroic Slave*, will be examined in chapter 5. See Yarborough 176–79 for an analysis of the texts by Brown, Hopkins, and Lydia Maria Child in relation to *The Heroic Slave*. See also note 7 to my afterword, on Child's story "Madison Washington."

10. "The Newspaper Press" 7. For an interesting contemporary discussion of the role of the news media see "The Newspaper Press" and "The Periodical Press."

11. Benedict Anderson argues that reading and absorbing the temporal and spatial structure of newspapers created a fertile environment for forming national identity in the United States. His interest lies not in the content of the papers, but in the concept of "news" and the notion of the nation with which it was aligned, an "imagined community" moving calendrically through time (33–36). Anderson's conceptually brilliant thesis influences my study to the extent that I understand the concept of news and the forum for its formation and representation, the newspaper, as together producing an important bond—which he calls national—among news readers, writers, and listeners. In contrast to Anderson, I focus on the historical moment of the emerging abolitionist and penny presses—the 1830s rather than the 1770s—and the way in which these new presses provided a forum for debate among variously empowered rival groups about who or what might constitute the national community.

12. See Mott 1962, esp. 193–208 on the "development of the news function" and 215–52 on the rise of the penny press.

13. See Schudson, chap. 1.

14. This description will be familiar to readers of *Benito Cereno*. Similarities between the *Amistad* and Melville's novella will be explored in chap. 4 below. For another consideration of these parallels, see Carolyn Karcher's sophisticated and extensive analysis (1992).

15. An explicit argument to this effect does not appear in the papers. Lieutenant Gedney never publicly justified his capture of the vessel, although several newspaper articles ask him to explain and defend the grounds on which he did so.

16. New Orleans *Picayune*, Washington *Globe*, Boston *Liberator*, Hartford *Courant*.

17. As Jones remarks, "the fate of the two sailors remains in question." The Africans asserted later that the sailors had drowned, and they appear not to have resurfaced later. 1987, 225 n. 31.

18. Many names were used in connection with the Mendians' apparent leader. I have chosen to use Cinqué because this name has come to be associated with this man over time. Various of his supporters, as well as news reporters, disagreed about how to spell and perhaps how to say his name. Some examples include the Spanish

name Cinquéz, Sinkwe (given him by the linguist, Professor Josiah Gibbs, whose analysis of the Mendians' names will be discussed later in this chapter), and Jingua (first given him by Lewis Tappan of the *Amistad* Committee but also used in the court documents). Most recently Arthur Abraham (1978) from Sierra Leone has called him Sengbe Pieh.

19. Oseola (1800–1838) was a leader of the Seminoles who never signed or recognized a treaty with the U.S. government. In 1837 he was seized by General Jesop and died in captivity shortly thereafter. His father was a white man named Powell. *New Columbia Encyclopedia* 2025.

20. See Roy Harvey Pearce (1965), still one of the best analyses of this theory of progress.

21. Although the reported response to this speech was that the Africans "leapt about and seemed like creatures under some talismanic power," yet they did not attack their captors. If the translation and transcription of this speech and the Africans' response is accurate, does it not seem odd that they did not repeat their act of rebellion in order to "avert bondage"?

22. Legal theorist Mark Kelman points to the apparently arbitrary uses of "time-framing," arguing, "Legal argument can be made only after a fact pattern is characterized by interpretive constructs. Once these constructs operate, a single legal result seems inevitable, a result seemingly deduced on general principle" (593). The authority of the competing claims in the *Amistad* case rests largely on the acceptance of its particular time-frame. I thank Wai-chee Dimock for introducing me to Kelman's article.

23. See Foster (1979) and Andrews (1988) for more on the conventions of slave testimony.

24. The argument that the *Amistad* Committee and other abolitionists supported the Mendians solely to further their own attack on slavery rather than to help fellow human beings—some asserted that they would not have helped a white man in similar circumstances, though it is hard to imagine how that could happen—was made at the time by slavery advocates and has since been made by historians of the *Amistad*, particularly Howard Jones. This argument is worth considering insofar as it connects Tappan and his associates to their larger project of abolition. Yet its very terms further marginalize the Mendians by suggesting that either (1) their accounts are merely what abolitionists wanted them to say, or (2) that their accounts of their experience have no importance or validity aside from a larger movement to end slavery in the United States.

25. To my knowledge there are no extant texts written by James Covey or John Ferry; nor are there interviews or more than brief descriptions of them in the texts I have examined. For a short biographical sketch of Covey, see *HAC* 15.

26. Jones makes a similar point but in relation to the Africans' criminal trial. He argues that the Africans were able to testify in lower courts and that their depositions had been accepted as testimony (1987, 193). This was indeed significant and unusual.

27. Litwack 93–97.

28. The case of the *Antelope* (1819) provides an illuminating example. The *Antelope* was captured by a U.S. naval ship off the coast of Florida, charged with illegal trade in native Africans, and brought into Savannah, Georgia. Originally hailing from Rhode Island under the flag of Venezuela, the *Antelope* changed its flag—and its captain—several times. Typically Georgia sold for the benefit of the state Africans that had been illegally imported. However the Africans of the *Antelope* were not sold because a new federal provision granted the president the power to return such Africans to Sierra Leone. It granted power, but insufficient funds, and the *Antelope* case languished in Washington for many months. Meanwhile, in Savannah the state marshall put the 280 surviving Africans to work, hiring some out, using others to help build infrastructure for the state. Many died during this time. Eventually it was determined that a certain number of the Africans had been legally held as slaves by Spain, while the rest had been illegally held by Portugal. The Africans were forced to draw straws to decide who would be remanded to Spain, and who would be returned to Sierra Leone. If the *Amistad* had been brought into port in a slaveholding state, it seems likely, especially given the efforts of President Van Buren's administration to return them (see below), that the rebels would have been immediately returned to the Spanish. See Noonan on the *Antelope* case.

29. The *Colored American* only sporadically covered the *Amistad* Africans during the early months of their captivity, typically reprinting articles from other papers. I have not been able to find any extant copies (in any form) of the *Herald of Freedom*. The *Colored American* provided the most extensive coverage of the Africans' activities after their release from jail, focusing in particular on efforts by the Reverend James Pennington to send African American missionaries with the Mendians back to Sierra Leone, and there to set up a Christian mission. Unfortunately consideration of this material lies outside the scope of this study. For more on the mission at Mendi and the role of African Americans in the American Missionary Association, see DeBoer.

30. "On the Names of the Captured Africans," New Haven *Palladium*, qtd. in NY *Ad & Ex* 11/9/39:1,3; rpt. *Lib* 11/15/39:184,2 and *Eman* 11/28/39:122,1.

31. On the versions of Cinqué's name, see note 18 above.

32. According to Barber in *HAC* (24), a Mendi and Gissi vocabulary was published in vol. 38 of the *American Journal of Science*.

33. The *Colored American* provided virtually the only coverage in the newspaper press of the Mendians' lecture tour. See, for example, 5/8/41:3,3; 5/22/41:2,1–2 and 2–3.

34. I am indebted to Ian Barnard for his clarifying thoughts on this topic.

35. See the deposition of Richard Madden, a British abolitionist who had been on the Anglo-Spanish commission to halt the slave trade in Cuba, in *Com Ad*, qtd. in NY *Semi-W Ex* 11/27/39:3,2; see also Jones 1987, 16–22.

36. The *Amistad* affair was not widely or extensively reported on in the Southern states because the incident of slave rebellion profoundly disturbed the security and identities of a slaveholding society. Apart from reprintings of judicial decisions, most of the reporting took place within the first weeks after the schooner's capture. These initial reports assessed a slaveholding perspective briefly and without argument.

37. Articles from this paper were translated and reprinted by those presses wanting to provide a forum for debate regarding the fate of the *Amistad* captives (NY *Ad & Ex*, *Eman*, Rich *En*, NY *American*).

38. Qtd. in Cinn *Gaz* 10/21/39; qtd. in *Eman* 11/21/39;117,3.

39. My discussion of time-framing is informed by Kelman. See note 22 above.

40. See Jones (1987) for a thorough consideration of this aspect of the case, esp. chap. 7. Apparently the administration dispatched the cutter *Grampus* to New Haven to take the captives back to Cuba as soon as the case was decided, thereby denying the abolitionists the right of appeal. John Quincy Adams's closing statement before the Supreme Court spent considerable time on this illegal action of (by then former) President Van Buren.

41. Attorneys for the Mendians opposed this "merging" by arguing that the United States had no stake in the matter and that Holabird's action was the administration's attempt to intimidate the court. This assertion of the defense attorneys points out the multi-branch system of the national entity called the United States and challenges the notion, implicit in Holabird's action, that one such branch (the executive) can claim sole rights to the national name and its authority.

42. Differentiation between the captives and the enslaved population in the United States also was made by writers without a clear stand on the appropriate fate of the captives. For example, one writer for the *Commercial Advertiser* argued that the Africans "are very far indeed from exhibiting the stolidity and lack of intelligence so generally characteristic of the Southern negro" (9/26/39:2,1).

43. Here is another example that asserts that race is of no consequence—so long as the subject is not the enslaved population in the United States: "I am very far from being tinctured with abolitionism, far from being disposed to resort to the common cant of the day on the subject of our domestic slavery. But on such an occasion as

this, I can really see and feel that the color of the skin makes no difference in natural rights" (*Com Ad*, qtd. in *Lib* 9/13/39:146,1).

44. The affidavit of Ruiz, taken after his arrest, asserts that he did not know Cinqué was African by birth (qtd. in *Lib* 11/1/39:176,2).

45. See, for example, "Africans at Home."

46. See, for example, *Com Ad* 10/4/39:2,3 and *Lib* 11/18/39:166,2.

47. An index of the effectiveness of this strategy can be found in the following attempt by the *Noticioso de Ambos Mundos* to undermine it: "who can believe that the language and meaning of these negroes, who speak none of the cultivated languages, and whose depositions have been taken through a negro interpreter, picked up by the abolitionists Lord knows where, have been truly and faithfully interpreted?" (Cinn *Gaz*, qtd. in *Eman* 11/21/39:117,3).

48. NY *Ad & Ex* 10/10/39:2,4 and 10/12/39:1,6; *Lib* 11/18/39:166,1.

49. See the passage from Judson's discussion in the Prudence Crandall case quoted as the epigraph to chap. 1. See also Angela Davis (1983, 34–36) for an insightful examination of this case.

50. Printed in *Eman* 1/23/40:154,3–6 and 155, 1–2; *Lib* 1/24/40:13.

51. See Jones 1987, 188–91.

52. No doubt the rebels' unfamiliarity with the language and culture in which they found themselves and their lack of access to literacy and print culture contributed to this absence. But perhaps even more significant, given that their firsthand accounts of their journeys from Africa to Havana and then on the *Amistad* were recorded and published in the newspapers, was the apparent unwillingness or lack of concern of even the Mendians' staunchest supporters to publish the Mendians' interpretations of "what happened." Given the patronizing attitude toward Frederick Douglass of both Garrison, characterized by his direction to "tell your story, Frederick," and John Collins, "Give us the facts . . . we will take care of the philosophy," it may be that the Mendians' supporters actively suppressed their interpretations of events. Qtd. in Stepto 1984, 175.

### CHAPTER THREE "THE CASE OF THE *CREOLE*" (1841)

1. News coverage of the "Case of the *Creole*" was less extensive than that of the *Amistad*, partly because the rebels left the United States and so could not be observed by reporters, and partly because the rebellion of enslaved people from the United States was inherently more threatening to the institution of slavery and to Euroamericans more generally. While the *Emancipator* and the *Liberator* covered this case extensively, as they had the *Amistad*, there was far less coverage of this

event in the penny and commercial presses of the Northeast, except for the *Journal of Commerce*, which had avowedly abolitionist leanings. Newspaper presses in the Southern states, including, for example, the New Orleans *Advertiser*, the Richmond *Compiler*, and the Charleston *Mercury*, in addition to the *Picayune* and *Enquirer*, covered events in conjunction with the *Creole* to a far greater extent than they had the *Amistad*. The subject of the *Creole* rebellion was important enough to slavery advocates to warrant an entire article in the *Southern Quarterly Review*, which I discuss below.

2. Depositions by the crew of the *Creole* may be found in Senate Documents, 27th Cong., 2d sess., II, nos. 51–46. These documents contain the "Protest" sworn to at New Orleans on December 2, 1841 (rpt. NO *Ad* 12/8/41; *Lib* 12/31/41:2,1–4; *Eman* 1/7/42:144,1–5), and individual depositions from the surviving crew of the *Creole* and the U.S. consul in Nassau.

3. See introduction and chap. 1.

4. Howard Jones makes a similar point. He argues that "the blacks on board the *Creole* were released by something approaching mob action" (1975, 31) and that neither British officers nor the crew of the *Creole* had any choice but to release the fugitives (33). My argument, while compatible with this assertion, has a different emphasis. The "Protest" rhetorically erases the agency of the people of Nassau, and this is part of a larger logic that denies a valid agency to any black people. One might argue that by using terms such as "mob action," Jones's article participates in a similar logic.

5. U.S. Congress, *US Serials Set*, vol. 397. 27th Cong. 2d sess. [137].

6. All quotations from the following debate are from *Lib* 1/21/42:2,1–3. Shorter versions appeared in other papers, such as Wash *Gl* 1/11/42:3,2; *H of F* 1/13/42:2, 4–6, and Ch *Mer* 1/15/42:2,1–2.

7. Calhoun mentions the article from the *Evangelist*, considered in the previous section, as one justification for his rewriting: "And recently he had seen extracted in a religious newspaper of the city of New-York, a justification of this atrocious murder, and the murderers compared to Washington."

8. Webster's dispatch was reprinted in numerous newspapers, including Wash *Gl* 2/23/42:2,3–4; Ch *Mer* 2/28/42:2,1–2; *Lib* 3/4/42:2,3.

9. Calhoun's actions were noted in *Lib* 3/4/42:2,5.

10. The dispatch supports its construction of the conflict by stating that "this is the substance of the case, as stated in two protests, one made at Nassau, one at New Orleans, and the Consul's letters, together with sundry depositions taken by him" (qtd. in *Lib* 3/4/42:2,3). Although I have reviewed all material now available to me, I have decided to base this study on materials that were made available to the public in the popular press. I therefore have not included in the main argument

the letters and depositions referred to here. These letters and depositions are available in *US Serials Set,* vol. 396. U.S. Senate Documents, 27th Cong., 2d sess., no. 38.

11. Webster's entry into the dispute on the side of slaveholders operates similarly to District Attorney Holabird's "merging" of the claims of Spanish slaveholders with those of the United States in the *Amistad* case. See chap. 2.

12. "No alteration of her own local law can either increase or diminish, or any way affect, the duty of the English government and its colonial authorities in such cases, as such duty exists according to the law, the comity, and the usages of nations" (qtd. in *Lib* 3/4/42:2,4).

13. For more on the relation between natural and positive law, particularly in regard to slavery, see Cover.

14. The newspaper press often returned to the case of Thomas Nash and the mutiny on the British brig *Hermione.* Marshall's opinion was offered in response to the execution of Nash, who had been extradited to Britain before he had proven his status as an American. See NY *Ad & Ex* 9/28/39:2,2 or *Eman* 10/10/39:93,6 and 94,1.

15. Characterizing the British as "hypocrites" refers to slavery having been abolished in the British West Indies in 1833. Slaveholders in the United States represented Britain's subsequent campaign to end the African slave trade and to emancipate any slaves that came within its territory as the height of hypocrisy, since it was customary for them to argue that, early in their history, the British had forced slavery upon the colonies against their will.

16. The *Colored American* ended publication just as the *Creole* case was being debated. Up until this time the *Colored American* had been the most consistently published and longest running African American newspaper in the United States.

17. All quotations are from the New York *Evangelist,* qtd. in *NASS* 12/30/41: 118,2. Also reprinted in *Lib* 1/7/42:1,4.

18. Most of the textual material in this section comes from abolitionist presses that do not identify themselves in terms of race. The one exception appears at the end of the section; this marking suggests that the other material was written by white people. It is likely that African Americans also wrote for abolitionist papers edited by whites, but it is impossible to know where and when except when noted explicitly.

19. For positive vs. natural law, see Cover.

20. On February 14, 1842, the House of Lords decided that there should be a formal agreement between the United States and Britain for the return of criminals; but there was no such agreement at this time. Furthermore, such an agreement would need to rest on the presumption that law in all nations is reasonable,

which they thought was not possible given the slave trade. Therefore no statute existed under which to return the *Creole* rebels to the United States, and because they had committed no crime under British jurisdiction, they had to be released. See *Eman & FA* 3/17/42:7,5. See also my discussion below.

21. Rich *Compiler* 12/17/41, qtd. in *Eman* 1/20/42:4.

22. All quotations from Wash *G.* 3/22/42:2,4–5. Also in *Lib* 4/1/42:2,4–5.

23. This quotation is Henry Clay's while speaking during the Senate debate over Calhoun's resolutions. Although "they" in this context specifically refers to the Senate, it might easily refer to the U.S. government as a whole.

24. Qtd. in Ch *Mer* 3/21/42:2,2.

25. Although Spanish diplomats continued to press for indemnification, and they were supported at different times by various U.S. Congressmen, no agreement was ever reached.

26. See Jones (1975) for a complete overview of the international debate and its effect on the Ashburton-Webster Treaty (1842).

## CHAPTER FOUR *BENITO CERENO* (1855) AND "THE SLUMBERING VOLCANO"

1. Douglass, "Slavery: The Slumbering Volcano" (*Lib* 5/11/49 and *North Star* 5/11/49).

2. Older examples include Stone (1949) and Scudder (1928). More recent examples of criticism that consider historical factors as primary yet still focus on the author include Rogin (1983), Karcher (1980, 1992), and Wald (1995).

3. My summary of criticism on *Benito Cereno* relies upon Lea Newman's excellent *Reader's Guide to the Short Stories of Herman Melville* (1986). Also see Burkholder for an overview of this critical history.

4. Schiffman, Glicksberg, and Fisher qtd. in Newman 133.

5. Critics who mention the *Amistad* and *Creole* rebellions include Jackson (90–91), Kaplan (14–16), Karcher (1992), Levine (181), Sundquist (1986, 104 and 115), Thomas (29–30), and Yellin (216–17).

6. My own analysis of the primary documents confirms Jones's already persuasive argument regarding Baldwin's primary significance. See Jones (1989), chap. 9, esp. 190–92.

7. Studies that compare *Benito Cereno* and *Voyages* abound; important ones include those of Dew, Jackson, Putzel, and Ward.

8. Sidney Kaplan simply says that *Voyages* "was apparently unknown to contemporary readers of *Benito Cereno*" (14). No review of *The Piazza Tales*, Melville's

1856 collection that included *Benito Cereno*, mentions *Voyages* (Hayford et al. 502).

9. *Benito Cereno* scholarship has been locked into a debate regarding Melville's racist or progressive views. Newman, in her very useful bibliographical essay on this material, notes that the criticism is notable for its extremes (144).

10. The Compromise of 1850 and the Kansas-Nebraska Act each used the principle of popular sovereignty to open to slavery the newly acquired territory above the boundary drawn by the Missouri Compromise.

11. See, for example, Garnet's "Address," Garnet's introduction to Walker's *Appeal*; and Douglass's speeches in Cork, Ireland, 4/23/48, in New York, 4/23/49, in Boston, 5/30/48, reprinted in Blassingame.

12. Parts of *The Heroic Slave* were published in *Frederick Douglass's Paper* 3/11/53. The first complete version was published in *Autographs for Freedom* (1853), a fundraising project for Douglass's paper edited by Julia Griffiths.

13. Mott 1957b, 423. *De Bow's Review* 22 (1857): 129.

14. For other comments on the antislavery character of *Putnam's*, see Yellin (1972, 216); Karcher (1980, 13–14 and 1992, 213) and Post-Lauria. Sheila Post-Lauria makes the strongest claim for that periodical's anti-imperialist and egalitarian stance, connecting the publisher, George Palmer Putnam, and the chief editor, Charles F. Briggs, to the antislavery movement (3).

15. In developing this historical analysis, I join a growing number of critics of both Melville's writing and of U.S. literature more generally who are interested in interactions within the discursive fields of a particular historical moment. In terms of *Benito Cereno* criticism, I see my approach as most similar to those of the following critics, although I also differ with each of them on a number of points: Karcher (1992) (who also analyzes *Benito Cereno* in relation to the *Amistad*); Levine (who considers the novella in relation to mutinies more generally); Post-Lauria (who gestures toward situating *Benito Cereno* within Putnam's editorial politics); and Sundquist (1986) (who analyzes *Benito Cereno* in relation to slavery in the Caribbean).

16. "Treating" was a term typically employed to describe the meeting and bartering of two ships at sea. Such intercourse was common and fraught to varying degrees with danger.

17. NY *Ad & Ex* and NY *MH* 8/24/39.

18. Although the quotation is from Leslie and Stuckey (291), their comment is only the most explicit assertion of an entire range of critics.

19. Robert S. Levine argues that most readers in the 1850s would have been complicit with Delano's perspective, based on his extensive analysis of tales of mutiny. His well-developed and convincing argument unfortunately elides too forcefully the contribution of racialism to Delano's perspective. See also my further comments below.

20. For example, Sterling Brown makes an implicitly gendered argument that the fierceness of the rebels in battle comes nearer the truth than the reputed gentleness of black people, and although the rebels are bloodthirsty he does not think Melville makes them into villains (13). Michael Rogin argues that Babo conventionalizes (and so disarms) the supposedly natural relations of master and slave by overthrowing slavery and then staging it as a play (211).

21. Jean Fagan Yellin is the only critic that I know of to connect *Benito Cereno* with slave narratives, commenting that it, "like the slave narratives," reveals these stereotyped faces to be masks (224).

22. Levine argues that Delano primarily perceived the Africans as mutineers, and as such responded quickly and without question the same way he would have had white sailors aboard another ship revolted against their captain (216). Certainly Levine's point carries weight to the extent that at sea a captain's word was law and his authority absolute; any resistance to this met with swift and brutal repression. But in effacing the racial character of this conflict Levine denies the influence of Delano's already well demonstrated racial prejudices.

23. *Voyages* spells Benito "Bonito." According to Delano's narrative, Don Bonito tried to refuse salvage to Delano once they had returned safely to Lima. Delano seems to have written this chapter largely to defend his position on this point, giving the text a specific agenda not unlike that of the "Protest" delivered at New Orleans in the case of the *Creole*. See chap. 3 above.

24. Although one might argue that the irreducible difference between the "blacks" and Delano and his crew portrays the situation more realistically than the logic of identification employed by abolitionist supporters of the *Amistad* captives and the *Creole* rebels, realism is not at issue here. Rather I am after the way in which representations interact within a discursive field, how they support or challenge specific positions within relations of power. Douglass's *The Heroic Slave* is not principally concerned with accurately portraying the life of a heroic slave rebel, but with creating a history, voice, and identity for a shadowy historical figure in order strategically to claim for him the trope of revolutionary struggle. What some might call Douglass's romanticizing of the *Creole* rebellion should not be understood as an uncritical or unwitting valorization of "slave ability" but rather as an important rhetorical and political strategy. Leslie and Stuckey remark that Melville cannot be accused of romanticizing slave ability as abolitionists often did (298). Yet how significant is such a criticism in a cultural environment in which romanticized visions of just about everything were normative?

25. Karcher argues that Melville exaggerates the savageness of the rebels and reduces that of the Spaniards in order to draw attention to the one-sided nature of the supposedly objective legal document, Cereno's deposition (1980, 134–35). I do not see how such changes lead to this conclusion. If this was the intention, would it not

have been more effective to include, for example, an incident of violence by the Spaniards in Delano's section of the tale that is then not recorded in the deposition?

26. F. O. Matthiessen makes a similar point in relation to the novella, arguing that *Benito Cereno* is relatively superficial because it does not take into account the fact that evil had originally been done to the enslaved rebels (508).

27. Gloria Horsly-Meacham more harshly judges than I will below Babo's transformation from *Voyages* to *Benito Cereno*, arguing that "the exceedingly clever Babo nonetheless in no sense undermines, as many have argued, Delano's judgment that the Black mind is limited, for movements and strategies attributed to any number of 'the Negroes' in the source are transferred exclusively to 'the Negro Babo' in Melville's deposition" (1991, 230). Although I agree with this assessment, I think Babo also continues to act in concert with his fellow rebels.

28. The deposition is somewhat confusing on this point. Early on, all those named in this paragraph are represented as the rebels (334), but near the end of the deposition are included these two statements: (1) "that the deponent has not seen the twenty negroes, from twelve to sixteen years of age, have any share in the execution of the murder . . . although they were all knowing to the insurrection"; (2) "that the twelve or thirteen negroes, from twenty-five to fifty years of age, were with [Jose], the principal revolters, and committed the murders and atrocities before related" (340).

29. Adler argues for the importance of Babo's figure by asserting that "he has the qualities of mind of a master psychologist, strategist, general, playwright, impresario," endowed with Melville's "own poetic insight" (88). Although I agree with this interpretation, my argument goes in another direction.

30. An as-told-to memoir written by Turner's proslavery lawyer, Thomas Gray, the "Confessions of Nat Turner," while mediated by Gray's recording and commented upon by the writer, nevertheless represents an articulate, intelligent, and unrepentant Turner who details both his motives and his actions. George's courtroom scene in *Clotel* will be considered in the following chapter.

31. Both reviews qtd. in Hayford et al. 505–6.


CHAPTER FIVE *THE HEROIC SLAVE* (1853)

1. Douglass 1975, II, 195. For more on Lincoln's and Woodrow Wilson's development of an official story with this argument, see Wald.

2. Douglass initially believed the Constitution to be a proslavery document, as did his abolitionist mentor William Lloyd Garrison. But he changed his mind in the late 1840s, claiming many of the strategies of political abolitionists. See, for exam-

ple, his views in "The U.S. Constitution," *FDP* 6/24/1851 (rpt. 1975, V, 191–99). For more on political abolition see Foner.

3. Scholarship on *The Heroic Slave* always mentions the rebellion on the *Creole,* and increasingly it attends to the textual materials through which this event is now available to us. I find Richard Yarborough's critique of *The Heroic Slave* primarily in the context of *later* versions of the *Creole* story the most problematic because it ignores the way in which the story enters into an already substantial dialogue about the meaning of the rebellion. Mary Kemp Davis (1984) takes her information from the historian Howard Jones's important, but secondary, "The Peculiar Institution and National Honor." William Andrews (1990) draws upon the Senate documents that contain testimony from passengers and crew of the *Creole* and at least one article from the *Liberator* speculating about Washington's past. Unfortunately Andrews uses the *Creole* crew's testimony as if it were a disinterested statement of the facts. Eric Sundquist (1993) has delved furthest into the primary documents, examining both William Jay's "The *Creole* Case and Mr. Webster's Despatch" and the proposed resolutions of Representative Joshua Giddings.

I draw my material from over ten major newspapers, which in turn reprinted articles from many other papers, both regional and national. In addition to journalistic accounts and editorial interpretations, the newspaper press printed transcripts of Congressional debates and diplomatic correspondence. This material gives far greater access to the breadth and contours of the public debate than government documents do alone, because government documents would have been available only to a very few. Newspapers were a primary site of mass cultural production and national identity formation. See, for example, Saxton 95–105, and Anderson 47–65.

4. Scholars of *The Heroic Slave* have debated the meaning and implications of Douglass's asserted equivalence among founding fathers and enslaved rebels. Mary Kemp Davis argued that Douglass "legitimizes the slave's use of violence to obtain his freedom by equating his violence with that which American colonists used to win their freedom from British tyranny" (46). Robert Stepto found praiseworthy "the signal idea that freedom for slaves can transform the south and the north and hence the nation" (1984, 182), but also dismissed as "overwrought" Madison Washington's speeches, "except perhaps in being much like some of Douglass's addresses and those of Virginia's other sons" (1986, 146). William Andrews (1988) then problematized Douglass's strategy with the question: what kind of exemplar can Madison Washington truly be, since he justifies his actions by appealing to "the authorizing mythology of an oppressive culture" (187), that of the slaveholding founding fathers? Joining Andrews, Richard Yarborough argued that Douglass's "celebration of black heroism was subverted from the outset by the racist, sexist,

and elitist assumptions upon which the Angle-American [*sic*] male ideal was constructed" (182). He concluded by noting that the novella "leaves us wondering whether the tools of the master can ever be used to achieve the complete liberation of the slave" (183). I entered the fray in an earlier article (1993) by asserting that "Douglass transforms [the model of the founders] by reinscribing it in the service of slave revolt as opposed to revolt among white men," simultaneously invoking and undermining the founders' authority (703). Eric Sundquist (1993) has suggested that to Douglass, as to other African Americans, "the ideology of the founding fathers unavoidably presented an ironic enigma," but nevertheless "the notion that the language of the Revolution was but a new form of totalizing imprisonment, a thorough mockery of freedom, is a view that would have been anathema to Douglass" (121). Russ Castronovo (1995) also has contested interpretations by Yarborough and Andrews, arguing that "As Madison Washington instructs, freedom does not descend from white-haired (or white-face) patriarchs; not does it constitute an inheritance granted solely to those sons society recognizes as the fathers' children. . . . Freedom, as exslaves repeated with ambivalence, is transgressive" (224). Robyn Wiegman's analysis (1995), like my argument here, asserts that "it is finally the masculinity of the slave that serves as the rhetorical ground for 'The Heroic Slave''s appeal to a common humanity," but also that the story demonstrates "the impossibility of uncovering an African (-American) presence where the universalized particularity of white masculinity routinely stands" (75).

As in a recent article (1995), in this chapter I argue that Douglass's claim to the legacy of the founders to authorize slave rebellion was deeply disruptive of the Union, bringing, as it does, the primary narrative of national emergence—the struggle for liberation against an unjust oppressor—directly into conflict with the Compact between the States, which was to keep slavery a state rather than a federal institution. Thus Douglass successfully changed the meaning of the Revolution, I assert, by refashioning it to suit the agenda of the event he (re)presents, an agenda which the founders would not have supported. Rather than understanding the notion of a struggle for freedom as *inherently* attached to a particular ideology, I conceptualize ideas and tropes as open to appropriation and transformation, and thereby acquiring *different* ideological import depending upon the context. Thus whereas Andrews and Yarborough question whether Douglass's approach can be effective, given the way in which they understand its relation to revolutionary rhetoric and middle-class ideals, I would second and extend both Sundquist's suggestion that Douglass would not have accepted the notion that the language of the Revolution was yet another entrapment, and Castronovo's idea that freedom does not inherently belong to any particular group. Douglass does not accede or assimilate to the founders' ideology; instead he claims a value—freedom—and redefines it for his own ideological purposes.

reveals the illogic of his perspective. This undermining of the mate's perspective enables readers to reach their own conclusions and challenges them to agree with Douglass.

26. Yarborough argues against Douglass's discursive erasure of violence on the *Creole* by noting that "revolution usually entails violence, and black self-assertion in the face of racist attempts at dehumanization often necessitates a direct and forceful assault upon the very structures of social power that provide most whites (especially white males) with a sense of self-worth, security, and potency" (181). As I hope this study has shown, Washington's claim to the trope of revolutionary struggle was an assault upon "structures of social power" that deeply disrupted the imagined security of dominant groups, despite Douglass's unwillingness to represent violence.

27. See Horsman, chap. 12.

28. For a perceptive analysis of gender in antebellum African American organizing, see Horton.

29. For more on Douglass and women's rights see Martin, chap. 6.

## AFTERWORD

1. See Karen Sánchez-Eppler for a brilliant and differently focused analysis of connections between abolitionist and feminist rhetoric, particularly having to do with women's ability—or lack thereof—to control the uses of their bodies.

2. Barbara Bardes and Suzanne Gossett (1990) survey nineteenth-century literature for those moments when women make their own "declarations of independence." Clustered primarily after the historical period examined in this study, most of the examples they have discovered entail white women's assertions regarding their desired access to property rights, education, the professions, and the political process. This independence, then, typically meant economic and social independence from men of their own class and race. None of the examples they cover include women claiming the right to violence in the service of their own liberation.

3. See chap. 1.

4. Jean Fagan Yellin has argued that Jacobs was assisted in her escape by a multiracial community of women that included slaveholders as well as slaves. Carla Peterson contests this notion, arguing that Jacobs satirized and criticized white women's sentimental sympathy (161–64). My argument differs from Yellin's in its emphasis on the connections between women and their children, rather than on those between women. See her introduction to *Incidents in the Life of a Slave Girl.*

5. Stowe's ambivalence, despite her apparent support, even more obviously shows through in her inability finally to interpret George's actions: "If it had been only a

Hungarian youth, now bravely defending in some mountain fastness the retreat of fugitives escaping from Austria into America, this would have been sublime heroism; but as it was a youth of African descent, defending the retreat of fugitives through America into Canada, of course we are too well instructed and patriotic to see any heroism in it; and if our readers do, they must do it on their own private responsibility. . . . When despairing African fugitives do the same thing [as Hungarian refugees],—it is—what *is* it?" (252; emphasis in original).

6. Brown's George Green removes first to Canada, then to Britain. Douglass's Washington ends his journey at Nassau. Delany's Blake makes most of his impact in Cuba.

7. I am indebted for reference to both of these articles to Karcher, the first through correspondence, the second through 1992, 225 n. 33.

8. Child did reprint the "Heroic Mutineers" article from the *Emancipator* (*NASS* 12/30/41:2,1), which translated "into the appropriate language of freedom" the words of the "Protest" delivered at New Orleans. Since this article explicitly invoked the trope in the service of the rebels, Child apparently supported this interpretation. But as I hope to have shown, Child was clearly ambivalent not only about violence, but about glorifying violence even if in what she otherwise understood to be a righteous struggle for liberty.

After the Civil War Child published her own version of the *Creole* rebellion, "Madison Washington," in *The Freedmen's Book* (1869). Child may have felt more comfortable writing what at that later point would have been understood as a sketch of an important historical figure in the fight against slavery, rather than what earlier might have appeared as a model for action. Even so, Child emphasizes Washington's limited use of violence, commenting that "he fought for freedom, not for revenge" (152), and noting how he stopped others from killing the white crew once they had obtained control of the vessel. Although Child follows fairly closely the story line established by Douglass, she removes both Listwell and Grant, and gives Susan a larger part although no more agency. Susan lives through Washington's return and recapture, and reappears on the *Creole* after the battle is won. Child's happy ending complicates the heroic isolation of Douglass's Washington and affirms the importance of heterosexual relations.

9. Other scholars, such as Pearce and Berkhofer, also document such observations. But they interpret this material differently. Pearce argues that Europeans simply used Native Americans as foils for their critiques of Europe. Berkhofer similarly argues these observations to be projections of European minds. These interpretations, while certainly true in part, do not take account of the real influence of cultural contact between natives of the Americas and Europeans, and, perhaps inadvertently, once again posit Europe and its peoples as primary and the Americas and its peoples as secondary, if important at all.

# Selected Bibliography

## NINETEENTH-CENTURY NEWSPAPERS

Charleston *Mercury* (Ch *Mer*)

Cincinnati *Gazette* (Cinn *Gaz*)

*Colored American* (*CA*)

*Commercial Advertiser* (*Com Ad*)

*Emancipator* (*Eman*)

*Emancipator and Freedman's Advo-cate* (*Eman & FA*)

*Frederick Douglass' Paper* (*FDP*)

*Herald of Freedom* (*H of F*)

*Journal of Commerce* (*J of C*)

*Liberator* (*Lib*)

*National Anti-Slavery Standard* (*NASS*)

New Haven *Daily Courant* (no abbrev.)

New Haven *Herald* (NH *Her*)

New Haven *Record* (no abbrev.)

New London *Gazette* (NL *Gaz*)

New Orleans *Advertiser* (NO *Ad*)

New Orleans *Picayune* (NO *Pic*)

New York *Advertiser and Express* (NY *Ad & Ex*)

New York *American* (NY *American*)

New York *Morning Herald* (NY *MH*)

New York *Semi-Weekly Express* (NY *Semi-W Ex*)

New York *Sun* (NY *Sun*)

*North Star* (*NS*)

*People's Press* (no abbrev.)

Richmond *Compiler* (Rich *Compiler*)

Richmond *Enquirer* (Rich *En*)

*Sunday Morning News* (*SMN*)

Washington *Globe* (Wash *Gl*)

In-text citations of newspaper articles use the following convention: *abbreviated title* month/day/year(in the nineteenth century):page,column. Example: *Lib* 12/14/41:2,1.

## OTHER SOURCES

Able, Annie Heloise, and Frank J. Klinsberg, eds. *A Sidelight on Anglo-American Relations, 1839–1858.* 1927. New York: Augustus M. Kelley, 1970.

"About Niggers." *Putnam's Monthly Magazine* 6 (1855): 608–12.

Abraham, Arthur. "Sengbe Pieh: A Neglected Hero?" *Journal of the Historical Society of Sierra Leone* 2 (July 1978): 22–30.

Adams, John and Abigail. Letters. *Heath Anthology of American Literature.* Vol. 1. Ed. Paul Lauter et al. New York: Heath, 1991.

Adams, John Quincy. *Argument of John Quincy Adams before the Supreme Court of the United States, in the case of the U.S. appellants, vs. Cinque, and other Africans, captured in the schooner Amistad.* New York, 1841. Rpt. *The Amistad Case* 3–135.

Adler, Joyce Sparer. "Benito Cereno: Slavery and Violence in the Americas." In Burkholder, ed. (1992), 76–93.

"Africans at Home." *Southern Quarterly Review* 10 (1854): 70–96.

Althusser, Louis. *Lenin and Philosophy.* Trans. Ben Brewster. New York: Monthly Review, 1971.

*The Amistad Case: The Most Celebrated Slave Mutiny of the Nineteenth Century.* New York: Johnson Reprint, 1968.

Anderson, Benedict. *Imagined Communities: Reflections on the Origin and Spread of Nationalism.* London: Verso, 1983. Rev. and extended ed., 1991.

Andrews, William L. "The Novelization of Voice in Early African American Narrative." *PMLA* 105 (Jan. 1990):23–34.

——. *To Tell a Free Story: The First Century of Afro-American Autobiography, 1760–1865.* Chicago: Univ. of Illinois Press, 1988.

*Appeal of Forty Thousand Citizens, threatened with disfranchisement, to the people of Pennsylvania.* Philadelphia, 1838. Rpt. Aptheker, ed. (1965), 176–86.

Appleby, Joyce. "Introduction: Republicanism and Ideology." *American Quarterly* 37 (1985): 461–73.

——. "Republicanism in Old and New Contests." *William and Mary Quarterly* 43 (1986): 20–34.

Aptheker, Herbert. *Abolitionism: A Revolutionary Movement.* Boston: Twayne 1989.

——. *American Negro Slave Revolts.* New York: Columbia Univ. Press, 1943.

——. *Essays in the History of the American Negro.* New York: International, 1945.

——. *"One Continual Cry": David Walker's Appeal to the Colored Citizens of the World (1820–30); Its Setting and Its Meaning.* New York: Humanities Press, 1965.

——. *To Be Free: Studies in Negro History.* New York: International, 1948.

——, ed. *Documentary History of the Negro People in the United States.* Vol. 1. New York: Citadel, 1965.

Arciniegas, German. *America in Europe: A History of the New World in Reverse.* San Diego: Harcourt Brace Jovanovich, 1986.

Baker, Jean H. *Affairs of Party: The Political Culture of Northern Democrats in the Mid-Nineteenth Century.* Ithaca: Cornell Univ. Press, 1983.

Baldwin, Roger S. *Argument of Roger S. Baldwin, of New Haven, before the Su-preme Court of the United States, in the Case of the United States, Appellants, vs. Cinque, and others, Africans of the Amistad.* New York: S. W. Benedict, 1841.

Banning, Lance. "Jeffersonian Ideology Revisited: Liberal and Classical Ideas in the New American Republic." *William and Mary Quarterly* 43 (1986): 3–19.

Barber, John Warner. *A History of the Amistad Captives. (HAC)* 1840. Rpt. New York: Arno, 1969.

Bardes, Barbara, and Suzanne Gossett. *Declarations of Independence: Women and Political Power in Nineteenth-Century American Fiction.* New Brunswick: Rutgers Univ. Press, 1990.

Beard, Augustus Field. *The Story of the Amistad.* New York: The American Mis-sionary Association, [n.d.].

Bell, Howard Holman. *A Survey of the Negro Convention Movement, 1830–1861.* New York: Arno, 1969.

Bercovitch, Sacvan. *The American Jeremiad.* Madison: Univ. of Wisconsin Press, 1978.

Berkhofer, Robert F. *The White Man's Indian: Images of the American Indian from Columbus to the Present.* New York: Vintage, 1979.

Bibb, Henry. *Narrative of the Life and Adventures of Henry Bibb, an American Slave, Written by Himself.* New York, 1849. Rpt. Wilmington, Del.: Scholarly Resources, 1970.

Blassingame, John W. *The Slave Community: Plantation Life in the Antebellum South.* New York: Oxford Univ. Press, 1972.

Blum, John M., et al. *The National Experience: A History of the United States.* 7th ed. San Diego: Harcourt Brace Jovanovich, 1989.

Bradley, David. *The Channeysville Incident.* New York: Harper and Row, 1981.

Brandon, William. *New Worlds for Old.* Athens: Ohio Univ. Press, 1986.

Brawley, Benjamin. *A Social History of the American Negro.* New York: Mac-millan, 1921.

Brown, Sterling A. *The Negro in American Fiction.* Washington, D.C.: Association of Negro Folk Education, 1937.

Brown, William Wells. *Clotel; or, The President's Daughter.* 1853. Rpt. *Three Clas-sic African-American Novels.* Ed. William L. Andrews. New York: Penguin, 1990. 71–283.

——. *Narrative of William W. Brown, a Fugitive Slave. Written by Himself.* Boston, 1847. Rpt. New York: Johnson Reprint, 1970.

Burkholder, Robert E. *Critical Essays on Herman Melville's "Benito Cereno."* New York: G. K. Hall, 1992.

Cable, Mary. *Black Odyssey: The Case of the Slave Ship Amistad.* New York: Penguin, 1977.

Carby, Hazel V. *Reconstructing Womanhood: The Emergence of the Afro-American Woman Novelist.* New York: Oxford Univ. Press, 1987.

Castronovo, Russ. *Fathering the Nation: American Genealogies of Slavery and Freedom.* Berkeley: Univ. of California Press, 1995.

Charleston, SC. (J. Hamilton, Intendant). *An Account of the Late Intended Insurrection Among a Portion of the Blacks of this City.* A. E. Miller, 1822. Rpt. *Slave Insurrections: Selected Documents.* Westport, Conn.: Negro Universities Press, 1970.

Chase-Ribold, Barbara. *Echo of Lions.* New York: William Morrow, 1989.

Child, Lydia Maria. "The Iron Shroud." *National Anti-Slavery Standard.* 3/3/42: 2,6; 3,1.

——. "Letter from New York—No. 12." *National Anti-Slavery Standard.* 12/2/41: 2,2–3.

——. "Madison Washington." *The Freedmen's Book.* Ed. Lydia Maria Child. Boston: Fields, Osgood & Co., 1869. 147–53.

Cordingly, David. *Under the Black Flag: A Romance and Reality of Life Among the Pirates.* New York: Random House, 1997.

"The Course of Civilization." *United States Magazine and Democratic Review* 6 (1839): 208–17.

Cover, Robert M. *Justice Accused: Antislavery and the Judicial Process.* New Haven: Yale Univ. Press, 1975.

"The *Creole* Case." *Southern Quarterly Review* 2 (1842): 55–72.

Dann, Martin E., ed. *The Black Press, 1827–1890: The Quest for National Identity.* New York: Putnam's, 1971.

Davis, Angela Y. "Reflections on the Black Woman's Role in the Community of Slaves." *Black Scholar* 3 (1971): 3–15.

——. *Women, Race and Class.* New York: Vintage, 1983.

Davis, David Brion. *The Problem of Slavery in the Age of Revolution, 1770–1823.* Ithaca: Cornell Univ. Press, 1975.

——. *The Problem of Slavery in Western Culture.* Ithaca: Cornell Univ. Press, 1970.

Davis, Mary Kemp. "The Historical Slave Revolt and the Literary Imagination." Ph.D. diss., Univ. of North Carolina, 1984.

DeBoer, Clara Merritt. *Be Jubilant My Feet: African American Abolitionists in the American Missionary Association, 1839–1861.* New York: Garland, 1994.

Delano, Amasa. *Narrative of Voyages and Travels in the Northern and Southern Hemispheres.* Boston, 1817. Chap. 18. Rpt. Hayford et al. 810–47.

Delany, Martin. *Blake; or, the Huts of America.* 1859–62. Ed. Floyd J. Miller. Boston: Beacon Press, 1970.

Dew, Marjorie C. "*Benito Cereno:* Melville's Vision and Revision of the Source." *A Benito Cereno Handbook.* Ed. Theodore L. Gross. Belmont, Calif.: Wadsworth, 1965. 178–84.

Dick, Robert Christopher. "The Rhetoric of the Negro Ante-Bellum Protest Movement." Ph.D. diss., Stanford Univ., 1969. Ann Arbor: UPI, 1977.

"Domestic Slavery." *Southern Literary Messenger* 5 (1839): 677–87.

Douglass, Frederick. *Frederick Douglass Papers.* Ed. John W. Blassingame. 5 vols. New Haven: Yale Univ. Press, 1979.

——. *The Heroic Slave. Autographs for Freedom.* Ed. Julia Griffiths. Boston, 1853. 174–239. Rpt. *Three Classic African-American Novels.* Ed. William L. Andrews. New York: Penguin, 1990. 23–69.

——. *Life and Writings of Frederick Douglass.* Ed. Phillip Foner. 5 vols. New York: International, 1975.

——. "Meaning of July Fourth for the Negro." Oration delivered in Corinthian Hall, Rochester, New York, 7/5/52. Rpt. 1975, II, 181–204.

——. *Narrative of the Life of Frederick Douglass, An American Slave.* 1845. Rpt. New York: Penguin, 1984.

——. "Slavery: The Slumbering Volcano." *Liberator* 5/11/49 and *North Star* 5/11/49.

DuBois, W. E. Burghardt. *The Souls of Black Folk.* 1903. Rpt. New York: New American Library, 1969.

Dumond, Dwight L. *Anti-Slavery: The Crusade for Freedom in America.* Ann Arbor: Univ. of Michigan Press, 1961.

Fisher, Philip, ed. *The New American Studies: Essays from Representations.* Berkeley: Univ. of California Press, 1991.

Foner, Eric. *Free Soil, Free Labor, Free Men: The Ideology of the Republican Party Before the Civil War.* New York: Oxford Univ. Press, 1970.

Foster, Frances Smith, ed. Introduction. *Minnie's Sacrifice; Sowing and Reaping; Trial and Triumph: Three Rediscovered Novels by Frances E. W. Harper.* Boston: Beacon Press, 1994. xi–xxxvii.

——. *Witnessing Slavery: The Development of Ante-bellum Slave Narratives.* Westport, Conn.: Greenwood, 1979.

——. *Written By Herself: Literary Production by African American Women, 1746–1892.* Bloomington: Indiana Univ. Press, 1993.

Foucault, Michel. *The Archeology of Knowledge and The Discourse on Language.* Trans. A. M. Sheridan Smith. New York: Pantheon, 1972.

Franklin, John Hope. *From Slavery to Freedom: A History of American Negroes.* New York: Knopf, 1947.

Frederickson, George M. *The Black Image in the White Mind: The Debate on Afro-American Character and Destiny, 1817–1914.* Middletown, Conn.: Wesleyan Univ. Press, 1987.

Garnet, Henry Highland. "An Address to the Slaves of the United States of America, Buffalo, New York." 1843. Rpt. *"Let Your Motto Be Resistance": The Life and Thought of Henry Highland Garnet.* By Earl Ofari. Boston: Beacon, 1972. 144–53.

——. Introduction. *Walker's Appeal . . . to the Coloured Citizens of the World . . .* 1843. Rpt. New York: Arno, 1969.

Gellner, Ernest. *Nations and Nationalism.* Ithaca: Cornell Univ. Press, 1983.

Genovese, Eugene D. *Roll, Jordan, Roll: The World the Slaves Made.* New York: Pantheon, 1972.

Giddings, Paula. *When and Where I Enter: The Impact of Black Women on Race and Sex in America.* New York: Bantam, 1985.

Gilroy, Paul. *The Black Atlantic: Modernity and Double Consciousness.* New York: Verso, 1993.

Gray, Thomas. *Confessions of Nat Turner.* 1831. Miami, Fla.: Mnemosyne, 1967.

Greenblatt, Stephen. *Shakespearean Negotiations: The Circulation of Social Energy in Renaissance England.* Berkeley: Univ. of California Press, 1988.

Grinde, Donald A., Jr. "Iroquois Political Theory and the Roots of American Democracy." In Lyons, ed. (1992), 227–80.

Grinde, Donald A., Jr., and Bruce Johansen. *Exemplar of Liberty: Native America and the Evolution of Democracy.* Los Angeles: American Indian Studies Center, 1991.

Gross, Bella. "Freedom's Journal and the Rights of All." *Journal of Negro History* (July 1932): 241–286.

Gross, Seymour L., and Eileen Bender. "History, Politics, and Literature: The Myth of Nat Turner." *American Quarterly* 23 (1971): 487–518.

Gutman, Herbert. *The Black Family in Slavery and Freedom, 1750–1925.* New York: Pantheon, 1976.

Harper, Frances Ellen Watkins. *A Brighter Coming Day: A Frances Ellen Watkins Harper Reader.* Ed. Frances Smith Foster. New York: Feminist Press, 1990.

Hayford, Harrison, Alma A. MacDougall, and G. Thomas Tanselle, eds. *The Piazza Tales and Other Prose Pieces, 1839–1860.* Evanston: Northwestern Univ. Press, 1987.

Hicks, Granville. "Dr. Channing and the *Creole* Case." *American Historical Review* 37 (April 1932): 516–25.

Hildreth, Richard. *Archy Moore, The White Slave; or Memories of a Fugitive.* 1856. New York: Negro Universities Press, 1969.

Horsley-Meacham, Gloria. "Bull of the Nile: Symbol, History and Racial Myth in 'Benito Cereno.' " *New England Quarterly* (June 1991): 225–242.

Horsman, Reginald. *Race and Manifest Destiny: The Origins of American Racial Anglo-Saxonism.* Cambridge: Harvard Univ. Press, 1981.

Horton, James Oliver. "Freedom's Yoke: Gender Conventions among Antebellum Free Blacks." *Feminist Studies* 12 (1986): 51–76.

Howard, Jean E. *The Stage and Social Struggle in Early Modern England.* New York: Routledge, 1994.

Huggins, Nathan I. "The Deforming Mirror of Truth: Slavery and the Master Narrative of American History." *Radical History* 49 (1991): 25–48.

Jackson, Margaret Y. "Melville's Use of a Real Slave Mutiny in 'Benito Cereno.'" *College Language Association Journal* 4 (1960): 79–93.

Jacobs, Harriet. *Incidents in the Life of a Slave Girl, Written by Herself.* 1861. Ed. Jean Fagan Yellin. Cambridge: Harvard Univ. Press, 1987.

Jay, William. *The Creole Case and Mr. Webster's Despatch: With Comments by the N.Y. American.* New York: N.Y. *American* Office, 1842.

Jervey, Edward D., and C. Harold Huber. "The *Creole* Affair." *Journal of Negro History* 65 (1980): 196–211.

Johansen, Bruce. *Forgotten Founders: How the American Indian Helped Shape Democracy.* Boston: Harvard Common Press, 1982.

Johnson, Charles. *Middle Passage.* New York: Atheneum, 1990.

Jones, Howard. *Mutiny on the Amistad.* New York: Oxford, 1987.

——. "The Peculiar Institution and National Honor: The Case of the *Creole* Slave Revolt." *Civil War History* 21 (1975): 28–50.

Jones, Jacqueline. *Labor of Love, Labor of Sorrow: Black Women, Work, and the Family from Slavery to the Present.* New York: Basic, 1985.

*Journals of the Continental Congress, 1774–1789.* Vol. II. 1778. Washington: Govt. Printing Office, 1908. Rpt. Johnson Reprint, 1968.

Kaplan, Sidney. "Herman Melville and the American National Sin: The Meaning of 'Benito Cereno.'" *Journal of Negro History* 41 (1956): 311–38; 42 (1957): 11–37.

Karcher, Carolyn L. "The Riddle of the Sphinx: Melville's 'Benito Cereno' and the Amistad Case." In Burkholder, ed. (1992), 196–229.

——. *Shadow over the Promised Land: Slavery, Race, and Violence in Melville's America.* Baton Rouge: Louisiana State Univ. Press, 1980.

Kelman, Mark. "Interpretive Construction in the Substantive Criminal Law." *Stanford Law Review* 33 (April 1981): 591–673.

Leslie, Joshua, and Sterling Stuckey. "The Death of Benito Cereno: A Reading of Herman Melville on Slavery." *Journal of Negro History* 67 (1982): 287–301.

Leverenz, David. *Manhood and the American Renaissance.* Ithaca: Cornell Univ. Press, 1989.

Levine, Robert S. *Conspiracy and Romance: Studies in Brockden Brown, Cooper, Hawthorne, and Melville.* New York: Cambridge Univ. Press, 1989.

Limerick, Patricia. *Legacy of Conquest: The Unbroken Past of the American West.* New York: Norton, 1987.

Litwack, Leon F. *North of Slavery: The Negro in the Free States, 1790–1860.* Chicago: Univ. of Chicago Press, 1961.

Locke, John. *Two Treatises of Government.* Ed. Peter Laslett. Cambridge: Cambridge Univ. Press, 1967.

Lott, Eric. "White Like Me: Racial Cross-Dressing and the Construction of American Whiteness." *Cultures of United States Imperialism.* Ed. Amy Kaplan and Donald E. Pease. Durham: Duke Univ. Press, 1993. 474–95.

Lowe, Lisa. *Critical Terrains: French and British Orientalisms.* Ithaca: Cornell Univ. Press, 1991.

Lyons, Oren, et al., eds. *Exiled in the Land of the Free: Democracy, Indian Nations, and the U.S. Constitution.* Santa Fe: Clear Light, 1992.

Martin, Christopher. *The Amistad Affair.* New York: Abelard-Schuman, 1970.

Matthiessen, F. O. *American Renaissance: Art and Expression in the Age of Emerson and Whitman.* New York: Oxford Univ. Press, 1941.

McDowell, Deborah. "In the First Place: Making Frederick Douglass and the African American Literary Tradition." *Critical Essays on Frederick Douglass.* Ed. William L. Andrews. Boston: G. K. Hall, 1991. 192–214.

McLaurin, Melton A. *Celia, A Slave.* Athens: Univ. of Georgia Press, 1991.

Mehta, Uday. "Liberal Strategies of Exclusion." *Politics and Society* 18.4 (1990): 427–54.

Melville, Herman. *Benito Cereno. Putnam's Monthly Magazine* (1855). Rpt. *The Piazza Tales.* New York, 1856. Rpt. Hayford et al. 46–117.

Miller, Perry. *Errand into the Wilderness.* Cambridge: Harvard Univ. Press, 1981.

*Minutes of the State Convention of Colored Citizens, held at Albany . . . for the purpose of considering their political condition.* New York, 1840. Rpt. Aptheker, ed. (1965), 198–205.

Morgan, Edmund S. "Slavery and Freedom: The American Paradox." *Journal of American History* 59 (1972): 5–29.

Morrison, Toni. *Beloved.* New York: Knopf, 1987.

Mott, Frank L. *American Journalism: A History, 1690–1960.* New York: Macmillan, 1962.

——. *History of American Magazines, 1850–1865.* Cambridge: Harvard Univ. Press, 1957.

Mott, Lucretia, and Elizabeth Cady Stanton. "Declaration of Sentiments." 1848. Rpt. *Feminism: The Essential Historical Writings.* Ed. Miriam Schneir. New York: Random House, 1972. 77–82.

Nash, Gary B. *Red, White and Black: The Peoples of Early America.* Englewood Cliffs, N.J.: Prentice Hall, 1974.

Nell, William C. *The Colored Patriots of the American Revolution.* Boston: R. F. Wallcut, 1855.

Nelson, Dana. *The Word in Black and White: Reading "Race" in American Literature, 1638–1867.* New York: Oxford Univ. Press, 1992.

Newman, Lea Bertani Vozar. *A Reader's Guide to the Short Stories of Herman Melville.* Boston: G. K. Hall, 1986.

"The Newspaper Press." *Southern Quarterly Review* 1 (1842): 1–25.

Noel, Donald L. "Slavery and the Rise of Racism." *The Origins of American Slavery and Racism.* Ed. Donald L. Noel. Columbus: Merrill, 1972. 153–74.

Noonan, John T., Jr. *The "Antelope": The Ordeal of the Recaptured Africans in the Administrations of James Monroe and John Quincy Adams.* Berkeley: Univ. of California Press, 1977.

Okoye, F. Nwabueze. "Chattel Slavery as the Nightmare of the American Revolutionaries." *William & Mary Quarterly* 37 (1980): 14–15.

Owens, William A. *Slave Mutiny: The Revolt on the Schooner Amistad.* New York: 1953.

Patterson, Orlando. *Slavery and Social Death: A Comparative Study.* Cambridge: Harvard Univ. Press, 1982.

Pearce, Roy Harvey. *Savagism and Civilization: A Study of the Indian and the American Mind.* Baltimore: Johns Hopkins Univ. Press, 1965.

"The Periodical Press." *Southern Quarterly Review* 1 (1842): 26–70.

Peters, R. *Reports of cases argued and adjudged in the Supreme Court of the United States.* Vol. 15. Philadelphia, 1841. 518–98.

Peterson, Carla. *"Doers of the Word": African-American Women Speakers and Writers in the North (1830–1880).* New York: Oxford Univ. Press, 1995.

Porter, Dorothy B. *The Negro in the United States: A Selected Bibliography.* Washington, D.C.: Library of Congress, 1970.

Post-Lauria, Sheila. "Editorial Politics in Herman Melville's 'Benito Cereno.'" *American Periodicals* 5 (1995): 1–13.

Putzel, Max. "The Source and Symbols of Melville's 'Benito Cereno.'" *American Literature* 34 (1962): 191–206.

Redding, J. Saunders. *They Came in Chains: Americans from Africa.* Philadelphia: Lippincott, 1950.

Richardson, Marilyn. Introduction. *Maria W. Stewart: America's First Black Woman Political Writer: Essays and Speeches.* Bloomington: Indiana Univ. Press, 1987.

Ripley, C. Peter, ed. Introduction. *The Black Abolitionist Papers. The United States, 1830–1846.* Vol. 3. Chapel Hill: Univ. of North Carolina Press, 1991.

Roediger, David. *The Wages of Whiteness: Race and the Making of the American Working Class.* New York: Verso, 1991.

Rogin, Michael Paul. *Subversive Genealogy: The Politics and Art of Herman Melville.* New York: Knopf, 1983.

Ryan, Alan. *Property and Political Theory.* New York: Basil Blackwell, 1984.

Said, Edward W. "Representing the Colonized: Anthropology's Interlocutors." *Critical Inquiry* 15 (1989): 205–25.

Sale, Maggie. "Critiques from Within: Antebellum Projects of Resistance." *American Literature* 64 (1992): 695–718.

———. "The Masculine Borders of the Republic." Unpublished MLA paper, 1993.

———. "The Slumbering Volcano: Recasting Race, Masculinity and the Discourse of US American National Identity." Ph.D. diss., Univ. of California, San Diego, 1992.

———. "To Make the Past Useful: Frederick Douglass' Politics of Solidarity." *Arizona Quarterly* 51 (Autumn 1995): 25–60.

Sánchez-Eppler, Karen. "Bodily Bonds: The Intersecting Rhetorics of Feminism and Abolition." *Representations* 24 (Fall 1988): 28–59.

Saxton, Alexander. *The Rise and Fall of the White Republic: Class Politics and Mass Culture in Nineteenth-Century America.* New York: Verso, 1990.

Schudson, Michael. *Discovering the News: A Social History of American Newspapers.* New York: Basic, 1978.

Scott, Joan. *Gender and the Politics of History.* New York: Columbia Univ. Press, 1988.

Scudder, Harold H. "Melville's 'Benito Cereno' and Captain Delano's Voyages." *PMLA* 43 (1928): 502–32.

Shalhope, Robert E. "Republicanism and Early American Historiography." *William & Mary Quarterly* 39 (1982): 334–56.

*Slave Insurrections: Selected Documents.* 1822. Westport, Conn.: Negro Universities Press, 1970.

Slavin, Arthur J. "The American Principle from More to Locke." *The First Images of America: The Impact of the New World on the Old.* Vol. 1. Ed. Fredi Chiappeli. Berkeley: Univ. of California Press, 1976.

Stanhope Smith, Samuel. *An Essay on the Causes of the Variety of Complexion and Figure in the Human Species.* 1810. Rpt. Cambridge, Mass.: Belknap, 1965.

Stanton, Elizabeth Cady, and Lucretia Mott. "Declaration of Sentiments and Resolutions, Seneca Falls." 1848. Rpt. *Feminism: The Essential Historical Writings.* Ed. Miriam Schneir. New York: Vintage, 1972. 76–82.

Staudenraus, P. J. *The African Colonization Movement, 1816–1865.* New York: Columbia Univ. Press, 1961.

Stepto, Robert B. "Sharing the Thunder: The Literary Exchanges of Harriet Beecher Stowe, Henry Bibb, and Frederick Douglass." *New Essays on Uncle Tom's Cabin.* Ed. Eric Sundquist. Cambridge: Cambridge Univ. Press, 1986. 135–53.

———. "Storytelling in Early Afro-American Fiction: Frederick Douglass's 'The Heroic Slave.' " *Black Literature and Literary Theory.* New York: Methuen, 1984. 175–86.

Sterling, Dorothy, ed. *We Are Your Sisters: Black Women in the Nineteenth Century.* New York: Norton, 1984.

Stewart, James Brewer. *Holy Warriors: The Abolitionists and Anti-Slavery.* New York: Hill and Wang, 1976.

Stewart, Maria W. *Maria W. Stewart: America's First Black Woman Political Writer. Essays and Speeches.* Ed. Marilyn Richardson. Bloomington: Indiana Univ. Press, 1987.

Stoler, Ann Laura, and Frederick Cooper. "Between Metropole and Colony: Rethinking a Research Agenda." *Tensions of Empire.* Ed. Stoler and Cooper. Forthcoming.

Stone, Geoffrey. *Melville.* New York: Sheed & Ward, 1949.

Stowe, Harriet Beecher. *Dred; A Tale of the Great Dismal Swamp.* 2 vols. 1856. Rpt. Grosse Pointe: Scholarly Press, 1968.

———. *Uncle Tom's Cabin, or Life among the Lowly.* 1852. Rpt. New York: Collier, 1962.

Strother, Horatio T. *The Underground Railroad in Connecticut.* Middletown, Conn., Wesleyan Univ. Press, 1962.

Stuckey, Sterling. *The Ideological Origins of Black Nationalism.* Boston: Beacon, 1972.

———. *Slave Culture: Nationalist Theory and the Foundations of Black America.* New York: Oxford Univ. Press, 1987.

Sundquist, Eric J. "*Benito Cereno* and New World Slavery." *Reconstructing American Literary History.* Ed. Sacvan Bercovitch. Cambridge: Harvard Univ. Press, 1986. 93–122.

———. "Slavery, Revolution, and the American Renaissance." *The American Renaissance Reconsidered.* Ed. Walter Benn Michaels and Donald Pease. Baltimore: Johns Hopkins Univ. Press, 1985. 1–33.

———. *To Wake the Nations: Race in the Making of American Literature.* Cambridge: Harvard Univ. Press, 1993.

Takaki, Ronald. *Iron Cages: Race and Culture in Nineteenth Century America.* New York: Knopf, 1979.

———. *Violence in the Black Imagination: Essays and Documents.* New York: Putnam's, 1972.

Tate, Claudia. *Domestic Allegories of Political Desire: The Black Heroine's Text at the Turn of the Century.* New York: Oxford Univ. Press, 1992.

Thomas, Brook. "The Legal Fictions of Herman Melville and Lemuel Shaw." *Critical Inquiry* 11 (1984): 24–51.

Thorpe, T. B. "Cotton and Its Cultivation." *Harper's Magazine* 8 (1854): 47–63.

*Trial of the Prisoners of the Amistad on the Writ of Habeous Corpus, Before the Circuit Court of the United States, for the District of Connecticut, at Hartford; Judges Thompson and Judson. September Term, 1839*. New York, 1839. (*TPA*)

U.S. Congress. House of Representatives. *Africans Taken in the Amistad*. (*ATA*) 26th Cong., 1st sess., H. Exec. Doc. 185. 1840. Rpt. *The Amistad Case*. 1–69.

Van Evrie, John H. *Negroes and Negro "Slavery": The First an Inferior Race: The Latter Its Normal Condition*. Baltimore, 1853. Revised and expanded, New York, 1863.

Wald, Priscilla. *Constituting Americans: Cultural Anxiety and Narrative Form*. Durham: Duke Univ. Press, 1995.

Walker, David. *An Appeal . . . to the Coloured Citizens of the World, but in particular, and very expressly, to those of The United States of America*. Boston, 1829. Rpt. Stuckey (1972), 39–117.

Ward, Robert J. "From Source to Achievement in 'Benito Cereno.'" *Anglo-American Studies* (1982): 233–40.

Weatherford, Jack. *Indian Givers: How the Indians of the Americas Transformed the Old World*. New York: Crown, 1988.

White, Shane. " 'We Dwell in Safety and Pursue Our Honest Callings' ": Free Blacks in New York City, 1783–1810." *Journal of American History* 75 (1988): 453–54.

Wiegman, Robyn. *American Anatomies: Theorizing Race and Gender*. Durham: Duke Univ. Press, 1995.

Williams, Raymond. *Keywords: A Vocabulary of Culture and Society*. New York: Oxford Univ. Press, 1983.

——. *Marxism and Literature*. New York: Oxford UP, 1977.

Wish, Harvey. "American Slave Insurrections before 1861." *Journal of Negro History* 22 (1937): 299–320.

Woodson, Carter G. *The History of the Negro Church*. Washington: Associated Press, 1921.

Yarborough, Richard. "Race, Violence, and Manhood: The Masculine Ideal in Frederick Douglass's 'The Heroic Slave.'" *Frederick Douglass: New Literary and Historical Essays*. Ed. Eric J. Sundquist. Cambridge: Harvard Univ. Press, 1990. 166–88.

Yellin, Jean Fagan. *The Intricate Knot: Black Figures in American Literature, 1776–1863*. New York: New York Univ. Press, 1972.

# Index

Maggie Montesinos Sale is Assistant Professor and
Undergraduate Director of the Women's and Gender Studies
Program at Columbia University.

Library of Congress Cataloging-in-Publication Data

Sale, Maggie.
The slumbering volcano : American slave ship revolts and the production of
rebellious masculinity / Maggie Sale.
p.   cm. — (New Americanists)
Includes bibliographical references and index.
ISBN 0-8223-1983-7 (cloth : alk. paper). — ISBN 0-8223-1992-6 (paper : alk. paper)
1. Slavery—United States—Insurrections, etc.—Sources.   2. National
characteristics, American—History—19th century—Sources.   3. Masculinity
(Psychology)—United States—History—19th century—Sources.   4. White
supremacy movements—United States—History—19th century—Sources.
5. Slavery in literature.   I. Title.   II. Series.
E447.S25   1997
305.896'073—dc21        97-7610